ENDSLEIGH

01224 625-868

LAURA

9-30/5-30.

FATAL STORM

THE 54TH SYDNEY TO HOBART YACHT RACE

Rob Mundle

ADLARD COLES NAUTICAL
London

Foreword

I clearly remember Rob Mundle's solemn news on his late-night Sydney to Hobart race update on television on December 26, 1998. He said he had spoken with meteorologist Roger Badham and reported the Sydney to Hobart race fleet, which was then flying down the NSW coast, could find themselves sailing into a severe depression that was forming in Bass Strait. It had the credentials of a cyclone, but worse still, the westerly winds it would generate would be in the opposite direction to the strong current.

I knew that could only mean huge waves and horrific sailing conditions. My mind immediately went back to August 1979 when I was the helmsman on the Australian Admiral's Cup yacht, *Impetuous*, in the disastrous Fastnet Race out of Cowes, England. That race claimed the lives of 15 fellow yachtsmen. After we rounded Lands End – the south-west tip of England – we received a weather forecast saying we could "expect a north-westerly change with wind gusts of 30 to 40 knots". The first gusts, which came in at around 10pm, were at 60 knots. They later rose to 80 knots.

It appears a similar thing happened in the 1998 Sydney to Hobart – gusts of around 92 knots were registered at Wilsons Promontory, a point due west of the fleet.

The carnage that resulted was for me, unbelievable, but in hindsight understandable when we saw on television the size of the waves and the strength of the wind. The rescue effort was remarkable and I say without hesitation that our nation is deeply indebted to those

Preface

It was always known that the ultimate storm might be delivered to the Sydney to Hobart yacht race one day. And that is exactly what happened in the 54th staging of the classic.

Since its inception in 1945 the race has stood as an Australian sporting icon. Each year, from the start on Boxing Day, December 26, until the yachts reach the finish line 630 nautical miles away, Australians have devoured news of its progress via television, newspapers and radio.

Like so many other "on-the-edge" sports, ocean yacht racing has always contained an element of danger. That is part of its appeal, especially in today's world where an ever increasing number of laws, rules and regulations have stripped our society of much of its spirit of adventure. The fact that the notorious waters of the Tasman Sea and Bass Strait are part of the challenge provides added excitement for competitors and spectators alike.

Having been a sailor all my life, and with this being the 30th time I had covered the classic, I knew soon after the start that there was a potential for disaster. That was confirmed the next morning when a weather station at Wilsons Promontory, a knuckle of land that juts out into Bass Strait, registered more than 90 knots of wind from the west.

This book details what happened in the ensuing maelstrom – literally a weather bomb exploded over the fleet. It led to the largest peacetime search and rescue effort ever seen in Australia. Of the fleet of 115 yachts

Part One

the years Campbell had learned that one of the many safety factors you apply to your personal equipment for ocean racing was oversize seaboots. If they are too big they are relatively easy to remove should you fall overboard. If they are too tight and can't be taken off, you might as well be swimming with a house brick on each foot. New boots were indispensable for this adventure and Campbell's priority in the precious little time he had left at home was to get to the marine store in downtown Seattle and buy them. He did just that. He bought size 12 boots – one-and-a-half sizes larger than he would normally wear.

At only 32 years of age, John Campbell had tried but failed to complete the Sydney to Hobart yacht race on two previous occasions. On the way to the airport, John and his father mused that this would be the third time lucky. John had been assured by his Melbourne-based sailing friend, Peter Meikle, that the yacht in which they would be racing, the 42-foot sloop *Kingurra*, was one of the more robust among the 115 entrants. *Kingurra*'s owner, Peter Joubert, was the designer, and the yacht's long racing record included no fewer than 14 Hobarts.

With nearly 20 hours of travel behind him, Campbell exited Sydney's international air terminal bleary-eyed and jet-lagged. The sky was clear and the new day was already warm. As he travelled to the Cruising Yacht Club of Australia (more commonly known as the CYC) on the eastern outskirts of the city's CBD, he was reminded Christmas was a very different beast in the Southern Hemisphere. A 28 degrees Celsius (82°F) day didn't seem to gel with the artificial snow and winter Christmas scenes painted on shop windows. There was one familiar thing though … effervescent and smiling children clutching their new toys.

The docks at the Cruising Yacht Club were among the busiest parts of Sydney at that early hour on Christmas

Day. The atmosphere was almost carnivalesque. Race yachts with colourful battle flags flying bobbed at the docks like impatient thoroughbred horses tethered to a rail. Crewmembers from out of town, who were staying aboard their race yachts, were shuttling to and from the showers in the clubhouse. Breakfast was also on the agenda on the wooden deck that extended out over the waters of the harbour. For most it was a hearty feed of bacon and eggs. For others it was a meal that helped soak up the liquid excesses of the Christmas Eve celebrations at the club.

John Campbell felt at home as he made his way along the narrow timber dock to where *Kingurra* was berthed. Campbell was warmly welcomed – old as well as new friends appreciated his effort in joining the crew for the big race. As he stepped aboard he quickly realised what Meikle had meant when he said it was the sort of yacht that would get them to Hobart. He took his bag below to be stowed and the dark timber interior, just like the exterior, said "solid". This was a sea-boat. He noted the sturdy bunks, the sensibly-sized navigation area and the compact overall layout. There was always something within arm's length to hang on to in rough weather. Even the toilet – the "head" in nautical terms – was as comfortable as it was well designed.

Seventy-four-year-old Melburnian Peter Joubert was taking part in his 27th Sydney to Hobart. Around mid-morning he and his crew guided *Kingurra* away from the dock and headed for a secluded bay on the harbour. Once the yacht was at anchor Joubert disappeared below to the galley and began preparing the massive roast meal he had been planning the previous two days. While the crew relaxed on deck and absorbed the peaceful surroundings – a tree-lined bay dotted with impressive terracotta-roofed homes – they talked about the great race that was set to

"Go easy on the Christmas dinner if you don't like sailing to windward." That was the early advice from leading yachting meteorologist Roger "Clouds" Badham in *The Australian* on December 17, 1998. "It all depends on a low that looks like forming off the New South Wales south coast late next week." Badham was basing his predictions on the current "American model" – a long-range weather forecast developed from a computer analysis of the existing world weather patterns. "Any forecast outside six days for these things can only be described as 'fuzzy' at best," Badham said. "There have been intense and sometimes cyclonic lows active in the Tasman Sea over the past six weeks."

★

It was mid-November 1998 when prominent Australian sailor David Witt went to Rarotonga, the capital of the Cook Islands and Witt's newly adopted home. He had an agreement to train young local sailors and in return he would be able to represent the Pacific island nation in the Sydney Olympics. He also had a sponsor for the entry of a maxi yacht for the Sydney to Hobart and he wanted the yacht to represent the Cooks. Witt and his Olympic crewman, Rod Howell, headed to the home of "Papa Tom" – the man who had opened the way for them to Olympic competition. His real name is Sir Thomas Davis and he had been the nation's Prime Minister for 10 years from 1978. He claims he still does not know why the Queen knighted him.

Papa Tom, a very large, powerful, grey-haired man is, to say the least, a colourful character. He has two passions – sailing and riding his Harley Davidson motorcycle.

Everyone knows him and everyone waves each time he blasts down the dusty roads. When not riding his Harley he drives an old Jaguar – the only one on the island. His home is at the edge of the foothills on what the locals call "the back of the island". It has been built in the style of a chalet with a high-pitched roof, and is sited on a large area of lush green lawn dotted with tall, coconut-heavy palms. The interior of the home is spacious and open, and surrounding it is a wide verandah – features that maximise the air-flow while minimising the heat.

On the day of their visit, Witt and Howell were warmly welcomed by Papa Tom onto the large verandah. The trio settled back into the comfortable chairs and within seconds the loquacious Witt was divulging his plan. Papa Tom liked the idea.

Witt then took it to the next stage, recalls Papa Tom.

"He came to me and said, 'If this plan succeeds will you sail with us?' I was stunned," said Papa Tom. "I said, 'Hey, I'm 81 years old. I'd only get in the way. I can't pull any ropes.' But inside me the sailor said, 'Do it'. If you have the ocean and sailing in your blood you cannot refuse an invitation to sail in a great race like the Sydney to Hobart – even if you are 81. For me it was a dream come true."

Papa Tom had been educated in New Zealand and Australia. In the winter of 1952 he sailed a small yacht with his wife, two children and two crew across the Pacific from New Zealand to South America, en route to Boston where he was to become a lecturer and researcher at Harvard.

"That was a horrendous trip. It was in a 44-foot ketch and we were sailing in mid-winter – the first small yacht ever to sail west to east in the roaring forties at that time of year. It was a 7000 mile voyage and we had 14 days of hell."

1998. "That gets nobody anywhere." Charles wanted boats with some potential that could be developed.

Olympic class sailing and offshore racing yachts soon became the mainstay of his life. He sailed for Britain four times in the Admiral's Cup, the unofficial ocean racing team championship. In 1997 however, he would change camps and race for Australia.

Steve Kulmar, the skipper of the Mumm 36 class Australian Admiral's Cup team yacht, *Sea*, and a veteran of 16 successfully completed Sydney to Hobarts and five Fastnet Races out of England, got to know Charles through prominent Sydney sailmaker and yachtsman Grant Simmer.

"I knew that as part of the Australian team, and wanting to do the best we possibly could, we would need some local knowledge for sailing on the waters of the Solent and off the coast of England," said Kulmar. "The perfect situation would have been for us to carry both a local navigator and tactician, but we realised the weight of two extra people would dull our performance. So we ended up looking for somebody who could navigate and also had really good local knowledge and great tactical skills.

"Grant mentioned Glyn Charles and gave me his number. I called him. It was about two months before the series. After a bit of to-ing and fro-ing he decided he would join us. He was an absolutely terrific person to have on the boat in that he would be there worrying all the time about making it go fast. He was always putting his heart and soul into it. We had a terrific series. Glyn was a very energetic guy on the yacht but laid-back in an almost Australian sort of way when on shore."

Glyn Charles' partner, Annie Goodman, was equally passionate about sailing. The comfortable cottage they shared in Bosham, on the shores of Chichester Harbour, reflected a lifestyle closely aligned to the sea. It was a perfect base for both because it was central to much of England's sailing activity.

Checking his emails one day, Charles found one from Steve Kulmar. Kulmar had committed to sailing on *Sword of Orion* in the 1998 Sydney to Hobart, and during some lead-up races it had become clear the crew needed more depth – someone who could comfortably slip into the role of tactician or supervisor.

"Ironically, I was talking to Grant Simmer again and he said Glyn was planning to come to Sydney to coach the British Olympic Soling contender, Andy Beadsworth, in preparation for the world championship," Kulmar recollects. "So I emailed Glyn immediately and asked, 'Are you interested in doing the Hobart?' He said he'd have a think about it. Information went backwards and forwards and in the end he said, 'OK, subject to final discussions in Sydney'."

Charles met with Kulmar and *Sword of Orion*'s owner Rob Kothe at the CYC the morning he arrived from London – December 10. They talked at length and outlined their plans for the race. About two days later Charles agreed to race – but only in the Hobart because he had the Olympic Soling coaching program organised from December the 11th to the 22nd.

Glyn Charles already had four Fastnet Races to his credit. He had now committed to his first Hobart.

★

Well-known sailing figure, John "Steamer" Stanley, had done it all. At 51 years of age, he had been a champion in the famous 16-foot and 18-foot skiffs that race on Sydney Harbour. His keelboat experiences had led him to the Admiral's Cup ocean racing championship in England, 16 Sydney to Hobarts, and the oldest trophy

1998 race. Steamer gathered the crew together when Winning confirmed right on the knock of closing date for entries that he did want to compete.

"I entered again just for the fun of doing it," Winning said. "We planned to do it every year until we got too old." Steamer assembled a group of sailors with considerable offshore experience. The crew included Jim Lawler and Bruce Gould, plus an enthusiastic 19-year-old, Michael "Beaver" Rynan, who worked weekends as a tender driver delivering crews to their yachts moored off Sydney's Middle Harbour Yacht Club. To race to Hobart aboard *Winston Churchill* with the likes of John Stanley and others was, he told friends, "the chance of a lifetime."

Yet again the grand old yacht was painstakingly prepared and by Christmas Eve the only thing left to do was buy the food and stock the galley. Winning and Steamer met at the marina at the northside suburb of Woolwich, borrowed a small open motor launch and headed for the waterfront supermarket at nearby Birkenhead Point. Shopping trolley after shopping trolley was loaded with the provisions needed to cater for the nine-man crew. As the little launch chugged back across the bay with its cargo, the two men chatted idly about the race and their plans for Christmas Day. Both intended to spend it with family and friends. Winning said he would go to the yacht late in the afternoon and touch up a couple of spots of varnish so the boat was positively glistening for the start.

More than 20 plastic bags filled with food and the essential utensils for cooking were stowed in *Winston Churchill*'s galley. This done, the grand old lady was gently motored across to the CYC's marina, attracting considerable attention as she went. This was after all the famous *Winston Churchill*, replete with gleaming cream topsides, timber made bright with many liberal coats of varnish, and a trim and tidy rig.

Docking complete, Winning and Steamer headed for the bar on the club's lower deck. It was packed with families, friends and of course excited and eager sailors. Many wore caps indicating that they'd raced overseas, done the Hobart before or simply that their yacht had a major sponsor; the faded red Mount Gay Rum caps were among the real collector's items. Present also were a large group of "punters" who had just come to ogle, and several young ladies – "racer chasers" – who were keen to meet the competitors.

Winning and Steamer met up with sailing rival Don Mickleborough and some of his crew and enjoyed a few beers and plenty of laughs. Later, the pair headed for Winning's Vaucluse home where they would enjoy a Christmas Eve dinner with his wife, Stephanie, and the children.

After dinner, Steamer headed back to the yacht to sleep. He would take a cab home the next morning then go on for Christmas Day drinks at Richard "Sightie" Hammond's with Mickleborough and other competitors, followed by Christmas lunch with his mother, Eve, and "all the mob".

★

Julie Hodder wanted an ocean racing yacht while her husband, Kerry, wanted a Porsche. The end result was that on Boxing Day 1998 Julie set sail in the 54th Sydney to Hobart as one of three owners of the 50-footer *Foxtel-Titan Ford*. Her husband was driving a family sedan at the time.

"He tolerates the yacht," remarked the dark-haired 45 year old. "I think he likes keeping me happy. When we discussed our options – the yacht or the Porsche – we

traffic; no hassled people; no news." The long trips also allowed Julie to expand and consolidate her navigational skills. She envisaged one day being the navigator on an ocean going yacht and held a dream of owning an offshore racer.

Back in Australia, Julie served her apprenticeship as an understudy navigator and general crewmember aboard *Diamond Cutter*, one of the more competitive yachts out of Middle Harbour Yacht Club. She was rewarded with wins in the club's offshore championship and a Brisbane to Gladstone race.

"Navigating was certainly the way to go for me," said Julie. "I love ocean racing but I hate sitting on deck and getting wet. I like doing anything on the yacht where I can actually move. Even the cooking appeals. You don't need great big strong muscles to go and navigate. There are two other pluses for me – I don't get seasick and I love dabbling with computers and electronics. So navigation's the ideal job."

It was almost inevitable that the Sydney to Hobart would become part of her offshore sailing agenda and by the 1998 event she was a veteran of no fewer than five races.

☆

After returning from Hong Kong, Julie sailed on a number of yachts, mainly in distance events. She also participated along with hundreds of other sailors mid-week in the summer twilight "beer can" races. It was during these Wednesday night races that she and the former world 18-foot skiff champion, Peter Sorensen, began discussing the possibility of buying an offshore race yacht.

"I always wanted a boat but I could never figure out why people wanted to own a boat by themselves. It's better to share the costs and the fun. Pete and I always got along well. I liked the way he ran a boat – the way he used it all the time, Wednesdays, Thursdays and weekends – Pete was always out there. I was sort of thinking about a 40-footer. I thought that might be something that we could handle physically and financially. Then I realised he was thinking more along the lines of a 50-footer or 60-footer. That thought became a little easier for me to accept when he brought Stan Zemanek into the equation."

Zemanek, Australia's most successful night-time talk-back radio show host, had known Sorensen since they raced skiffs on Sydney Harbour decades earlier. With the syndicate formed, Hodder, Sorensen and Zemanek went out and purchased the 50-footer *Morning Mist III* from Melbourne in 1998. Their desire was essentially straightforward – to race hard and have a good time. Their initial target was the exclusive, invitation only Big Boat Series at Hayman Island in Queensland's Whitsunday region in August. *Morning Mist III* collected first prize in its division. The trio had a winner.

They were hoping their good fortune would continue the following week at Hamilton Island Race Week, but just eight miles out of Hayman their luck ran out. *Morning Mist III* ploughed into a reef travelling at a speed of eight knots. The structural damage to the hull and keel was so extensive that the insurers went close to considering it a write-off. Chastened but by no means defeated, Hodder, Sorensen and Zemanek decided that they should turn their attention to the Hobart race. The yacht was duly trucked back to Sydney for major surgery.

"The damage was massive," said Julie. "The hull had to be stripped of everything then turned upside down in a shed at McConaghy's boat yard. Almost the entire bottom of the hull had to be cut out and rebuilt."

The work took longer than anticipated. Plans to have *Morning Mist III* – now named *Foxtel-Titan Ford* – tested in lead-up races in late December evaporated. The keel was bolted back on and the yacht relaunched only days before the start.

The 1998 Hobart race would be its first sea trial.

☆

In August 1979 Paul "Tanzi" Lea was one of many people acclaimed as a hero in Britain. For three days he piloted a Royal Navy Sea King helicopter through a vicious storm over the Irish Sea, searching for disabled and sinking yachts and plucking survivors from the decimated fleet in the Fastnet Race. Fifteen competitors died that year along with two other sailors who were accompanying the fleet on a non-race yacht.

"I was actually on leave ... summer leave because it was August. I was sitting at home in the garden talking to some friends when the phone call came. They said, 'Look, there's a problem with the Fastnet Race. Can you come on out and help?'. Off I went and I think we were about the third Sea King to launch out of the air station at Culdrose."

The rescue effort was a distressing yet poignant climax to an impressive career which had begun at the age of 17. Lea had joined the Royal Navy in 1964 despite harbouring a desire to head for the skies rather than the sea. Eight years later his dream was realised when he was assigned to train with a Sea King squadron. In 1981 he came to Australia with his wife, Gill, and their two young children, Daniel and Joanne.

"I came on an exchange posting for just over two years," he said. "It was an opportunity we really looked forward to accepting. I did 10 months on the Sea Kings and then 15 months as an instructor with 723 squadron. It was a very enjoyable period in our life, so much so that when we went back to the UK the lifestyle that I'd experienced in Australia began to nag at me. In the end it got to me so much that I had no alternative but to sit down with my wife and children and talk about living in Australia."

Subsequently Lea re-established contact with the Royal Australian Navy and, after two years of negotiation, was offered a permanent job with the primarily land-based Sea King squadron at HMAS *Albatross* at Nowra, south of Sydney. He would go on to become the Chief Pilot and Commanding Officer.

In mid-1990, when they arrived in Australia, Lea and his wife were feeling confident about their new life. The children weren't so sure.

"After a few months however my eldest son, Daniel, said 'Dad, I want to stay here now'. Australia was home."

Just three years after arriving in Australia, Lea was called on to act as a guardian over the Sydney to Hobart fleet in the punishingly rough 1993 event. Having enjoyed a considerable amount of dinghy sailing over the years, the Sydney to Hobart rekindled an interest and he began to follow the race each year. When it came to the time for the 1998 race Lea was on leave, not stand-by, from HMAS *Albatross*.

"I remember hearing there might be a bit of dodgy weather around for the yachts but thought, oh we're covered, [even though] we only get twelve hours notice on an emergency. Sunday was a normal day for me. I went kayaking on the local river in the morning as I often do. In the afternoon it was the usual gardening ... that sort of stuff. At around seven o'clock the phone rang. The message was simply 'come on in'. Luckily I hadn't had a drink ... so I was at the base by 7.30pm."

Lieutenant Commander Tanzi Lea was again on his way to becoming a hero.

★

Rob Kothe was a relative newcomer to the Grand Prix level of ocean racing, but that didn't stop him from wanting to be a winner.

"I was always interested in sailing, so much so that in the fifties and sixties I was one of the young kids who listened to everything I could on the radio that had anything to do with sailing. I always listened to the call of the America's Cup on radio. You've got to be nutty to do that sort of stuff. The problem was that I lived out in the bush, on the other side of the Great Dividing Range, at Tumbarumba, down towards Canberra. I couldn't go sailing in the seventies so I was a sail plane competitor – a glider pilot. When I came to Sydney I realised that sail planing was out and sailing was in."

Kothe would later learn, as he increased his profile at the CYC, that he and fellow member George Snow, the owner of the maxi yacht *Brindabella*, used to share the same airspace gliding over the Brindabella Ranges near Canberra.

★

After a year away, Steve Kulmar had decided it was time to return to offshore racing.

"I needed a year away from the sport after sailing in the Admiral's Cup in England in 1997," Kulmar said. "I'd sailed boats every year of my life since I was eight. There had been little else in just about all of my social life and available time. I needed a break. I told a friend, Ron Jacobs, I was thinking about doing some casual sailing again. He encouraged me to meet with himself and Rob Kothe at the Oaks Hotel at Neutral Bay in late September. I found Kothe to be a nice enough bloke, and as keen as mustard. I thought, well I'll do a couple of races with them and see.

"I made it clear that I wasn't available all the time because I didn't want to get caught up in the full-on racing scene and immediately find myself back where I was a year earlier. If we thought we all liked each other, well, then I'd commit to a Hobart. It was a pretty casual arrangement." Kothe, Kulmar and the *Sword of Orion* crew did strike a chord and Kulmar committed to do the Hobart as a principal helmsman.

Kulmar and his wife Libby had been childhood friends in the Sydney waterfront suburb of Hunters Hill. Both sailed out of the local sailing club. Friendship blossomed into romance and they married in 1983 – but not before Steve had sailed in the Admiral's Cup that year. Libby knew she was marrying a man and his sport.

"I never had any qualms about Steve going ocean racing," she said. "Never. Not even in 1984 when I was pregnant with Pip and it was a rough race did I worry. I'd lie in bed at night, listen to the storm outside and say, 'Yeah, it's windy' but that was it. [Steve was aboard the eventual race winner, *Indian Pacific*, that year.] I didn't even worry about this race when we heard what it was going to be like."

It was the Kulmar family's turn to host Christmas lunch at their modern flat-roofed home overlooking Manly and the waters of the northern part of Sydney Harbour. The huge ceiling-to-floor windows afforded spectacular views and large doors ensured that summer sea breezes kept the occupants cool. A large swimming pool, aside from providing instant refreshment from the summer heat, was also a great benefit to daughters Pip, 13, and Madeline, 10, who were competitive swimmers.

"We had 33 people for lunch; family, friends and some sailors," recalls Libby. "It was glorious. The kids were in the pool all day having a great time. Everyone was talking about the race, they were keen to follow it, especially with Steve racing again."

Mindful that he probably wouldn't get much sleep over the ensuing days, Steve Kulmar slipped quietly away from the Christmas celebrations around mid-afternoon and went to bed. When he returned to the party after his "power nap" there were few guests left. The day wound down in a relaxed and convivial fashion and before long the entire Kulmar clan, including Libby's parents who were staying over, turned in as well.

Just 48 hours later Steve Kulmar would unwittingly be part of Australia's largest ever peacetime search and rescue operation.

Two
The Great Race

It was around VP Day – Victory in the Pacific Day for the Allies in 1945 – when a small group of offshore sailing enthusiasts decided they would hold a dinner one evening at Usher's Hotel in Sydney. Little more than 12 months earlier they had formed the Cruising Yacht Club of New South Wales (which would later become the Cruising Yacht Club of Australia). Prior to and during World War II Usher's was one of the classiest hotels in energetic downtown Sydney. It was where successful businessmen relaxed over a chilled ale at the end of a busy day and where ladies enjoyed being wined and dined in the plush comfort of the first-level dining room. The five-storey, dark-brick building was classically proportioned, and was located on one of the city's bustling thoroughfares, Castlereagh Street. Its robust design, with windows, doorways and awnings heavily highlighted, was typical of the colonial architecture of the time.

One of the CYC's founders, Peter Luke, knew that the Royal Navy's Chief Engineer at its wartime Sydney Harbour base at Woolloomooloo, Captain John Illingworth, was a pre-eminent ocean racing yachtsman from England. In fact it was said of Illingworth in one prominent Sydney magazine at the time: "He was perhaps the greatest exponent of sailing and ocean racing yet to visit Australia, and he greatly impressed Australian yachtsmen with knowledgeable lectures substantiated by victories in leading offshore and harbour events." Little wonder that Luke invited him to be the guest speaker at the dinner.

In its embryonic days, CYC members would hold what they described as "very informal and low-key" club meetings in the photographic studio owned by Peter Luke's father, Monty. It was next door to Usher's Hotel. When there was a need for members to get together over dinner it was usually at a small place near Wynyard, the mid-city rail and bus terminus. "It was called Sue's Café," Peter Luke said, "but the food they served was sufficiently bad for us to always call it the Greasy Spoon."

The dinner at Usher's was obviously a very special occasion. The small audience was captivated by Captain Illingworth's vivid stories of offshore racing in England. Later, as they relaxed over port and quality cigars, Bert Walker – who was the club's first president – remarked somewhat casually to Illingworth, "Jack Earl and I are cruising down to Hobart after Christmas. Why don't you join us?" Illingworth thought it a splendid idea and accepted the invitation. Enthusiastic conversation followed until someone in the group piped up, "Let's make a race of it."

The great race was conceived.

Until the proposal for the Hobart race surfaced most of the CYC's sailing activities had been short coastal hops out of Sydney. Over the Christmas–New Year period of 1944, Earl, Luke and a few others had ventured some 200 miles south on a cruise to the beautiful little coastal town of Eden, near the NSW–Victorian border. The success of that adventure had excited Earl and his family and they began talking about a casual cruise farther south the following Christmas. The plan was to sail aboard their stout ketch *Kathleen Gillett* – a veritable floating home.

It was pure coincidence that Earl and Walker – who were CYC founders – planned to cruise to Tasmania together. Earl, who later became a marine artist of international acclaim, was also the second Australian to cruise around the world. One weekend, when he and his family were aboard *Kathleen* and anchored off an isolated beach on Sydney Harbour, their plans took another step toward fruition.

Anchored nearby was Bert Walker's yacht, *Saltair*. Earl knew that Walker, a Tasmanian, would have charts of the Tasmanian coast so he rowed his small dinghy across to *Saltair* and asked permission to step aboard. "I thought I'd ask him about 'Tassie' [Tasmania] and the Derwent River. He got very excited about that and said he would like to join us, to make it a cruise in company." For the next hour the pair enjoyed a few drinks, checked charts of Tasmania and planned their voyage. Jack then rowed back to his yacht and revealed to his family the exciting new developments. It wasn't long before Peter Luke heard of the plans for the cruise and he asked if he could join them with his yacht, *Wayfarer*.

☆

Once the decision had been made at Usher's Hotel, there was no slowing the momentum. The start date was December 26, Boxing Day in Australia. It was considered to be an ideal time as it was the height of summer and it would allow competitors and their families to enjoy Christmas Day at home. Unfortunately, for Earl's family, their enthusiasm for the cruise to Hobart was soon replaced with the realisation that it was now a race. They would not be going along for the ride.

The first time the general public became aware of the event was via a printed addendum to a small article in the

October, 1945 edition of *Australian Power Boat and Yachting Monthly Magazine*. It was so small it could easily have gone unnoticed.

> **"Yacht Race to Tasmania; it is expected that an Ocean Yacht Race may take place from Sydney to Hobart probably starting on December 26, 1945. Yachtsmen desirous of competing should contact Vice President Mr P. Luke, 62 Castlereagh Street, Sydney, for information. Entries close December 1, 1945."**

The article preceding the addendum announced the results of a race conducted by "the Cruising Yacht Club of NSW" over 17 nautical miles from Sydney Harbour to Palm Beach. The sturdy 35-foot cutter *Maharani* (later abbreviated to *Rani*) and skippered by Captain J. Illingworth, was the winner.

The Notice of Race for the Sydney to Hobart was soon issued. It reminded competitors that "the setting of spinnakers is not permitted" – something in keeping with the cruising attitudes of those first entrants. A method of measuring and handicapping yachts was devised and a starting line chosen " from Flagstaff Point, off Quarantine Bay, 200 yards in length, with the starter's boat identified by a white CYC flag." The practice of the white CYC flag remains a club tradition to this day. The line was actually just inside the entrance to Sydney Harbour – to the north. In later years the race would start on the south side, closer to the CBD.

Contacted by the CYC, the Royal Yacht Club of Tasmania, in Hobart, agreed to manage the finish line while the Royal Australian Air Force agreed to schedule "flying exercises" for Catalina flyingboats over the course so they could report the position of any yacht sighted.

Word of the race was greeted with great enthusiasm by the daily press. The Australian public, still weary after five years of war, was in need of fresh excitement and adventure. This was it – a perfect panacea in the form of a daring 630-nautical mile voyage from NSW to Tasmania. Brave men, and at least one woman, would be fighting unpredictable and often tempestuous seas aboard small boats all in the name of fun.

As the start date approached there were 10 yachts registered to compete. At the last minute the Livingston brothers advised that their yacht, *Warrana*, was unable to get away from Melbourne in time to reach Sydney. In years to come, though, the Livingstons would leave an indelible mark on the history of the classic. They raced the famous yachts carrying the name *Kurrewa* with considerable success and they also donated a magnificent perpetual trophy, the F. & J. Livingston Trophy, for the first yacht to be positioned south of Tasman Island at the entrance to Tasmania's Storm Bay.

The first race provided the avid Australian newspaper readers and radio listeners with all the high drama and exhilaration they wanted. Front-page news headlines told of the fleet's plunge into the face of a fast-approaching southerly gale and the possibility that the storm had claimed *Rani*, Captain Illingworth and his crew. The Catalina flyingboats could only locate the 56-footer *Winston Churchill* at the head of the fleet. There was no sign of *Rani*. The flight crew didn't realise that Captain Illingworth had pushed on into the jaws of the storm while his rivals had slowed or even stopped. Lashed to the mast by ropes when on deck, Illingworth and his crew pressed on and sailed out of the blue into Storm Bay, 44 miles from the finish. They reached Hobart unscathed and received a tumultuous welcome from the people of the city. *Rani* claimed both the line honours trophy and the prize for being first on handicap.

Jack Earl, in his biography, saw that first race this way:

"We had a wonderful sail down the coast until we got to Montagu Island when a southerly buster hit us. Illingworth, we heard later, had reefed down and fore-reached *Rani* through it. He just refused to take any of the gear off her. His attitude was 'we will only have to put it back on again'. We reefed down and nursed our ship along in a very conservative fashion, and hove-to through that gale. Some of the boats actually put into the south coast ports. The crews of *Saltair* and *Abermerle* are supposed to have spent time ashore shooting rabbits and going to the movies.

"Illingworth just kept plugging away. He was out of radio contact for quite a few days and at one stage we all presumed he'd been lost. Well, of course, the rest is history. Illingworth won by a day. We were still mooching down the Tassie coast when we heard that he had suddenly popped up in Storm Bay. When we got right up into the Derwent there was a tremendous north-westerly gale. It blew 74 knots and really knocked the fleet about. We had a triple reefed main, a jib and a mizzen. But within a quarter of a mile of the line the breeze suddenly dropped and the Derwent was as flat as a millpond. It wasn't worth putting all that gear back on again so we just concentrated on getting across the finish. We came in third just behind *Winston Churchill*. We learned a few tricks from that first race and when I went down the following year as mate in Bob Bull's *Christina*, we pulled out all stops and we won."

Illingworth's remarkable effort in ploughing on through the worst of the gale and trouncing his opponents stimulated an enormous tide of public interest in the future of the event. *Australian Power Boat and*

Yachting Monthly's report on the race noted: "The hope that an ocean race would be held annually was expressed at a civic reception given by the Lord Mayor (Mr Soundy, MHA) at the Hobart Town Hall on January 8, 1946."

Responding to a speech by the Governor of Tasmania, Admiral Sir Hugh Binney, Captain Illingworth said he and his crew "had been deeply impressed by the welcome given them in Hobart, which was an ideal place at which to end an ocean race."

The race report continued: "The Cruising Yacht Club at Sydney and the Royal Yacht Club of Tasmania had launched the sport of ocean racing on a firm basis. A next step was for an Australian yacht to visit Great Britain and 'take the ashes away'. Every other branch of Australian sport had been represented in contests in Britain. The president of the CYC (Mr Walker), who sailed *Saltair*, said that nowhere else could yachtsmen have received a better welcome."

Walker was quoted as suggesting that when the next race was held it was likely to attract between 30 and 40 boats. "At no far distant time Australia should challenge the USA," he said. "We have the men in Hobart now who can steer a boat as well as and better than Mr Vanderbilt [the famed America's Cup defender]."

★

The Sydney to Hobart was soon confirmed as an annual event and it took only a few years for it to be acclaimed as one of the world's three "majors" in offshore racing – the others being the Fastnet Race out of England and America's Newport to Bermuda. All three events demanded the highest level of skill and endurance, regardless of the conditions.

In many respects the Sydney to Hobart is perhaps the greatest of them all. From the colourful start within the natural amphitheatre that surrounds Sydney's magnificent harbour, through to the finish at the waterfront dock area of the beautiful and historic city of Hobart, it is a race of guts, determination, majesty and splendour.

The 630-mile course is seen to have four distinct and always challenging components. There is the unpredictable and often savage Tasman Sea off the NSW south coast; the notorious Bass Strait crossing between mainland Australia and the island state of Tasmania where wild winds and shallow water can compress waves into massively powerful, foaming liquid mountains; the challenging stretch down the Tasmanian coast and across the often appropriately named Storm Bay where bitterly cold winds can sweep in from the Antarctic region and bring a freezing winter chill to high summer, and finally there's the test presented by the last stretch, the 11 nautical miles up the Derwent River

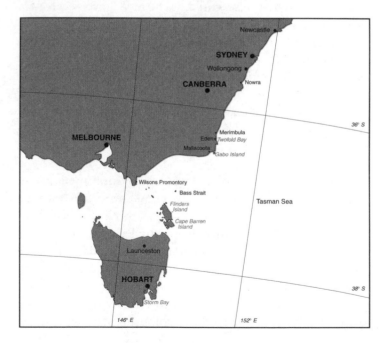

to the finish line. Anywhere on this course the whim of the wind gods can take you from calm to calamity in a flash – even on the river.

The Sydney to Hobart is an unpredictable race, at times serene at others terrifying. A gentle spinnaker ride down the coast with the sun warming one's back is like a sleigh ride across smooth new snow. The first light of the new day, where the darkest of nights ever so slowly gives way to dawn's palette of pastels, is an experience few could forget.

Roger Hickman, a highly experienced offshore racer and race veteran, sees the appeal of ocean racing in general, and the Hobart race in particular, this way: "Ocean racing takes place in the stadium of life. It's not as though you're inside some artificially heated and lit stadium. It's got all the features of 'why do people climb Mount Everest'. It's something you just have to do. There is this wonderful challenge to complete the race and be safe. Thrown in with this is the most romantic environment in the world. You get all the benefits of the wind, the sea, the sun, the moon and the stars plus the spectacle of marine life. It's all rolled into something that is competitive. It's the absolute classic situation where man, or woman, is pitted against the elements.

"It is certainly an 'on-the-edge' sport like skydiving, motor racing, football and so many others. You cannot be under the illusion at any time that it is safe. Like any other 'on-the-edge' sport, ocean racing can be extremely dangerous. That is an aspect we all accept. Unbridled dangers have always been a vital part of life. Ocean racing delivers those dangers plus moments of beauty that will be with you for the rest of your life."

While Mother Nature will always create the rules and decide the result, it's the competitors, the camaraderie, the teamwork and the stamina which make the race what it is. For some sailors, like Sydney's Richard "Sightie" Hammond, you cannot get enough of the Sydney to Hobart. The 1998 race was his 40th start. A record. For him and so many others, Christmas Day is more like Boxing Day eve – the eve of the start of the Hobart. Hammond has a host of Hobart race stories, but the one he recalls with the most clarity is his first race in 1952. It was baptism by fire – or more specifically, ice. He was aboard the aging Tasman schooner *Wanderer* that year and he remembers that both the yacht and its owner, Eric Massey, were very old.

"I went for the adventure. To race to Hobart was something just about every young sailor wanted to do. I was one of the lucky few to secure a ride."

Hammond thought his initiation was complete when a howling southerly buster with winds gusting up to 40 knots swept across the fleet off the NSW south coast. Massey considered the conditions to be so bad at the height of the storm that he ordered that the yacht ride it out with all sails lowered.

Worse was to come.

First it was torment. *Wanderer* had made such slow progress south that on New Year's Eve it was caught in a windless hole just off the coast at St Helens, near the north-east corner of Tasmania. The crew could only listen to the celebrations on shore. The torment turned to torture soon after *Wanderer* entered the appropriately named Storm Bay and was blasted by a wild sou'westerly gale.

"It was blowing 60 knots, the seas were raging and the spray was near horizontal," Hammond said. "To say it was bitterly cold was an understatement – there was bloody ice on the mast. Without doubt it was the most memorable Hobart race I have ever done, partly because it was my first and partly because it was so rugged and cold."

It wasn't enough to turn Hammond away from the sport. He went on to become one of Australia's best ocean racing navigators – hence the nickname "Sightie" because in the old days he was always taking sun sights with his sextant.

Another yachtsman who wasn't deterred from going back to the Hobart race after a horrific experience was Sydneysider Jim McLaren. In 1956 he competed for the second time, on this occasion aboard his own yacht, the 30-footer *Vailima*, a tiny double-ended yacht that had been built by its original owner in a suburban backyard. According to McLaren, it was a race in which "not much happened". For most sailors it would have been a race where plenty happened. "We had a southerly when we cleared Sydney Heads, another southerly change off the NSW south coast then a third, a beauty, as we entered Bass Strait. Three bloody fronts before we got to halfway.

"The last one was from the south west. The wind got to 86 knots – bloody hard. I don't think the seas were as big as what they experienced in the 1998 race, but the same wind and rain were certainly there. You couldn't sail in it. We had to go down to bare poles. We did manage to set the sea anchor but it took only one big wave to break the rope attached to it. The same wave took out the forward hatch. After that we could only run with it. We felt like we were heading for New Zealand. I was getting a bit worried because we could only hang on and hope. We were like that for 24 hours."

McLaren and his crew set sail again and eventually crossed Bass Strait unscathed. Then, off Tasmania's east coast they suffered the indignity of having the wind evaporate completely. Finally they reached Hobart – almost eight days after leaving Sydney. But they weren't last to finish. Another entry, P. S. Parry's *Renene*, took almost 10 days. McLaren declared he would never race south again.

He finished up building his own yacht and competing in four more. His love of the sea spread to his children. In June 1988, his daughter, Kay Cottee, became the first woman to sail single-handed, non-stop and unassisted around the world.

★

The Sydney to Hobart has attracted a vast cross-section of competitors over its long history. It has fascinated a Prime Minister and a Premier, numerous media magnates, millionaires and billionaires and countless average "Joes" from Struggle Street. Edward Heath, who was later to become Britain's Prime Minister, won the race in 1969 with his 34-foot sloop *Morning Cloud*. Heath thought it was appropriate that on the 25th anniversary of Illingworth's victory, another "Brit" had taken the honours. Three years later, high profile American media man Ted Turner posted a rare double in being both first to finish and then being awarded outright victory – the corrected time, or handicap, trophy.

Rupert Murdoch competed with his own yacht, *Ilina*, in the early sixties but would have to wait until 1995 before he experienced the thrill of victory. He was aboard the sleek, white-hulled maxi *Sayonara* owned by friend and business associate Larry Ellison, head of the Oracle computer software company. Murdoch's son Lachlan was to be aboard the same yacht for the 1998 race.

★

While an addiction for some, the Sydney to Hobart has cured many sailors of the desire to ocean race. There is of course only one certain cure for seasickness – sitting under a tree!

The 1998 race was the 34th pilgrimage south for 74-year-old Sydneysider Don Mickleborough. Surprisingly, when asked why so many people kept going back, he had trouble answering. "I'm buggered if I know why we keep doing it," said this carefree man with a permanent grin on his face. "I guess it's the camaraderie. It's just that you are out there with your friends. You face the best and the worst of the conditions and have to work hard to get through. I suppose if I couldn't sail to Hobart with my mates I wouldn't bother going." Then, after pondering the question a little longer, "OK. Yes. It's the parties. Sure the race is there as a race. But it also gets you from one good party to an even better one."

One party stands out in the memories of many. It was back in 1962 when the Sydney to Hobart really went international for the first time. Wealthy New York ship broker, Sumner A. "Huey" Long, had brought over what was then the world's ultimate racing yacht, *Ondine*, to challenge Australia's best. It was a truly exceptional piece of boat building possessing a unique aluminium hull painted pale blue. It was dubbed the "Yankee yawl". Huey Long was justifiably confident.

But much to his dismay, and to the surprise of almost all observers, *Ondine* didn't get it all her own way. It was only when the big Sydney schooner, *Astor*, had her billowing spinnaker deflate after the massive wooden spinnaker pole that was holding it aloft splintered, that Long managed to bring his state-of-the-art yacht from behind to win. He made it home by just 100 yards. It was a sweet victory indeed for Long because *Ondine* also established a new mark for the 630-mile course – three days, three hours, 46 minutes and 16 seconds. But Long's hope for the double victory went as limp as *Astor*'s spinnaker when Vic Meyer's powerful steel racer, *Solo*, sailed in and claimed the ultimate handicap trophy – the prize for having the best corrected time for the course.

Long was not happy. He was certain *Solo* had broken race rules. He flew to Launceston in northern Tasmania seeking aerial photographs he believed were in existence. He was sure these photographs would show *Solo*'s life raft was not, as required under race rules, carried on deck. At five o'clock the morning after Long left for Launceston there was a party still in full swing aboard *Astor* on Hobart's historic waterfront. It included a young Rupert Murdoch (who had just moved to Sydney from Adelaide and taken over the ownership of the *Daily Mirror* newspaper) and many of the crew who had been with him for the race aboard his yacht *Ilina* – "Thunder", "Rawmeat", "Curley" and Don (who went under the nick name of "Don Two" because there already was a "Don Juan"). While they partied, *Ondine* sat silently at the dock nearby, devoid of all signs of human activity.

Long's actions became the subject of much debate with the revellers aboard *Astor*. The consensus was that instead of hunting for *Solo*, and the win he felt he deserved, he should be enjoying life as a hospitable host in post-race celebrations aboard his yacht. It did not take much for some of those aboard *Astor* to decide they would help out. An *Ondine* party would happen – with or without Huey Long.

Murdoch, ably assisted by one of his newspaper managers, "Curley" Brydon, convinced a local printer he was *Ondine*'s owner and had a thousand impressive party invitations printed. They were "Ondine blue" and advised of a celebration taking place aboard the yacht at 8pm the next evening. The "planning committee" moved to the local hotel that afternoon. There Murdoch, Mickleborough, Brydon and friends hand-addressed the invitations to everyone from the Lord Mayor of Hobart to the local pipe band; the Marine Board, the nurses' quarters of the Hobart hospital and owners of other competing yachts.

"They were signed 'hope you can make it, Huey'," Mickleborough recalled. "And just to cover our bases I had my brother in Launceston send a telegram to *Ondine*'s sailing master, Sven Joffs, in Hobart, asking him to ready the yacht for the party. He signed it 'Huey'."

By 8pm there were spectacular scenes around Constitution Dock. Murdoch and company had sufficient 18-gallon kegs of beer delivered to the area in front of *Ondine* to satisfy the considerable thirst of the assembled guests. With no sign of Huey Long, Joffs, an extremely dedicated yacht manager, stood on the deck looking bemused if not bewildered. All the time he was easing out the dock lines to make it impossible for those onshore to step aboard. As the pipe band played the Lord Mayor's car slowly made its way through the crowd. The Lord Mayor alighted to be greeted by the call for "three rousing British cheers".

It soon became apparent this was a "no-host party". But in Hobart you don't need a host, in fact you don't really need a reason for a party. Eventually Huey Long arrived and it took him no time to realise what was happening. He retreated rapidly to his hotel and spent the next few hours trying unsuccessfully to charter an aircraft out of town.

"Sadly, Huey missed a great party," Mickleborough said. "Even the police joined in."

Huey Long suffered no long-term effects after the 1962 post-race celebrations, and the magic of Hobart brought him back again and again with successively bigger yachts in the years that followed.

★

The second Sydney to Hobart, in 1946, attracted a fleet of 19 starters and confirmed the race's future. Once again the colourful comments and plaudits flowed following its completion. *Seacraft* magazine's headline read: "Small Yacht Wins Again ... *Christina*'s great victory proves that the present generation can provide its full quota of iron men to sail the wooden ships."

The following year the fleet expanded to 28, but further growth stalled until 1956. From that year on the Sydney to Hobart continued to grow through to 1985 when a fleet of 180 set sail. Nothing could compare though with the 50th anniversary race in 1994. In what was to be one of the greatest assemblies of ocean racing yachts and talent the world had seen, a staggering 371 yachts lined up on Sydney Harbour. It was an unprecedented show of strength even by international standards.

Accompanying the growth of the race over more than five decades has been the steady development of one of the best safety and communication networks covering any of the world's major offshore events. Due to the probability of inclement, if not downright ferocious, weather, the Sydney to Hobart has become an annual testbed for race organisation, yacht design and hull construction. Top international sailors like New Zealander Geoff Stagg do this race as often as possible "for a reality check". Stagg, who is the representative-at-large for the world's most successful ocean racing yacht designer, Bruce Farr of Annapolis in Maryland, was aboard the 1997 race winner, *Beau Geste*. He reckons the Sydney to Hobart stresses just about everything – the structure, rig, sails and crew. "The Hobart is a bloody great race. I think it's actually tougher than an around-the-world race because I don't think the around-the-world racers get anything like the extreme conditions you get in a Hobart race. The Hobart race also demands a good all-round boat. One-way machines rarely do any good. In fact very few of them actually finish." Stagg said that one of the most difficult aspects lay with the crew and what was demanded of them.

"You need a real balance. It's hard for the crew in the middle of the boat to understand that in a race like the Hobart they have to stay on the rail [sitting on the windward side of the deck] around the clock when you are belting upwind. Their weight is crucial to the performance of the yacht. It doesn't matter how tired you are, you have to stay there. At the same time we have to get the helmsman and [sail] trimmer who are off watch down below to rest. Having them rested for their next watch is just as crucial as having the remaining crew on the rail. When the moment presents itself, when we crack off or set spinnakers, that's when the bulk of the crew can catch up on a lot of sleep. That's the key to winning races. It's a team effort. If you don't do that you're not serious about winning."

★

There are numerous impressive statistics associated with the Sydney to Hobart. Prior to the 1998 event, a total of 4230 yachts had faced the starter and they had carried more than 35,000 competitors. Considering the extreme dangers, it was remarkable that only two sailors had died as a result of injuries suffered aboard their respective boats. Incredibly no one had been lost overboard and not recovered – a fact that many saw as evidence of solid safety procedures and rigid race organisation – plus an occasional dose of good fortune.

The most remarkable stories of survival came out of the 1993 event – one of the toughest on record before the 1998 race. A southerly gale with winds gusting up to 50 knots and a fast-flowing opposing current combined to whip up mountainous waves off the NSW south coast. Conditions were so severe that of the 104 yachts that started, only 38 finished.

Around midnight on the second night a huge breaking wave overwhelmed the 35-foot sloop *MEM*. The yacht capsized and owner–skipper John Quinn was hurled into the sea after the sheer force of the broken water caused his safety harness to break. Quinn surfaced and was faced with the horror of seeing his yacht sailing away. The crew knew he was overboard and were desperately searching, but they could not see him. Other race yachts and ships rushed to the area to search but Quinn was rated as having very little chance of surviving in the horrendous conditions. Every 15 minutes or so a colossal breaking wave more than 40-feet high would sweep through the area, so powerful that it would hurl a man around like a soggy rag doll. After four unsuccessful hours of searching, the worst was feared. Race officials discussed writing his obituary. They were unaware Quinn, aided by a light buoyancy vest, was still alive and was duck-diving under each immense breaking wave.

"The only time I really started to get a bit desperate was right at the end and that was for a very short period of time," Quinn said. "At that stage the buoyancy vest I was wearing was losing some of its buoyancy and I was starting to take water and get tired. A while later, as I rode to the top of one big wave, I saw it – the most beautiful Christmas tree you have ever seen. It was a bloody big ship with all lights blazing coming ever so slowly towards me. At one moment I thought the ship was going to pass without anyone spotting me because it was coming down the drift at an angle and the stern, where all the lookouts were gathered on the bridge and using searchlights, was the most distant point from me. My heart began to sink.

"Then a big wave picked up the stern and knocked it sideways towards where I was. Suddenly the ship was right there, just metres away. I started to yell my lungs out 'Hey, hey, hey!' I shouted. Brent Shaw, who was manning a searchlight, first heard my yells then spotted me. He was fantastic. After hearing me shout he got the searchlight on me and started to shout out 'I've got you. I can see you.'"

While the searchlight was trained on Quinn, the race yacht *Atara*, which was just astern and damaged but still searching, moved in to drag him aboard. It had been five freezing hours since he'd fallen overboard. He was 50 miles offshore.

There was a wry link between this incident and the very first Sydney to Hobart. John Quinn's father Harry had bought *Rani* from Captain Illingworth soon after it won the first race and in 1959 he had taken John and two family friends on a fishing trip to Port Stephens, north of Sydney. A storm moved in so they anchored *Rani* off the deserted Broughton Island and went ashore to spend the night in an old fisherman's hut. Battered by the fierce waves, *Rani* dragged its anchor that night and was wrecked on a coastal beach a few miles away. With no sign of survivors an aerial search was mounted and eventually the four were spotted on Broughton Island, but with conditions so severe, they had to wait four days to be rescued by a boat.

The 1993 Quinn incident brought yet another review of race safety standards and search and rescue operations. Yet again it was the Hobart race that would lead the world towards new standards.

Former Sydney to Hobart race director, Gordon Marshall, told of one big change that the Hobart race brought to international yacht design: "We heard alarm bells in the early to mid-seventies when the lightweight, skiff-type yachts arrived on the scene. In one race only one of six of these lightweights reached Hobart. It was apparent they couldn't handle rough conditions. In fact they were dangerous because they carried the minimum amount of ballast and the maximum amount of crew weight to keep them upright. The yachts were also extremely wide so the crew could sit out on the side and have their weight contribute towards keeping the yacht as level as possible. At one stage the hulls were becoming so wide and the keels so small they probably would have stayed upside down had they capsized.

"We had no option but to introduce stability factors into race rules. Yachts had to prove they were stable and self-righting before being allowed to compete. It was one rule that went on to become universally accepted around the world and in turn ocean racing became safer."

Even in the early 1990s some people did not like the trend they were seeing in the design of yachts. In December 1990 the late Alan Payne – a legendary Australian yacht designer – had his thoughts printed in a story in *The Weekend Australian*. "Bad weather could turn Sydney–Hobart into a racing catastrophe. Modern yachts not safe in heavy seas." He referred ominously to "the 100-year storm".

"I'm not talking about the blows they normally experience in a race where the wind gets up for a few hours then abates and everyone gets to Hobart and says how tough it was," Payne said. "I'm talking about the extreme conditions where huge seas break. These waves can really happen in the worst conditions on these race courses [he was referring to the Melbourne to Hobart and Melbourne to Devonport races]. These are the conditions where the yachts will fail structurally, where they will be capsized and where rigs break. The problems are that they aren't strong enough, or in the event of a capsize are so stable in the inverted position that they don't want to come upright."

Eight years later, in the 1998 race, much of what Payne predicted *could* happen *did* happen. His theories were based on considerable research into what sea conditions would be developed by a 35-knot gale in Bass Strait over a 24-hour period. He said that it was inevitable in those conditions that every yacht would see a wave of at least 33 foot (10 metres) in height on the 150-mile fetch from Gabo Island, off the mainland, across to Flinders Island, off Tasmania's north-east corner. In fact many of the 1998 Hobart fleet saw winds of around 70 knots – twice as strong as those on which Payne based his predictions. His calculations suggested three yachts would completely disappear, taking 22 people with them; six crew would be lost overboard; three life rafts containing 12 people would never be found and a rescue helicopter would crash while on a mission.

It was apparent after the 1998 race that if it hadn't been for the herculean rescue effort and the fact that much of the drama occurred in relatively close proximity to the south-east corner of the Australian mainland, Alan Payne's predictions could well have come true. While generally accepting his comments, ocean racing authorities have always been quick to stress that the standards covering design, construction, communications and safety equipment are among the most stringent in the world.

In the early days of racing to Hobart the oft-heard comment was "wooden yachts and iron men". Today, many of the sailors who manned those heavily timbered craft look at the modern yachts made of fibreglass and space age materials and mumble "plastic yachts and plastic men". One of the greatest sailors to come out of the Hobart race, Magnus Halvorsen (who with brother Trygve won three consecutive races aboard *Freya* between 1963–65), refers to contemporary offshore yachts as "cocktail shakers".

But modern ocean racing yachts represent the very latest in design technology, materials and equipment. Instead of starting life as a series of pencil sketches, drawings and half models that are eyeballed by the builder, the yachts more often than not germinate within the "mind" of a powerful computer. Working within basic parameters determined by the owner (primarily length and budget), the designer and his team begin formulating a shape based on the limitations of the handicapping rule and the optimum performance attainable for a yacht of the desired size. The general rule of thumb is that the greater the waterline length of the yacht and the larger the sail area, the faster the boat will be. Hull shapes are usually analysed by a computer then tank-tested before a decision on the final shape is made.

Engineers must design the structure using proven laminate information and calculations which are generated by a computer that tests the loads on the hull, deck, keel and rudder. Apart from fibreglass, other exotic materials such as carbon fibre, Kevlar and honeycomb or foam cores are used. Often the hulls are baked in a huge oven to achieve maximum strength.

Indeed the technology and techniques used are not that far away from those employed in spacecraft construction. Almost the entire vessel, from hull to rig to sails, is handcrafted, a painstaking process that can take up to six months. Because of the intricate nature of the construction, the yachts are extremely vulnerable if not built to precise specifications. Modifications which disrespect the very nature of a one-piece structure – a monocoque – are usually catastrophic. This type of structure is literally only as strong as its weakest part, a principle which was clearly illustrated in the 1988 race.

Rod Muir's new spare-no-expense, space-age maxi *Windward Passage II* was deemed to have a mortgage on line honours and probably the course record. Approaching Bass Strait the yacht was doing everything expected of it – leading the fleet and bettering the record pace set by *Kialoa* in 1975. But Mother Nature threw a spanner in the works in the form of a howling sou'westerly gale. Initially the *Windward Passage II* crew answered the challenge of the rising seas and howling winds and kept the race record in their sights. Without warning, in the middle of the night, the entire crew heard a sickening crack. A quick check found an ugly split had developed across the deck near the cockpit which, if the yacht had continued in the race, could have expanded and led to total structural failure.

In an instant *Windward Passage II* had gone from brilliant to busted. It turned out someone had cut a small hole in the deck laminate to accommodate a compass, hadn't reinforced the area and thus the structural integrity of the hull had been compromised. As one crewmember put it, if *Windward Passage II* had continued in the race there was a chance "the back half of the boat would have fallen off".

Compare that incident with *Rani*'s problems in the first race. Its crew stuffed a blanket into a gap in the planks to slow a leak so they could continue!

Improvements in design, construction and materials have seen a steady increase in the speeds at which the yachts travel. Interestingly, it took 21 years for the record set by the now vintage American maxi ketch *Kialoa* in 1975 – where she took just two days,

14 hours, 36 minutes and 56 seconds – to be bettered. In 1996 the German giant, *Morning Glory*, owned by Hasso Plattner, scraped a mere 30 minutes off the record. *Kialoa* and the rest of the fleet had a dream run in 1975. Spinnakers were set as soon as they cleared the Sydney heads and from there on it was smooth sailing all the way down to Hobart. Such ideal conditions are rarely encountered.

A telling comparison can be drawn between the first race in 1945 and the gale-lashed 1993 event where only 38 of the 102 starters finished. The 1993 fleet struggled against headwinds and mountainous seas all the way south in what was considered a slow race. Of the 1945 fleet only the fastest yacht, *Rani*, had an elapsed time which would have positioned her before the slowest yachts in 1993 – she would have crossed the line 34th. Compared to the 1992 race *Rani* would have finished one and a half days behind the slowest yacht.

★

International media interest in the Sydney to Hobart race has always ensured it receives prominent publicity. At the same time, Australia's general media – television, newspapers and radio – have elevated the event to the status of prime-time, compulsory Boxing Day entertainment. Its start is the subject of a two-hour national live television coverage; it is always front page and headline news; and hundreds of thousands of spectators either watch from home, headlands and beaches on the harbour shores or cram the omnipresent and colourful flotilla of boats that gather to farewell the fleet.

The media's enthusiasm for procuring first-hand and exclusive information from the fleet stretches back to the earliest races. There have been many industrious, almost ingenious efforts, to get "the scoop", and none more so than that hatched by the Sydney *Sun* newspaper's yachting writer, Lou D'Alpuget (father of writer Blanche), and the then young journalist Frank McNulty back in 1947.

D'Alpuget wanted an exclusive and he saw McNulty, who was crewing on the yacht *Moonbi*, as his source. D'Alpuget didn't want to use radio communications because they were then subject to consumption by anyone who was listening. So, when *Moonbi* set sail on Boxing Day that year, it had on board three additional guests – homing pigeons! After two days at sea McNulty did as planned. He pencilled onto cigarette papers a report on the yacht's progress and attached them to the legs of the birds.

"I took the pigeons onto the deck and released them, but they refused to leave," he said. "I think they were seasick. I held them up and they just fluttered back to the deck. Eventually I took a bird in my cupped hands and began swinging it towards the sky. After a few swings I let the bird go and sure enough it flapped off towards the coast."

D'Alpuget got his scoop.

In the nineties the media's thirst for Hobart race news has not abated. It starts weeks before the event every year. The official television network treats viewers to a one-hour special on preparations some 10 days before Boxing Day.

★

In 1998 the Christmas Eve pre-race briefing was big news. Roger Badham had been quoted in *The Australian* as saying there was plenty of wind brewing for the fleet.

"A high casualty rate is the likely scenario when a forecast southerly buster hits the fleet within 24 hours of the start of the Telstra Sydney to Hobart yacht race on Boxing Day." He went on to say the approaching front that was originally expected on Christmas Day had slowed dramatically. It now appeared it would pummel the fleet during the first night at sea or early the next morning.

"I'm beginning to wonder how God knows it's time for a Hobart race," Badham said. "The pattern looks like it will be very similar to what we have seen in most of the recent Hobart races. That means a nor'easterly wind for the start and a fast spinnaker run down the coast before the fleet hits a brick wall in the form of a southerly buster. It's still a little early to make an accurate prediction on whether or not the conditions will give the frontrunners a shot at the race record, but if I had to stick my neck out now I'd say it won't happen. The indications from all the computer models we have available say that it looks like the wind will be quite soft off the Tasmanian coast. That will slow the leaders for some time."

Badham said the southerly buster was likely to deliver winds of between 25 and 30 knots for between 12 and 24 hours. The wind was then likely to change direction towards the east and abate.

The forecast conditions for the first 24 hours of the 1998 event were uncannily similar to those experienced in the 1996 event. George Snow's maxi *Brindabella* led Hasso Plattner's *Morning Glory* for the first three hours of the race before losing its mast soon after the southerly hit. The *Morning Glory* crew reacted to the change in a remarkably conservative fashion – fearing dismasting or structural problems they lowered the mainsail completely and set a headsail. It was a wise move and they survived under that configuration until the wind began to ease then went on to set the record.

☆

At the 1998 pre-race briefing the official weatherman, Ken Batt, injected some Christmas spirit when he appeared in front of his eager audience wearing a Santa Claus hat. He was short on weather "gifts" however and admitted the pattern was becoming a little difficult to predict. It appeared the southerly buster would certainly hit the first night out, but there was also a low lurking off the east coast and it was showing signs that it might move south. The competitors and the media left the briefing room faced with a lot of "ifs and maybes".

"It was really the first Hobart race that I'd done in a number of years where I felt there was an unresolved, an absolutely unresolved, weather pattern," recalls Steve Kulmar. "There was a divergence of opinion. Ken had started by saying the three models disagreed. The only thing they could agree upon was that we'd run into the change in the first 24 hours. The computer models were saying, 'We think there's a low pressure system somewhere up off Coffs Harbour, which is going to have an influence over here but we can't agree on the direction it will travel.' I think the European model was saying there's a low pressure in the [Great Australian] Bight and it's the major influence. So I guess I left that weather briefing thinking we'll just have to catch up and look at it in detail on Boxing Day morning."

Unknown to everyone, Mother Nature was setting a trap.

Three
The Anticipation

A magnificent summer day dawned over Sydney Harbour on December 26, 1998. Steve and Libby Kulmar awoke around 6.30am to the first silver shafts of sunlight dancing on the glassy waters of the harbour off Forty Baskets Beach. Steve noticed that a heavy dew had settled on the lawn during the night. In Sydney that could only mean that a strong nor'easterly sea breeze would develop in the afternoon, a breeze that would make for great racing under spinnaker.

As always Steve's mother had made a boiled fruit cake for the crew. While breakfast was being prepared Libby cut this moist and dark homemade treat into sections so everyone on board could enjoy two slices each. She was tempted to taste it but resisted out of superstition and tradition. Meanwhile Steve methodically packed his gear, and went to great lengths to ensure everything would stay dry.

Libby's parents, John and Nerolie – "Noo" to everyone – were also up for breakfast. John planned to go to the club with them to enjoy the sights and farewell Steve. After that he and Noo would head north to the central coast where they would holiday at picturesque Avoca Beach.

"Why don't you come up for a few days while Steve's away?" Noo asked Libby over breakfast.

"Oh, I don't think I'll come up. I think I'm going to have to pick up Steve." Libby's response shocked her after she'd said it. In recalling those comments Libby did not know what had prompted her. "I've never ever said anything like that before Steve had gone to do any other ocean race. We've always expected him to finish in Hobart and he has. I just can't explain why I said it."

The latest weather forecasts confirmed nothing much had changed. There would be a nice nor'easterly for the start, then a south to sou'westerly change during the night – a typical southerly buster for what was shaping up as a typical Hobart race. There was, however, still an element of uncertainty about the intentions of a low that was lingering off the NSW coast and what impact an upper air disturbance might have on conditions in Bass Strait. Roger Badham was already well on his way to the CYC from his home at Coledale, south of Sydney. He had been up almost the entire night analysing the very latest local and international computer models of the developing weather patterns.

Badham had outlined what he expected to happen, what to look out for and what the many potential scenarios might be. Most of the race's high profile competitors were relying on him to provide them with the answers to the mysteries of meteorology – answers that would give them the best possible chance of winning. Badham's briefcase carried satchels with the name of each yacht he was servicing written on the outside: *Sayonara*, *Brindabella*, *Wild Thing*, *ABN AMRO Challenge*, *B-52*, and many others.

"This is a typical Hobart race – with the southerly change – but this is one of the most

difficult in recent years to accurately pinpoint the wind changes due to an intense low that looks set to develop near Tasmania," he said.

"The low is associated with an upper cold air trough [and fast moving fronts] that will produce heaps of breeze south of Tasmania and things look pretty reasonable on the Tassie coast. Over Bass Strait – well it depends exactly where the low develops – how close to Tasmania ... but best guess is not too far south and the forecast at the time of writing this [early hours of December 26] is for quite strong winds across Bass Strait on the 27th and slowly moderating winds on the 28th.

"This afternoon/tonight, 26 December: nor'easterly sea breeze in the afternoon ahead of a southerly front expected around midnight. This is a sou'westerly change through Bass Strait and a southerly (180°) change along the NSW coast. This is really a trough system and thunderstorms are likely with and ahead of the trough. Late yesterday, storms gave short wind squalls of 50 to 60 knots across Victoria – this will be the case again this afternoon, so be prepared. A low in the Tasman looks like being absorbed into the trough/front and sliding down the front to be off Tasmania tomorrow.

"Sunday 27 December: high pressure must wait over the Great Australian Bight while a low pressure system spins up south east of Tasmania. The high will ridge along the Victorian coast and north Bass Strait around the NSW corner, but if the low really spins up, then it will be the cyclonic circulation around this that will dominate Bass Strait."

The one word that stood out was "cyclonic". Americans call it a hurricane.

There was plenty already happening when Badham and his wife Margaret arrived at the CYC to deliver the eagerly-awaited forecasts. The weather predictions would determine the planned sail inventory for the race, the yacht's course and tactics for the first 12 hours, and how the yacht might be configured for maximum performance. The docks were jammed with sailors, supporters, spectators and media. Wheelbarrows laden with supplies, ice, crew bags and yacht equipment were being deftly guided through the crush to their respective destinations. High in the forest of masts and what seemed to be the tangle of rigging supporting them, crewmembers were swinging around like monkeys on strings, scanning for potential problems. Television crews with bulky cameras on their shoulders panned, tilted and zoomed in and out to capture the pre-race atmosphere. Reporters were busy interviewing the race identities.

Tom Sobey, a 17 year old from Albury on the NSW–Victorian border, was attracting a lot of attention. His efforts the previous day to hitch a ride aboard a race yacht had failed. Undaunted, he decided to give it one more shot on Boxing Day. From 7am he had walked the docks at the CYC with signs pinned to the front and back of his shirt. The scrawled red writing read "Crew available". Sobey had just finished his final year of high school and had come to Sydney on the off chance that he might be able to snaffle a ride to Hobart. Like so many young sailors raised in a world of dinghy racing, Sobey regarded the Hobart as the ultimate event. But 1998 was not to be his year, and as the fleet set sail, Tom Sobey watched from the shore.

★

As Steve Kulmar was leaving for the CYC on Boxing Day morning, he stopped by his daughter Pip's room, gave her a kiss on the cheek and whispered goodbye. A muffled grunt from a head firmly buried in a pillow was the only response he received. Later, as Steve and the other family members drove towards the Sydney Harbour Bridge, a personal concern unrelated to the race or the weather conditions niggled him. He hated the fact that the yacht was at the crowded club on race day and much preferred it when the preparations were done elsewhere. He didn't enjoy having to struggle with his bags through a crowd just to get to the yacht. But just like the weather conditions, this was something that was out of his control.

Sailors, wannabes, socialites, media types and countless curious spectators had been gathering at the club since the early hours of the morning. For some, but not everyone, navigating through the throng had indeed become a tricky business. Paul Borg, from Mooloolaba in Queensland, confidently made his way along the dock with a white cane in one hand and a friendly arm to hang onto. He was heading for *Aspect Computing* – the yacht manned by the group competing under the banner "Sailors with DisAbilities". Borg had lost his sight two years earlier yet was determined to continue sailing. Also in the *Aspect Computing* crew was 12-year-old Travis Foley, a dyslexic from Mudgee and the race's youngest competitor.

The smell of breakfast – bacon and eggs cooking on the club's outdoor barbecue, toast and freshly brewed coffee – filled the air as sailors clad in their colourful T-shirts and shorts mingled with the punters wearing their best summer attire. In the small carpark at the side of the club, crewmembers waited anxiously for representatives from the Bureau of Meteorology to arrive with the official race forecast. Out on the street others were paying

$10 and throwing their excess baggage, cruising sails for the trip home, inflatable dinghies and spare equipment into the back of the large truck that was heading to Hobart. Excess weight would slow a yacht down and only the bare essentials could be taken on board.

George Snow, property developer and owner of Australia's glamour maxi, *Brindabella*, was having his hand shaken and his back slapped as he struggled through the crowd to get to his 75-foot racer at the end of the marina.

"Good luck, mate. Make sure you beat those Americans," came a call from the crowd. It was a nice thought, but deep down Snow and his enthusiastic supporter both knew that the odds were against his "old girl" beating the triple world champion *Sayonara*. A few hundred metres to the north, at d'Albora Marinas, *Sayonara*'s owner, the trim, fit and energetic Larry Ellison, had arrived and was attracting a fair amount of attention. But one of his crewmembers was stealing the show. Lachlan Murdoch, the 27-year-old CEO and Chairman of News Corporation in Australia, stood with his fiancée Sarah O'Hare. Needless to say, the photographers were having a field day.

Sayonara was both an impressive piece of yacht building and a beautiful boat to look at. From its sleek white hull and aerodynamic carbon fibre mast through to the crew's crisp white T-shirts – complete with the bold red and black *Sayonara* logo – it was arguably one of the finest yachts in the world and was wholly justified in being the odds-on favourite. Larry Ellison was a spare-no-expense campaigner and had assembled an experienced and highly accomplished crew. It was headed by New Zealand ace and principal helmsman Chris Dickson, an America's Cup, match racing and around-the-world racer who had come straight from taking his marriage vows in Auckland. Californian Mark Rudiger was navigator and had guided Paul Cayard's *EF Language* to a crushing victory in the Whitbread round-the-world race earlier in the year.

Steve Kulmar and family arrived at the club, squeezed their car into the already packed temporary carpark, unloaded the gear, then prepared themselves for the annual dock dance – the ducking, weaving and dodging necessary to reach the yacht.

"We'd never been aboard *Sword of Orion* so we all hopped on and had a bit of a look around," recalls Libby Kulmar. "I hadn't met Glyn [Charles] and some of the crew so we chatted while they were getting ready."

The family didn't want to stay for the start, preferring instead to be at home in time to watch it live on television. They decided they would all go to the clubhouse with Steve, but not before Madeline took a photo of her father with the new waterproof camera he'd been given for Christmas. They met up with friends, Bob and Sue and Matt Fraser. Bob had an update on the weather – the southerly buster was definitely brewing and on current indications would greet the fleet off the south coast of NSW some time between 2am and dawn. He confirmed the anticipated wind strength in the change was around 35 knots and added that it might back to the west. The low that was looming was still an unknown quantity. Kulmar thought they would probably have a quick beam reach for the crossing of Bass Strait. But he was getting impatient. It was time to go. He walked Libby, Maddie and John back to the car.

"We wanted to get back home, cool off with a swim then watch the start on television," said Libby. Steve was about to say goodbye to Maddie when she produced a surprise gift for him.

"Dad, I got this in the Christmas stocking. It's a good luck charm for you. I've got one and this one's yours."

She handed him a loop of thin luminous yellow cord. Hanging on it like a pendant was a small plastic ball, one-third the size of a golf ball. It was a pink piglet's head. When you squeezed it the piglet's mouth opened and shut and made a clacking sound.

"You have to wear it," Maddie said.

Steve bent down and Maddie put it over his head.

"Maddie, it's beautiful. Thank you, darling," he said as he kissed her goodbye. He waved as they drove off, and then, with the piglet pendant secured around his neck, battled his way back to *Sword of Orion*.

✯

The CYC was not the only hive of pre-race activity that Boxing Day morning. All around the harbour, other yacht clubs, marinas and private docks were buzzing with last minute preparations. In pretty Mosman Bay two well-known and well-respected yachting figures were busy getting their charges set for sea.

Ian Kiernan, better known as "Bik", or "Captain Yucky Poo" to his mates (he earned the latter nickname through his prodigious environmental activities), had in recent years become an Australian household name. More than a decade earlier Kiernan's love for Sydney Harbour had motivated him to organise the successful "Clean Up the Harbour" community campaign. It soon grew into "Clean Up Australia" and then the United Nations-backed "Clean Up the World" campaign.

"It started with 40,000 people cleaning up Sydney Harbour in 1989," Kiernan recalls. "It has now grown to 40 million people in 120 countries cleaning up the world. I'm proud of every one of them."

Kiernan's yacht, the classic Alan Payne-designed 36-footer *Canon Maris*, had an historic link with the Hobart race. Its original owner Jack Earl – a man whom Kiernan regarded as a father-figure and mentor – was one of the event's founders. That link was strengthened with the inclusion of Earl's grandson, Matthew Tomaszewski, in the *Canon Maris* crew. Also aboard was Jonathan "Gibbo" Gibson, son of John "Gibbo" Gibson, who was aboard *Winston Churchill*, and Richard "Sightie" Hammond, the most experienced competitor in the race, who was navigating. And to top it all off, 1998 was *Canon Maris'* 40th birthday.

Canon Maris was a tidy, low-wooded little timber yawl with clean white topsides, a teak deck and an immaculately varnished cabin. It was meticulously maintained and, according to Kiernan, "probably better than the day it was built". A lot of water had passed under its keel since it came into Kiernan's hands in 1970. "I've sailed her twice to the United States, done four Hobarts in her plus a single-handed Trans Pacific and a single-handed Trans Tasman." If that wasn't enough, Kiernan had also completed a single-handed around-the-world race, and had crewed for Australia in the Admiral's Cup in England and Clipper Cup in Hawaii. His vast experience told him this was going to be a tough race.

"For some reason I just picked it. Regardless, you should always be ready for rough weather. For us, with the boat being 40 years old, we always take our race preparation very seriously, but this time we were even more prepared. At the last moment I had a new storm trysail made and we were attending to all of the issues for a heavy race. I ordered a new life raft and had an EPIRB [Emergency Position Indicating Radio Beacon] fitted to that. All of our crew were provided with full sets of Musto HPX wet weather gear together with flotation vests and integrated safety harnesses. I wanted everyone to be dry and comfortable because on *Canon Maris* we just live, eat, sleep, sail and breathe the race. No one gets out of their sailing gear during the race. Everyone is ready to go on deck at all times. That way there's none of the frigging around with guys saying, 'Who's got my seaboots and my safety harness?'"

The six *Canon Maris* crew were at Mosman Bay Marina, as required, at 9am, resplendent in their red shirts, white shorts and the traditional *Maris* beret, a tribute to artist and original owner Jack Earl. *Canon Maris*, *Winston Churchill* and *Southerly* were set for a veteran's race among themselves. Beers and rum 'n' Cokes were the wager and the bets would be paid and collected at a waterfront hotel in Hobart.

As *Canon Maris* headed out of the bay the crew enjoyed some light banter with the team preparing one of the hottest contenders for handicap honours – Syd Fischer's 50-footer, *Ragamuffin*. Fischer, at the ripe old age of 73 had, without question, been Australia's most successful ocean racing yachtsman. He had won just about everything that mattered, including the Hobart race, the 600-mile Fastnet Race, the Admiral's Cup and the Kenwood Cup. He led the Australian team to victory in the disastrous 1979 Fastnet Race. This was to be Fischer's 30th Sydney to Hobart.

Docked at the harbourfront doorstep of Fischer's three-level dark-timber residence was a fleet of yachts including his 1995 America's Cup race entrant and of course the mighty "Rags". The large room on the lower level of the home had been given over to yacht racing memorabilia and photographs covering Fischer's near 40 years of offshore competition. Minutes before *Canon Maris* glided past, Fischer had assembled the crew – a powerful blend of experience and raw, young energy – in the "racing room" so sailing master Grant Simmer could brief them on race weather and tactics. For 21-year-old crewmember Nathan Ellis this was his initiation to the classic. Once the briefing was over the crew moved outside to make the important final checks.

✸

Immediately adjacent to the CYC, the Royal Australian Navy's headquarters at Garden Island was also bristling with pre-race activity. The Navy's youth training vessel, the 144-foot *Young Endeavour*, Britain's bicentennial gift to Australia in 1988, was being prepared to go to sea. The classically proportioned brigantine was to act once again as the radio relay vessel. The previous week the CYC's chief radio operator Lew Carter and his team of technicians had installed the bank of radios needed to communicate with the fleet.

It was a symbolic Hobart race for Carter. He had completed no fewer than 16 races aboard yachts and had done an additional nine as radio operator which took him to the magic number of 25. Lew's two volunteer assistants, Michael and Audrey Brown, were also entrusted with a highly demanding job. Despite having retired to Mooloolaba, in Queensland, they would provide strong support for Carter in what is an around-the-clock task. When the trio arrived at Garden Island on Boxing Day and were welcomed aboard by the ship's captain, Lieutenant Commander Neil Galletly, Carter had two concerns.

"I always thought it was going to be a rough year, just by looking at the weather patterns that you could see leading up to it, even over a couple of months. I was at the race briefing and after listening to Ken Batt deliver his forecast I thought he was pretty sceptical about the whole thing. He didn't seem to be able to say what he thought we were going to get. I sensed he glossed over a few things without giving his true opinion. He seemed to have a bet each way."

Carter was also worried about the radios that had been installed for the race.

"The radios are checked while the ship is at the dock but I have said for a number of years I considered the procedure insufficient. My opinion is that the radios should be tested at sea probably a fortnight prior to the race and preferably during some of the club's short ocean races. I think it would be a good idea to incorporate skeds [from *schedule*; the position reports from all race yachts] into those short ocean races to acclimatise ourselves and the yachties again with procedures. To test the radios on *Young Endeavour* at Garden Island is very difficult. You don't get out properly because there are so many buildings and other areas of interference. This time I wasn't happy with the radio right from the start, right from when we were in Garden Island. I didn't appear to be getting to some of the places that I thought we should have been able to contact."

★

Back at the CYC, the atmosphere was electric. John "Steamer" Stanley and Michael "Beaver" Rynan had been driven to the club and young Michael's eyes were like golfballs and his mouth agape as he took in the excitement of the morning of his first Hobart race. The pair made their way to *Winston Churchill* and met up with the rest of the crew. Crisp new boldly-striped shirts and shorts were issued and once everything had been readied, most of them paraded back along the dock in their new attire to enjoy a few drinks with mates before they put to sea.

Steamer spotted race meteorologist Ken Batt. He sat down with him and showed him some old photographs of *Winston Churchill* in the first Hobart race in 1945.

"Ken had some relations racing on the yacht that year and I was trying to see if he could identify them." Naturally they also discussed the weather and Batt confirmed what he had said at the briefing – there was a chance the fleet would be buffeted by winds up to 50 knots and that it was going to be sou'west turning west. Steamer thought, "hang on, this doesn't sound right," but Batt could offer nothing more due to the instability of the pattern.

Meanwhile Ian Kiernan was easing *Canon Maris* into "The Pond" next to the outdoor bar. Kiernan's wife, Judy, was put ashore so she could join a spectator boat. The bar was buzzing and among the myriad faces, Kiernan recognised plenty of mates, including Stanley and Mickleborough. "We had to put up with the bloody ragging of Mickleborough and his bloody larrikin *Southerly* crew – 'we'll be on the dock with a beer for you, and all that shit'," recalls Kiernan. "Then I looked across and there was Steamer just sipping on a schooner. I gave him the finger and he knew what it meant – the race was on. He smiled, gave me the Hawaiian Salute – the thumb and the little finger – and continued drinking. Jim Lawler was nearby and I shouted out 'hi' to him. He was looking just like a bloody prince of a man in his sailing hat. I exchanged calls of 'good luck' with Gouldy and Richard Winning. They had brought *Winston Churchill*'s performance right up and we knew they were going to be bloody hard to beat."

The *Canon Maris* crew pushed their yacht away from the dock, Kiernan slipped the engine into gear, eased the throttle forward, turned his charge away from the marina and motored off towards the start line.

On the way out they had an impromptu team meeting so Kiernan could remind them of what was expected. "Guys, I think we're going to have a heavy and wet weather race," said Kiernan. "We've all got plenty of experience but I want to remind you that the executive decisions are made by Dick Hammond and myself. We want your feedback all the time but we don't want chatter in times of decision. Keep yourselves clipped on. Sail conservatively but quickly and enjoy the bloody race." Hammond confirmed the heavy weather theory and outlined what he expected for the run down the coast that afternoon and when the blow might arrive that night.

The *Winston Churchill* crew had also decided it was time to move. They returned to the yacht, farewelled their support team, including Stephanie Winning and the children, then guided their historic and graceful lady out onto the harbour.

Peter Joubert's *Kingurra* was one yacht that had gone out onto the harbour early. Crewman Peter Meikle recalls it was for a very good reason.

"Peter always makes us put up the storm jib and the trysail before the start. He does it every year so that the old-timers are reacquainted with the settings and any new guys know where it all goes – and learn how not to scratch the varnish. I remember distinctly sailing past a few race boats with lots of people wearing smart matching shirts. They were all pointing at us, laughing and carrying on. The same blokes would probably be saying later on that what we did should be a compulsory pre-start practice."

The team from North Queensland aboard Wayne Millar's yacht, *B-52*, departed the CYC marina and headed out onto the harbour grinning from ear to ear. The forecast nor'easterly for the first half-day of the race should allow them to produce their secret weapon – a blooper. The youngest generation of sailors in the race would never have heard of a blooper. To them the word meant an embarrassing mistake, nothing more. It was, in fact, a special offshore racing sail that was in vogue 20 years earlier. In the Hobart race it was deemed illegal for the Grand Prix division, the IMS (International Measurement System) yachts. But as the boys from Townsville discovered, it was quite legal in their division, the CHS (Channel Handicap System) section.

Curiously, it was due to that ignorance that the sail came into existence. *B-52* crewmember and Townsville solicitor John Byrne had discovered the blooper loophole in the CHS rule just before the Hobart. "I mentioned tallboys and bloopers to a group of young sailors and they looked at me with blank stares," Byrne recalls. "They'd never heard of those sails. For some reason that sparked my interest. I knew the blooper was illegal under the IMS rule but I wasn't sure about CHS. I checked the rules then went to the committee in England that controls CHS racing. They agreed it would be legal."

Byrne told Millar of the breakthrough and the pair swiftly contacted North Sails in Sydney, stressing the need for total secrecy. North Sails management researched the project and found that their loft in South Africa still had designs for bloopers from 20 years ago. The sail was ordered from there and air freighted to Sydney just before the start. The blooper was a lightweight headsail that was attached to the bow and set outside the leech (trailing edge) of the mainsail when the yacht was sailing directly downwind under spinnaker. Their secret tests showed that speed increased from eight knots to 9.5. That could mean a gain of 18 very valuable miles over their rivals if it could be used effectively in the first 12 hours.

★

Don Mickleborough's sloop *Southerly*, aka "The Floating Hotel", was probably the least conspicuous race yacht on the CYC dock. Built in 1939, she was one of the grand old ladies in the fleet. She boasted the oldest and most experienced crew with an average age of somewhere around 60 and between them over 100 Hobarts. Mickleborough had done 33 while Tony Cable topped the list with one more. The professionally presented sign swinging in the breeze on *Southerly*'s mast revealed this team's attitude towards their younger rivals: "Old age and treachery will overcome youth and skill."

Over the years Mickleborough had become a bit of a traditionalist. Being aboard the oldest yacht it was important that they saw "the youngsters" – that is everyone else – off. So two hours before the start, when most other crews were clambering aboard their yachts while families and friends stood on the dock to wave goodbye, the senior citizens from *Southerly* were still firmly ensconced in the bar enjoying perfectly poured beers. It was not until 12.15pm, 45 minutes before the start, when they were certain all others had departed, that they decided it was time to leave. They walked leisurely down the dock to the yacht, laughing and appearing casual and carefree. The dock lines were cast off and they motored the old girl out into the fray.

It seemed that just about anything that floated was out on the harbour that glorious Boxing Day morning; everything from large luxury vessels to ferries, yachts and powerboats and even canoes, surf skis and paddleboards carrying some of the more adventurous. Waterways authorities, water police and volunteer groups patrolled the boundaries of the course in small boats keeping watch over the no-go zone. At this stage their job was relatively easy, but once the post-start stampede towards the harbour entrance began they would be tested to their limits.

Sydney's harbour is undoubtedly one of the world's most beautiful. The modern and vibrant city sits superbly on its southern shore some seven miles from the heads. The famous Opera House with its sail-like roof, and the gunmetal grey "coathanger" – the Harbour Bridge – recline like a proud guard of honour at the entrance to Circular Quay, the bay that is the city centre's maritime doorway. The harbour takes the form of a magnificent natural amphitheatre and the surrounding hills are an appealing mix of bushy parkland and seaside suburbs dotted with a broad spectrum of homes. Ribbons of golden sand, backed by grassy covered picnic grounds, give the city folk, lovers of the outdoor life, excellent access to the water.

Thousands of moorings, marina berths and private docks are filled with every conceivable type of craft, from multi-million dollar mega yachts to the tiniest of "tinnies" – small aluminium dinghies. On Boxing Day the surrounding homes, hills and headlands are packed with people waiting eagerly to witness the spectacular start. It is estimated that more than 300,000 people watch the event live. On South Head, the rocky bastion that marks one side of the entrance to the port, the outside broadcast television unit from Network Ten was already on the air. Overhead, between 15 and 20 media helicopters were buzzing around like dragonflies.

At the controls of one of them was Gary Ticehurst, chief pilot with the ABC television network in Sydney and a man who had become somewhat of a race legend over the previous 16 years. Flying helicopters was his first love and his pet assignment each year was to shadow the Hobart fleet and be the aerial camera platform that supplied the vision to the television news pool. His efforts had resulted in spectacular footage being beamed around the world of the 1984 and 1993 events, two of the roughest races on record. In 1993 Ticehurst took part in a number of search operations that successfully located upturned and badly damaged yachts. Each year he would spend up to two months planning the filming and communications strategy – how the signals would be sent back ... what frequencies would be used ... would Merimbula be used as a base to transmit all the signals ... how he would talk to the yachts. Prior to the actual start, preparations for the 1998 event had been running smoothly.

"I went out to the ABC and readied the helicopter. The frustration really started because the fuel pump at the ABC failed. We couldn't fuel the chopper and it was less than 30 minutes before we had to be in the air. There was no way the pump was going to be fixed by the time I was due to do the coverage. Eventually we went to Channel 9 and did the shuttle service over there all day. It was tiring but at least we got the chopper going." This was the first of a number of long and tiring days for Ticehurst.

☆

While many yachts stayed in the vicinity of the start line off Nielsen Park Beach – about three miles up-harbour from the heads – some of the more serious contenders for line and handicap honours cruised to the harbour entrance. The aim was to let everyone on board get a feel for the conditions that were developing out on the ocean – and to help settle any pre-race jitters. They were greeted by a sparkling blue ocean which had gently rolling swells coming in from the north east. Some of the more commercially-inclined yachts sailed the five miles inside the harbour up to Manly, turned, then set the spinnaker that was plastered with their sponsor's logo and cruised back to the start line.

Half an hour before the official 1pm start, most of the 115 contenders had manoeuvred themselves into the starting area. Large circular Telstra decals on the bow, plus flags fluttering from the stern, identified them as race boats. The yachts left a lattice-like pattern of white wakes on the blue water as they crisscrossed the harbour with only mainsails set. It was the aquatic equivalent of thoroughbreds parading in the ring before the start of the Melbourne Cup. The massive maxis with their towering rigs were the most easily identifiable. Sail number US17 was *Sayonara*, C1 *Brindabella*, M10 was Grant Wharington's exciting new *Wild Thing* and 9431 was *Marchioness*. The *Marchioness* crew looked as pleased as punch, for they knew the strengthening nor'easterly breeze during the day could give them an edge on the downward run. They also knew that a southerly would hamper their progress – *Marchioness* was far from fast when sailing to windward.

One yacht that certainly stood out was David Witt's *Nokia* – a ketch with a bright blue hull and the sponsor's name written proudly on the side. *Nokia*'s sail number, COK1, revealed that this yacht was the first big boat to be racing internationally under the flag of the Cook Islands. Papa Tom could be seen standing on the deck absorbing the excitement, his long, shiny grey hair flowing in the breeze.

The dark-hulled radio relay vessel *Young Endeavour* with its crew of 12 officers and 18 trainees aged between 18 and 23 made a magnificent sight as it moved slowly down the harbour past the race yachts and spectator craft. It would wait for the race fleet outside the heads. Lew Carter didn't take in the scenery. He was in the radio room, still frustrated by poor communications.

"I found it difficult to contact some of the yachts. We probably kidded ourselves [about the problem] at the time, thinking, it's only because of where we are. Then, when we got outside the heads we still had problems.

I noticed that the squelch button on the radio wasn't working at all. It acts as a sort of fine tuner on the radio to give you your best possible signal. I then tried to contact Penta Comstat, a land-based communications station located north of Sydney, but the signal that I was getting from them was non-existent. I had to do something about it."

Carter started to weigh his options.

★

The nor'easter meant it would be an upwind leg from the "invisible" starting line (a line between the start boat on the east side of the harbour and a buoy to the west) to the heads and beyond. This would in turn necessitate tighter manoeuvring and skilled handling. Collisions were a distinct possibility. A downwind start where the harbour became a concentrated blaze of brightly-coloured spinnakers would have been a visual bonus on such a beautiful summer day. It wasn't to be.

The smallest yachts racing, those around 30 feet (nine metres) in length, like Jim Dunstan's tiny 1981 race winner, *Zeus II*, had just six crewmembers aboard. The maxis, measuring some 78 feet (24 metres) in length, had around 26 aboard – the equivalent of two rugby league teams.

At 12.50pm the *boom!* from a cannon aboard the start boat and the raising of flags signalled the 10 minute countdown. Every 30 seconds the helmsmen would ask the crew how much time there was to the start gun. The helmsmen and tacticians were talking, fine tuning their start strategy while the man on the bow and others amidships warned of any yachts that might be in close proximity.

Boom! Another cannon shot signalled five minutes to go. Most crews were by now starting to line up their yachts, hustling for a good position. As well as being a lookout, the man or woman on the tip of the bow was beginning to send hand signals back to the brains-trust in the cockpit. Three fingers up – three boat lengths from the line; two fingers – two lengths; one finger – one length; closed fist – on the line and holding. The calls differed according to position, but one thing was for certain – no one wanted to cross the line early.

On the dot of 1pm Australia's golden girl of swimming, Susie O'Neill, tugged the cord that fired the cannon signalling the race was underway. It was a clean start. But there was already drama. On the eastern shore the race's biggest boat, the 83-foot *Nokia*, had collided with *Sword of Orion* and Hugh Treharne's cruiser-racer, *Bright Morning Star*.

Sword of Orion had been damaged. Some stanchions supporting the lifelines – the safety fence around the yacht's perimeter – had been torn out of the deck and there was a small crease in the aluminium mast. Treharne checked his boat and discovered the damage to *Bright Morning Star* was superficial. *Nokia*'s only wounds were scarred topsides near the bow. The crews heatedly debated who was right and wrong and protest flags – bright red squares with a dovetailed trailing edge – were hoisted. But there was nothing more to do but get on with the racing and sort out the rest in the protest room in Hobart.

The incident didn't detract from the stunning spectacle of 115 yachts powering their way towards the Sydney heads in a strengthening sea breeze. The armada of spectator craft joined the charge, churning the narrow laneways reserved for them along the harbour shores into a blur of whitewater. The race yachts tacked from one side of the harbour to the other and after only minutes of racing the maxis, *Sayonara*, *Brindabella* and *Wild Thing*, were at the head of the pack.

Less than 15 minutes after the start, *Sayonara* showed the fleet the way around the first buoy off South Head. She continued in this authoritative manner, rounding the offshore mark ahead of the rest before turning south, setting her spinnaker aloft and accelerating away in perfect downwind sailing conditions.

"Sayonara Sydney."

Four
Sailing towards a brick wall

A southerly buster is a summer-time weather phenomenon that spreads its influence over much of the NSW coast. It is a bit like Mother Nature turning on the air-conditioning to bring relief from the oppressive heat and humidity. Its name was originally a southerly *burster* and has its origins in the early days of European settlement. For many decades inner-city residents of Sydney called it the "brickfielder" because the change brought with it clouds of red clay dust from the St Peters brickyard.

> **"It is a particularly vicious form of a cooler southerly change – a shallow cold front that becomes trapped on the eastern side of the Great Dividing Range that runs down the Australian east coast," says Roger Badham. "It is locally enhanced by the strong temperature gradient across the front. The most violent southerly busters arrive in the Sydney region in the afternoon or evening, enhanced by the afternoon heating ahead of the change. They move up along**

the coast with clear or partly cloudy skies, sometimes with scattered thunderstorms.

"Southerly busters are most vigorous on the Illawarra and Central Coasts, particularly between Ulladulla and Newcastle. Immediately ahead of the buster the wind dies, then the southerly winds build very quickly (usually over 10 to 15 minutes) to be 30 to 40 knots and occasionally with gusts of up to 50 or 60 knots as it passes. However, the strong winds are generally short lived, easing to be less than 30 knots within a few hours."

Sometimes a southerly buster is nothing more than a slight glitch in the Sydney to Hobart, a chilly whisper blowing only 20 or 30 knots and disappearing almost as quickly as it arrived. But occasionally they charge up the coast gusting up to 80 knots. They often follow strong nor'easters and the challenge for everyone racing is to try to pick just when they will hit. When the change does arrive the yacht must be converted from a downwind racing configuration into one which will cope with the approaching blast. The wind effectively rotates through 180 degrees.

Sometimes the front's arrival can be quite daunting. It is heralded by a rolling, cigar-shaped, lead-coloured cloud that stretches from horizon to horizon. Often there will be no visual warning in a clear sky. The only thing to be seen will be a sudden darkening of the ocean surface ahead – the influence of wind on water. In just minutes conditions can go from being near windless, from astern, to having more than 40 knots on the bow.

It's like sailing into a brick wall.

There is another unpredictable and challenging element that comes into the racing equation when a southerly buster blows – the fast-flowing southerly current that streams down the NSW coast, bringing warm tropical water from Queensland's Coral Sea. It can run like a river at three or more knots. Pit that massive current against a 40-knot gale from the opposite direction, and the ocean soon swells into liquid mountains.

✸

The *Sayonara* team had impressed everyone with some slick work after the spinnaker blew apart just south of the Sydney heads. In less than three minutes a new one had been set. It was obvious in those conditions that the American entry wouldn't get everything its own way. *Brindabella*, sporting a powerful new asymmetrical spinnaker, was pushing out to sea in search of the strongest current. She had drawn level with *Sayonara*, but close behind, the syndicate-owned *Marchioness* was making its move.

Together with *Wild Thing*, the big trio headed the race at speeds approaching 20 knots. It was exciting and satisfying racing but every crew was fully aware they were now at the business end of proceedings. Speed maximisation was paramount. Sails were continually trimmed while the helmsman worked the yacht down the lingering blue swells in an effort to promote surfing. Long white wakes streamed astern like vapour trails. There was constant talk about the weather, especially when the menacing grey and white clouds of the thunderstorm, forecast for the evening, could be seen building to the south. Below deck, navigators were watching weather fax machines disgorge the latest meteorological information.

✸

Aboard *Young Endeavour* radio operator Lew Carter and his assistants, Michael and Audrey Brown, were still being hampered by communication problems. Just south of Sydney, Carter decided to contact the technician who'd installed the radio. His advice to Carter was to "continue with it for a while and see how you get on". That didn't sit too comfortably with the trio. Carter realised the last opportunity to correct any problems would be off Wollongong, 45 miles south of Sydney. Once again he contacted the technician.

"I wanted him to know that I wasn't happy at all," said Carter. "We thought we were going to get a hectic Hobart this year and we needed everything to be spot on with the radios. The guy said that he had another radio at home. My problem was how the hell was I going to get it on board. Fortunately for us the police launch *Nemesis* was proceeding down the coast with the fleet as far as Eden. The obvious option was to have the technician drive from Sydney to Wollongong with the new radio. He could be picked up by *Nemesis* there and be brought out to us.

"There was quite a swell running – about three metres – and a strong wind blowing, but still the *Nemesis* crew did a marvellous job. The technician was worried about how he would get both on and off *Young Endeavour* in those conditions, so I did a bit of a con job on him and told him all would be OK. I knew that once I had him on board I had no more worries. It wouldn't worry me if he couldn't get off because we had our new radio and that was all we wanted. He could come all the way to Hobart with us as far as I was concerned. As it was we did get him off and home. Four minutes after he left we had our first 'sked' with the fleet – loud and clear."

⭐

By 3pm, two hours after the start, Roger Badham had returned to his home south of Sydney. The moment he arrived he went straight to his office and hurriedly downloaded the latest weather prognosis from the international computer models.

He didn't like what he saw.

That afternoon the author spoke with him.

"Mundle ... Clouds here. I've just looked at all the latest charts and there's only one thing I can say. If I were on half those yachts out there this afternoon I'd be taking my spinnaker down right now and turning back to Sydney. They are going to get hammered. There's a bomb about to go off in Bass Strait. A low is going to develop and intensify. They are going to get 50 knots, maybe more, and huge seas. This race is going to be worse than 1993."

The low pressure zone formed over Bass Strait as a result of a sharp cold upper air trough that slowed, tilted and deepened as it engaged warm humid air drawn in from the north east. Badham described it as "a text book frontal low pressure development", quite common across the waters immediately south of Australia. The region of cold upper air could be seen clearly on satellite images as it crossed the Great Australian Bight on the days immediately before December 26. The "cold pool of air" became cut off from the upper westerly flow when the system deepened to the surface during the early hours of Sunday the 27th. It was this region of cold air that brought summer snow to the high country of Victoria and NSW that day.

The official race forecast issued from Sydney at 1450hrs on the 26th read as follows:

SYNOPTIC SITUATION: A high near New Zealand is ridging onto the central NSW coast.

A low 995hPa near Lord Howe Island is slow moving. A cold front is over central Victoria.

WARNINGS: Storm Warning is current south from Merimbula.

Gale Warning is current south from Broken Bay.

WIND: North to north-east wind 20/25 knots ahead of a W/SW change 25/35 knots, with stronger gusts, expected near Jervis Bay around midnight–2am and then near Sydney around 3am–5am Sunday. Wind may tend briefly north west 15/20 knots prior to the change.

WAVES: 1 to 2 metres, rising to 3 metres offshore with W/SW change.

SWELL: 1 to 2 metres.

WEATHER: Scattered showers and thunderstorms developing tonight ahead of the change then clearing tomorrow.

OUTLOOK FOR NEXT 48 HOURS: Winds moderating north of Jervis Bay Sunday night. Gale to storm force W winds south of Jervis Bay expected to moderate Monday evening.

The Bass Strait forecast issued from Victorian Bureau of Meteorology Office at 1646hrs read:

EASTERN BASS STRAIT: North-easterly wind 20/30 knots in the far east at first. A west/south-west change at 20/30 knots extending throughout this evening and increasing to 30/40 knots tomorrow morning and to 45/55 knots during the afternoon. Seas/swell 2 to 4 metres increasing 3 to 5 metres during the morning and 4 to 6 metres during the afternoon.

According to that forecast there was going to be one hell of a battle in Bass Strait.

Sydney to Hobart race headquarters – the Cruising Yacht Club of Australia (CYC) on the shores of Sydney Harbour. The outside deck is the favourite spot for pre-race festivities.

High profile crewmember Lachlan Murdoch and then wife-to-be Sarah O'Hare relax on the deck of *Sayonara* at the dock just hours before the start. There is always an air of anticipation hanging over the fleet at this time.

Meticulous effort goes into the preparation of the hull and keel of a race yacht. The keel is moulded out of lead with most of its weight concentrated at the bottom.

Amid a forest of masts crewmen hang like monkeys while making final checks of rigging before the race start. Most masts are aluminium and the rigging stainless steel rod or wire.

It was a "brochure day" for the start on Sydney Harbour on December 26, 1998. Hundreds of thousands of spectators followed the excitement either from boats or vantage points along the harbour foreshores.

Gary Ticehurst, the man who became a vital cog in search and rescue operations, at the controls of the television news helicopter that followed the race. This was the 16th Sydney to Hobart he had covered.

The classic old yacht *Winston Churchill* sets off on her fateful passage south. This yacht was one of nine that contested the very first Sydney to Hobart race in 1945.

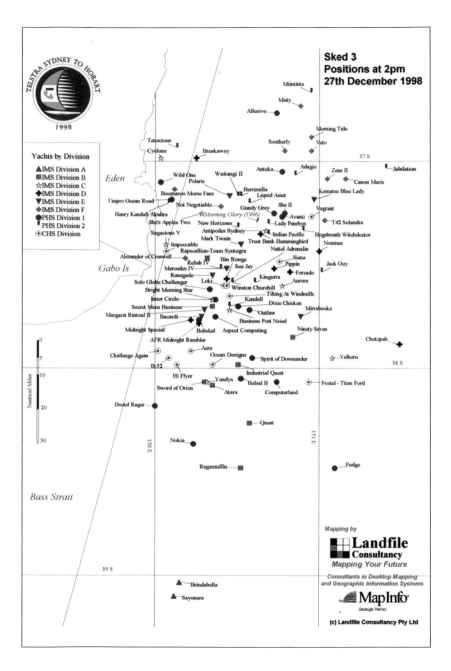

The way we were. This is the position report for the race fleet just when the "weather bomb" was exploding in Bass Strait.

The Australian Maritime Safety Authority (AMSA) search and rescue headquarters in Canberra. This is the Rescue Control Centre (RCC) from where the search and rescue operation was coordinated.

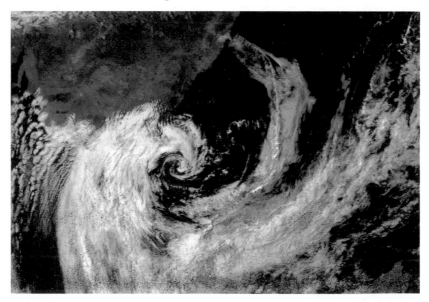

The eye of the storm in Bass Strait. This satellite photograph reveals the intensity of the storm south east of the Australian mainland.

✫

At that point the crews hadn't heard the latest reports, but already the experienced sailors suspected something big was brewing. The north-easterly wind was strengthening all the time and was now well above the predicted velocity of around 25 knots. The sea breeze and favourable current remained so strong throughout the afternoon and evening that the entire fleet was ahead of the race-record pace set by the state-of-the-art German maxi, *Morning Glory*, two years earlier. Lew Carter, Michael Brown and the *Young Endeavour* skipper, Lieutenant Commander Neil Galletly, noted the fleet was flying. They were twice as far from Sydney as they were most years.

"We discussed with the skipper what we would do," recalls Carter. "We always talk our own tactics throughout the race because it's important for us to be in a position where we can be of assistance if needed, even though that's not our primary role. We always try and keep ourselves about mid-fleet, maybe with a leaning towards the back. We were up on the bridge and had a bit of a chat about the weather patterns and the current. We'd had a look at the chart and were talking about the problems that we might experience down the bottom, off the south-east corner of the mainland. The depth of the water drops dramatically as soon as you get beyond the 100 fathom line down there. We were thinking about the convergence of three to four knots of very warm current against waves from a south-westerly change. We decided if we were going to have any problems it would be in that area."

They were right.

✫

By mid-afternoon Gary Ticehurst had reconfigured the ABC helicopter so that it was ready to cover the race and he and his two passengers, Scott Alle, a producer for the ABC and cameraman Peter Sinclair, began their chase of the yachts down the coast.

"The plan was, as in most years, to position at Merimbula for the night," recalls Ticehurst. "We usually leave so we can arrive in Merimbula about half an hour before last light – it's 185 nautical miles south of Sydney. With such a strong following wind I was hoping we could cover the lead yachts and then come back in. On the way to them, and while going through the smaller yachts, we were listening to the weather forecasts. They were predicting 40 to 50 knots. They said the change would come around about midnight with local thunderstorms all the way down to the coast.

"Sure enough, they were spot on with the latter part. You could see the lightning. It was that typical sultry grey afternoon and you could feel that it was going to happen. One thing that was pretty impressive was the speed at which the entire fleet was travelling south. The forecast

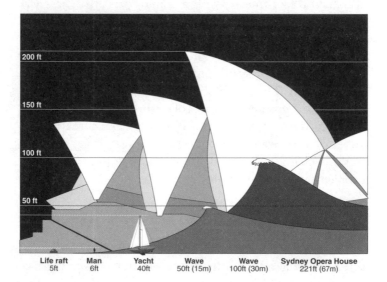

Life raft	Man	Yacht	Wave	Wave	Sydney Opera House
5ft	6ft	40ft	50ft (15m)	100ft (30m)	221ft (67m)

for 40 to 50 knots the next day didn't concern us. In fact it excited us. I thought, this is going to be a little bit tougher than just a southerly buster. This is going to last a day or two. We're going to get some action – great vision.

"When we arrived at Merimbula that evening we literally had to poke our way around the thunderstorms just to get to the airport. There were so many of them. It was pouring with rain, torrential rain. We were certain then that the fleet was going to cop it overnight – there'd be a few things going on. We wanted to be out over them at first light."

☆

Throughout the afternoon and early evening the crews were enjoying exhilarating rides. Then, as darkness closed, they had the added spectacle of the huge thunderstorms that Ticehurst had encountered. They were moving out from the land and across the course.

"What we saw was almost unbelievable," said John Messenger, sailing master of the maxi *Marchioness*. "The lightning was all over the place – horizontal and vertical. It was horrific. It just lit up the night. It was incessant. The trouble was we didn't know if the storm was going to bring the change or just stay as a storm. We were always on full alert. There was a bit of apprehension on board." *Marchioness* was then at least level and possibly ahead of *Sayonara* and *Brindabella*, which were farther out to sea. That situation changed in an instant.

"The wind was coming from around 035 degrees and blowing at around 20 knots. We had the spinnaker on and were really flying. We were surprised that the wind didn't drop when the thunderstorm got to us. Instead it held and began flicking between 035 and 350. We were forever chasing it – changing course all the time to keep the wind at the right angle over the stern. It was as though the wind couldn't make up its mind as to what it wanted to do. Suddenly one big wave got under our quarter and lifted the stern. We lost control and broached wildly. Now this is a big boat, but she stayed down, on her side, for what I guess was between three and four minutes."

Two burly blokes were hanging onto the wheel, keeping the rudder hard over in a desperate bid to get *Marchioness*' bow back towards course and give it a chance to come upright. A brief lull in the wind and the influence of another wave were enough for the rudder to bite the water – but all too quickly. With most of the 22 crewmembers hanging on to a near vertical deck, *Marchioness* bolted back upright then took off downwind out of control at 20 knots. This time it speared off course and the opposite way – to leeward. A classic "Chinese Gybe" ensued.

The wind filled the mainsail from the opposite side and the boom went whistling across the yacht like a giant scythe. At the same time the spinnaker went aback. *Marchioness* was knocked flat once more. The spinnaker was then filled with water instead of wind. Sheets and lines were tangled across the deck and under the hull.

John Messenger called for a cessation of racing activities. All sails were lowered and the spaghetti-like mess of sheets, wires and lines was tidied up. It was 30 minutes before sails were hoisted and *Marchioness* rejoined the race.

☆

With the north-easterly wind approaching the 40 knot mark Geoff Ross' *Yendys* (Sydney spelled backwards) was starting to do things a Beneteau 53 cruiser-racer had not done before – it was vibrating and humming and at times hitting 20 knots. By 10pm the crew knew it was time to take down the 1.5-ounce spinnaker. If they didn't there was a chance the rig might be ripped from the boat, especially if they broached and were knocked down. Just as the drop procedure started *Yendys* went out of control and did broach.

"We were knocked well over," said Ross. "I was up to my thighs in water in the cockpit. The guy at the front of the boat for the drop, Peter Seary, wasn't clipped on and was just sucked clean off the bow by the force of water. He was gone. What happened next was almost unbelievable. He shot down the side of the boat in the water and before you could even blink a huge wave picked him up, lifted him over the lifelines and dumped him on the deck at the back of the cockpit. We were in a hell of a mess by then and it would have taken a long while to turn back if we'd lost him."

By that time the spinnaker had all but taken itself down – blown to bits – except just a small piece that fluttered like a flag from the halyard near the top of the mast. Seary went straight to the mast as though nothing had happened, clipped onto a halyard and was hauled to the masthead to retrieve what was left of the spinnaker.

✸

Surprisingly, there had so far been no retirements. But this was soon to change. One of the race favourites, Ray Roberts' bright yellow 46-foot sloop *ABN Amro Challenge*, was the first to come to grief. It was spearing through the night when there was a sudden and sharp jolt, first on the keel and then on the deep blade of the spade rudder. They had hit either a large sunfish or floating debris. The yacht careered out of control in an instant. The rudder had been ripped off and their race was run. It was a bitter disappointment for co-designer Iain Murray who was aboard and hoping for a big win.

Around the same time another of the handicap honours contenders, Ron Jones' near new *Sledgehammer*, was limping back to port. The steering system had failed, the result of chafing.

Other crews, like that aboard Charles Curran's 60-footer, *Sydney*, were revelling in what had been a great running race. But *Sydney*'s race end was nigh. At 11.30pm, after averaging 18 knots for the previous 10 hours, the crew heard a massive bang from the stern area.

"We had the spinnaker up and were absolutely flying," said sailing master Dave Kellett. "While we were searching for the cause of the first bang there was another. We discovered that the lower rudder post bearing had shattered. The rudder post was wobbling around. It didn't take much thought to realise that if we pushed on, the rudder post could break free and be like a can opener. It would have opened up the hull."

The spinnaker was lowered, then the mainsail. The *Sydney* crew then sat and waited patiently for the forecast south-westerly change. When it did arrive they set a small headsail, turned the bow northwards and headed for home.

☆

Champion offshore yachtsman Roger Hickman, skipper of *Atara*, had completed 20 of the 21 Hobart races he had entered.

"The first night we had one of the most wonderful runs downwind you could want," recalls Roger. "There was more lightning in the sky than I'd ever seen. At one stage I asked Peter Gardner, who's an extremely experienced sailor, if he wanted to have a drive. He said, 'No, Hicko. It's your boat so you play with it.' So play I did. I have to say that at the same time the situation was starting to concern me. I kept recalling what Ken Batt, the meteorologist, said not long before we left, 'You're going to have a lot on Hicko'. He does a wonderful job representing the Bureau of Meteorology for the race but unfortunately he's shackled by enormous bureaucracy. He and the other forecasters can't come out and make a punt on weather and give us a good guide. It always has to be so substantiated.

"What he said left me in no doubt that we were going to have plenty on once the change came. So we were already gearing up for sort of 45 or 50 knots. We have a policy on *Atara*, and any other boat I race for that matter, that at 40 knots you get the mainsail down, roll it up on the boom and then put the cover on it so that it can't catch the water or blow away. That way you're as safe as houses. We just run with the headsail because you can get it down quickly if you have to and it doesn't go anywhere, like blow over the side. Our plan in a blow is to go to the storm trysail, with a No. 4 headsail, whereas most boats go to the storm jib and then to the trysail."

Different styles of yachts employed different techniques going into that first night. The strengthening nor'easter, which was registering more than 35 knots on some sections of the course, was surprising a growing number of experienced sailors. Even *Winston Churchill* was bowling along with a bone in her teeth – a big white bow-wave that was being cut and curled away before disappearing into the night. John Stanley was enjoying it.

"We set the spinnaker at a gentlemanly pace after turning south at Sydney then proceeded down the coast, knowing all the time that we were going to be hit somewhere along the line that night. We were out to make the most of the nor'easter while it was on and get down the track as fast we could. The breeze got fresher and fresher to the point where we couldn't overload the old *Winston Churchill* too much. So we took the spinnaker off. It was probably blowing around 30 knots at that stage. We then poled out a No. 2 headsail until that too proved to be too much. We pulled that headsail off and gybed inshore when the wind started to back towards the north and north west. It was around 35 to 40 knots then."

The *Kingurra* crew was also concerned with the way the weather was developing.

"It was just beautiful sailing through the afternoon and the early evening," said Peter Meikle. "We were doing 12 knots over the ground with between two and three knots of current assisting us. At that point we knew we were in for a little bit of a belting but all the time things were beginning to not add up. We had no idea what we were in for – it just didn't seem quite right. It certainly seemed strange that the north-easterly was continuing to build in strength. I remember thinking when we got down to the 2.2-ounce spinnaker that things were a bit odd.

"The one good thing about it all was that on the first night out, as is always the case on *Kingurra* in a Hobart race, there was a roast coming up. We had this enormous hunk of beef in the oven with all the trimmings. The game for Peter was to see if he could get this very nice roast out of the oven and served before the change came through. That was probably the thing that was occupying the minds of at least half the crew. The other half weren't planning on eating."

Up front, *Sayonara* and *Brindabella* were surfing down wave after wave and maintaining amazing average speeds. At the same time the conditions were no longer concurring with the forecast. Larry Ellison sensed things were changing, and changing fast.

"We thought things were getting a little bit screwy when we were hitting 42 knots of wind running away from Sydney. We were doing 24 to 26 knots under spinnaker."

The downwind rollercoaster ride continued well into the night. As midnight approached many yachts had replaced their spinnakers with poled-out headsails – a more snug rig that was easier to control. The Grand Prix boats were still hanging onto their "kites" until the wind began its steady change in direction towards the west then sou'west. It was between 1am and 3am that the south westerly hit the entire fleet with a vengeance.

"At 0230hrs the wind went to 350 degrees from 020 degrees, the sea became difficult," recalls Roger Hickman. "We had hit speeds of 19 knots plus, and had done 86 miles in 4 hours and 10 minutes with between two and three knots of favourable current. I felt the fun was up. We downed the 0.9-ounce chute [spinnaker] then put up the jib-top and poled it out. We gybed and then settled down. All boats our size were either behind us or retired. *Ragamuffin* was out of sight and *Ausmaid* was a white light out seaward. The breeze moved quickly in to the west around 20 to 25 knots. With the No. 4 and two reefs we were in good shape."

★

"Mayday, mayday, mayday," was the chilling call that penetrated the airwaves at around 0230hrs on December 27. Crews on race yachts right across the course scrambled to listen to their radios. "This is *Challenge Again, Challenge Again, Challenge Again*. We have a man overboard!"

The incident had begun when the 41-foot fibreglass production yacht went into a wild broach – a near capsize. The moment the shout went out the very experienced crew did everything they could. Owner Lou Abrahams, a Sydney to Hobart race veteran out of

Melbourne and one of Australia's best offshore sailors, had been hurled across the cabin from his seat at the navigation station during the broach. He was slightly dazed but immediately clambered back to his seat. His index finger went straight to activating the "MOB" (man-overboard) button on the GPS (Global Positioning System) unit. At least that would define the search area and increase the chance of recovering the man. Watch Captain Fraser Johnston, a similarly experienced ocean racing sailor and professional yacht delivery captain, was jolted from a light sleep.

"I'd just dozed off after finishing my watch," Johnston recalls. "We'd had very little sleep that night because we'd been sailing so hard downwind. The next thing I knew the boat was broaching and I was pinned in the aft quarter berth. I heard 'Man Overboard' and thought, oh Christ here we go."

As he struggled to free himself from the bunk and fight his way to the cockpit his mind flashed back to the 1993 race. He was aboard *Atara* that year, the yacht that extricated John Quinn from his five-hour, death-defying battle with the ocean in about the very same spot. Like the rest of the crew, Johnston knew that everything needed to go like clockwork if the man was to be recovered. They would probably only have one chance to get him. "I ripped straight up on deck and asked in haste who it was. There was uncertainty, but that didn't matter. Someone shouted out, 'We think it's young Nick'." Johnston knew that the helmsman, Col Anderson, was well in control.

"All I saw was a blur go across the boat in front of me," recalls Anderson. "This body was being hurled through the air. It happened in such a way that he went from the weather side and through the gap between the deck and the boom. Then, with the yacht heeled over so far, he missed landing in the leeward rail. He went straight through the gap and into the tide. I just pulled the boat straight up onto a reach so we could turn and go back to him on a simple reciprocal course when we were ready. I started the motor and called on the guys to make a quick check to see if there were any lines over the side. We didn't want to foul the prop.

"Fraser was over the back trying to sort out the man-overboard buoy. It was a tangled mess with thin cord going everywhere. I shouted that there was only one thing to do – get all the bloody mess on board before we put the engine into gear because even a little bit of shit cord is enough to wreck your prop if it happens to get around it. I remember seeing some of the crew coming on deck still half asleep wondering what the hell was going on. All I could do was shout to them to get the mainsail and the jib down."

Although the crew were trying desperately to get the main and headsail down, somehow the long cord lines keeping all the components of the man-overboard system tied together had tangled around the rudder while the yacht had been lying on its side. When he called for a knife Johnston heard someone finally identify the man overboard. It was "Skippy" – Victorian policeman Garry Schipper – and he had a torch.

Johnston cut the man-overboard buoy free and let it down, then headed for the next most important thing – the engine control. He called on crew to check they had ropes to throw to Schipper when they got close to him. He doubly checked there were no lines in the water then engaged the gear lever. "It was terrific that Skippy still had the torch. But just as with the Quinn rescue, there was much excitement going on – the adrenalin was running. You must make sure you don't make a silly mistake under those circumstances."

One crewman, Richard Grimes, had remained with his eyes glued to Schipper from the moment he hit the water. He pointed to him at all times so Anderson knew where to steer to get back to him.

"We'd pulled down a headsail and stuffed it downstairs, so everyone below had been disturbed," recalls Garry Schipper. "They were all awake – which turned out to be a good thing. We'd changed from the reacher to the No. 4 – no real drama – and were flogging along with probably 25 to 35 knots coming across the deck from the west. I was coming back to the cockpit from the bow. I had a safety harness on and it was attached to the jackstay. The problem was that there were sheets and stuff across the jackstay so I couldn't get all the way back. I decided to unclip myself off the jackstay and then re-attach the harness strop to something closer to the cockpit. I wasn't concerned about doing that because the boat was sailing nicely – we hadn't broached at any stage.

"Wouldn't you know it, just as I unclipped we got hit by a rogue wave right at the stern, under the boat. It knocked the stern to leeward, caused the boat to go into a broach and laid her over on her side. I had been on my knees, with my knees against the cabin side. As soon as we broached I overbalanced – I slid across the cabin top on my stomach – straight over the safety rail and into the piss. I didn't even touch the rail. I was flying. I remember grabbing hold of a winch as I went but it was slippery and I lost my grip. It's hard to stop my weight in full flight – 147 kilos. What I didn't realise at the time was that I had a waterproof torch in my hand and took it with me.

"I was fully rigged in my full wet weather gear, thermal underwear and seaboots. The first thing I realised though was that the water was warm. It was a small consolation. One of the crew thought quickly enough to grab another floating torch, turn it on and hurl it into the water towards where I was. That would also help identify where I was when they could turn back."

While some crewmembers struggled to release the man-overboard buoy and life ring, others concentrated on keeping Schipper spotted. To lose sight of him could well cost him his life.

"When I surfaced the boat was probably 10 or 15 metres from me and moving away, still at a reasonable pace. The first thing I could think of was that the weight of water in my boots and gear would be pulling me under. I just knew I wasn't going to be able to swim for the boat. My immediate thought as soon as I hit the drink was, don't panic. For an instant I remembered what John Quinn said after he'd spent five hours in the water in the 1993 race – he just tried not to panic.

"After about 10 or 15 seconds I realised I had the torch in my hand. I had held onto it as I went over the side. I turned it on, and it worked. Hallelujah. I was able to shine the torch on the boat. They had stopped probably 250 metres from me. I knew they'd see me with the torch – but that wasn't my thought at the time. I wanted to get my harness off and my other gear so I could tread water more easily. But it was bloody impossible to get my harness off because every time I stopped using my arms to tread water I started to sink. I just had to continue breast stroking.

"I eventually got one boot and a sock off. That was bloody difficult because, like so many others, I'd taped my boots on to keep the water out. It was a lot of effort for a small result. Every time I tried to do something with the harness or my boots I started going under. The guys seemed to take forever to get back to me. Obviously they'd had their problems getting sails down and trying not to get any lines over the side and around the rudder or propeller. All I can say was that I was feeling very, very lonely. I was already exhausted. I was breathing heavy, probably because of the adrenalin rush. I was tiring but I just kept treading water.

"When I saw the boat coming towards me I was still worried. I didn't know if they could still see me. I kept trying to shine the torch at them from above my head. The rest of the time it was just under the surface. Before long I realised they had me spotted. That was a relief. But the first time they made a run at me to pick me up I thought I was going to get the bloody bow right through my head. Fortunately it missed."

"It was pretty scary for Skippy," recalls Col Anderson, "but I had to get the boat really close to him. I had to be really certain that I had positioned the boat almost on top of him so the guys could grab him. It ended up that getting the yacht there was the easy bit. Getting him back aboard was hard."

Strong, eager hands grabbed whatever they could that was attached to Schipper and clung desperately to it. Their arms were now his lifelines. The crew were lying on their stomachs on the deck, leaning out over the side and all the while the yacht was bucking like a bronco and the waves were trying to tear him away. If he was ripped from their grasp he would almost certainly drown.

"A couple of the young guys grabbed me," Schipper recalled while wiping away tears. "Suddenly I saw them as my kids. They were clinging onto me; they didn't want to let me go. They were going to save me. They were terrific. They were all over me, leaning down over the side, hanging onto me, attaching bloody ropes everywhere so they wouldn't lose me."

The dramas continued. The rough seas, Schipper's bulk, and problems with a special sling designed to lift crew back onto a yacht's deck made it a perilous and daunting task.

"The biggest problem for everyone was that I was so bloody exhausted I just couldn't help them. Every time I got near to being in the sling I slipped out. Eventually they clipped a halyard onto my safety harness as well as the sling and finally winched me up to deck level. Then, while I was still suspended, they guided me into the cockpit and lowered me into the cabin. I just collapsed." Schipper was back on deck little more than 10 minutes after going over the side. Abrahams checked with him and the rest of the crew on how they felt about the drama. The decision was to continue in the race.

"The crew was fantastic. Bloody professional. I was very, very fortunate. I had nine good guys backing me up in an extremely difficult situation."

Five
The cauldron
begins to boil

On December 27, 1998 Mother Nature dropped a meteorological bomb on the hapless Sydney to Hobart fleet. Many of the crews, and even some of the weather services, had little comprehension of what was brewing in the north-east corner of Bass Strait. Weather faxes were beginning to confirm that the low, which for days had deliberated over where it would unleash its brutal winds – south of Tasmania, west of Tasmania, or in Bass Strait – had now made up its mind. The race forecast issued from weather forecasters in Sydney at 0213hrs read as follows:

> **WIND: W/SW winds 25/35 knots, with stronger gusts. Winds increasing to the south of Merimbula offshore, reaching 40/50 knots this afternoon as low deepens.**
> **WAVES: 2 to 3 metres, rising to 4 to 5 metres offshore in the south.**
> **SWELL: 1 to 2 metres, rising to 3 to 4 metres offshore south of Merimbula.**

From the time the fleet had experienced the south-westerly change in the early hours of the day through to mid-morning, sailing conditions had been deteriorating markedly. As forecast, the wind was increasing in strength to between 30 and 40 knots and the waves were growing in stature and number. The first 12 hours of racing had seen hard downwind running, then, after the change, the yachts were reaching across the wind. Little wonder that the two leaders, *Sayonara* and *Brindabella*, were now well into Bass Strait and setting a race record pace. There was speculation by some pundits that if the speedy conditions prevailed the magical two-day barrier might be broken – more than 14 hours would be carved off the record.

At around 9am Roger Badham reported on the worsening weather to a media contact.

The situation is starting to look very grim, especially for the boats that will enter Bass Strait later this afternoon and night. The 6am observations showed Wilsons Promontory with 71 knots of mean wind speed. The Prom. over reads some 25 per cent to 33 per cent in wind speed but regardless, this was a very significant observation. Fifty to 60 knots seems certain.

Badham suggested the "nastiest" winds were probably in a thin elongated band on the western flank of the low pressure system which would be dragged over the fleet as the system moved east into the Tasman Sea later in the day. The strength of the west-sou'westerly winds had forced the majority of yachts east of the rhumb line – the 585-mile direct passage between Sydney and the first corner in the course, Tasman Island, at the entrance to Storm Bay. They were all benefiting from the south-flowing current.

Some navigators and tacticians had purposefully set a course that was well offshore because they believed it would prove to be the fastest. Other crews had found themselves 30 and 40 miles offshore simply because of the influence of the wind and waves. Regardless, all these yachts now had their last remaining sanctuary before Bass Strait – Eden – almost directly upwind. Some crews were already discussing their options – to continue racing or to head for a safe haven on the NSW coast. Others, like the maxi *Marchioness*, had the decision made for them through equipment failure. John Messenger had had trouble slowing his yacht down, even with a No. 4 headsail and three reefs during the morning. They finally came to grief when the baby stay (the baby stay extends from around halfway up the mast to the middle of the foredeck and controls the pumping action of the mast in rough weather) broke. They considered fixing the fitting but after reading the latest weather fax they decided their race was over. *Marchioness* was tacked and steered back towards Sydney.

Grant Wharington had seen a crack develop in the carbon fibre mast of his new yacht, *Wild Thing*, when it nose-dived. Race control was advised at 6.30am that the maxi had retired and was heading for Eden. It was a disappointing result for what had been considered a line honours favourite.

By mid-morning Roger Badham was becoming increasingly concerned. Wilsons Promontory, in Bass Strait and less than 100 miles to the west of the rhumb line, had recorded a wind gust of 92 knots. It reaffirmed his belief that the yachts would be hit with strong winds and terrible seas right off the south-east tip of Gabo Island – the area where the confluence of the currents would be at its worst. He again confirmed that the fiercest conditions would be between 3pm that day and 3am the following morning and predicted that more than half the fleet would be knocked out.

This is Badham's explanation of how the storm developed:

> Intense low pressure systems frequently develop across the waters around eastern Australia and the Sydney to Hobart storm was right up there among the worst of them. This particular low pressure system was a classic text-book development of a "frontal" or "secondary" low pressure system. The original front and associated upper trough and vorticity centre burst up from the Southern Ocean into the western region of the Great Australian Bight on December 23. On Christmas Eve and during Christmas Day the system began to intensify as it became strongly baroclinic – the associated jet stream winds becoming much stronger and wrapping around the whole vorticity centre.
>
> Late on Christmas Day, tell-tale cirrus "leaf" type cloud began to appear on the NE side of the towering cumulus and thunderstorm clouds – these so called "leaf" type clouds indicating strong upper shear and that surface convergence was guaranteed to follow. A low pressure system would develop in 24 to 30 hours, but where? Even at this time, the computer forecast models were not 100 per cent certain on the exact location; it was still most likely to develop just off the Tasmanian coast ... most probably between Flinders Island to the north and Maria Island to the south. At no stage, right up to when the low actually began to develop, did any of the models indicate that the low would "spin-up" within Bass Strait, west of the rhumb line.
>
> On Boxing Day, as the race started, the

complex meteorology was unfolding. Only during Boxing Day, as the upper low and vorticity centre entered western Bass Strait, did it become apparent that the surface low was actually going to form in eastern Bass Strait and not off the Tasmanian coast. The surface low pressure system deepened as air aloft was drawn away in the jet stream at a faster rate than the air could feed in at the earth's surface. The barometer readings over east Bass Strait were already quite low and continued to fall, but at Wilsons Promontory between 3am and 6am on the morning of December 27, the surface pressure fell 8.1hPa in three hours. Good sailors would be aware that such a severe pressure fall heralded Force 10 – or 50 knots of wind speed.

The morning of the 27th over south-east Australia was no normal summer morning. As the cold upper air spread across the highlands of Victoria and NSW snow began to fall; good falls! The computer models gave forecasters exceptionally good guidance on every aspect of this weather system, except for the exact location of where the low was going to develop. With hindsight, the USA global model (the MRF standing for Medium Range Forecast) picked the development many days ahead of time. As far back as December 21, the MRF model output for December 27 indicated that a 986hPa low would develop immediately east of Flinders Island with SW winds of 40 to 45 knots over eastern Bass Strait. In fact, the MRF model consistently went for this development, while the other major models were much more uncertain in both the timing and position of the developing low pressure system. It is certainly unusual for such an intense and rapid development to take place over Bass Strait during December, so it was logical for forecasters to expect the actual location (of development) to be further south. It is useful to gain an insight into how the forecasters can be lulled into false thinking. For the two week period leading up to Christmas, the ECMWF (European global model) had been the preferred model on nearly every day but in the days leading up to the race, this model did not offer consistent guidance with the low pressure system. Both the GASP (Australia) and ECMWF models showed that the development would be weaker and more likely to be east or sou'east of Tasmania and certainly not the intense system that actually developed over eastern Bass Strait.

✸

John Quinn, the man who was rescued after spending five hours in a horribly turbulent and storm-ravaged ocean off the NSW coast in the 1993 race, decided that he and his crew aboard *Polaris* would seek shelter and see what developed before deciding to continue or retire. Quinn was a veteran of 17 Sydney to Hobart races.

"We knew before the start that we were going to get a little bit of a blow. Initially we were talking about 30 to 45 knots, but as we went south the expectations went up to 45 to 55. We'd had a good run down the coast on the first day with a good set [current] behind us. The old *Polaris* was going like a bloody bullet actually. We were being pushed a bit out to sea probably because the set had a bit of an easterly component. After the front came in we changed to two reefs in the main and a No. 4 jib. We were just slightly 'sprung' because I was sailing higher than course. I really wanted to be back on the rhumb line or just inside it by the time we got to Gabo.

"I suppose the wind was maxing out at a little bit above 30 knots at that stage. We ran the weather fax which gave us a prognosis for 11am the next day and immediately saw it had changed a lot from the previous day's prognosis. It showed a low in the same position, but instead of being at 990hPa it was down at 984hPa. I just said to the guys, 'Oh shit, this is not good. This is another '93. There's going to be a lot of damage tonight'. The fax just showed this bloody tight little bloody eyeball, down at 984, just squashed between a high and the land. In reality it looked as if it was going to be a bit worse than '93. I added only one comment, 'We're going for shelter'. I passed the weather fax around, and there was nobody who disagreed."

Quinn knew the best option was to tack the yacht and aim it directly at the coast. A bay just south of Eden was the eventual target. The new course meant *Polaris* was sailing away from the low toward hopefully better conditions, after which they would continue on to Hobart. Quinn had been enjoying a race within a race as there were two sisterships to *Polaris* competing – Tony Mowbray's *Solo Globe Challenger* and Peter Heanley's *Ruff N Tumble*, both from Lake Macquarie, north of Sydney. They were fibreglass Cole 43 designs – sweetly proportioned 43-foot yachts that were around 20 years old. Mowbray, a sailmaker from Newcastle, had once owned *Polaris*. In 1984 he sailed it non-stop around Australia with one other crew "just for the heck of it". It was a 54-day voyage.

He had bought *Solo Globe Challenger* in Melbourne six months before the Hobart race but at that stage had no intention of competing. His goal was considerably greater – to set sail in October 1999 on a single-handed non-stop odyssey around the world. He planned to follow the course taken by Australia's Kay Cottee in 1988 and intended to use the voyage to raise money for the local John Hunter Children's Hospital. While he was preparing the yacht friends suggested he enter the Sydney to Hobart and offered to help with the substantial financial requirements. It was an offer he couldn't refuse.

The yacht's rig came out for five weeks and was completely rebuilt to the standard required for the circumnavigation. In the end the engineering specifications far exceeded what the average Hobart race could dish up. Mowbray decided to combine experience and youth in the race crew. His mentor, Bobby Snape, who was to make this his 23rd trip south, was his first choice for the team of eight.

"We weren't going out there with guns ablaze and trying to win," said Mowbray. "We were going to have a go, for sure, but really we we're only just in there to make up the numbers. At the same time I spent a lot of time getting the boat ready because I'm not the sort of person that goes to sea undercooked."

After a great run down the coast that saw them ahead of their arch rivals, the *Solo Globe Challenger* crew were justly content. Early on Sunday morning, when the breeze started to clock around to the north and north west, they gybed the yacht and headed back inshore to maximise their advantage. Mowbray noticed the wind strength was beginning to fluctuate. Towards the end of the morning, they were south east of Gabo Island, approximately 30 miles into Bass Strait and had done a respectable 210 miles in 25 hours.

★

Rob Kothe and the crew of *Sword of Orion* had been closely monitoring two concerns overnight and into the morning of the 27th – the crease in their mast and the weather. Kothe found weather analysis and application very satisfying. It was a bit like reading a good book – the more you got into it the more you enjoyed it. He was using the SatCom C unit and weather fax and was keeping close tabs on the reports on the radio channels. When the wind began to move towards the north then north west around midnight, they dumped the spinnaker and went to a poled-out No. 3 headsail. The best current was along the edge of the continental shelf and by 2 or 3am they were still making good time. When the wind started to move towards the west then south west early in the morning, they went to a double reef sail.

At around 3am a problem was discovered aboard *Sword of Orion* – bananas! Young crewmember Sam Hunt was rummaging through the galley looking for a snack when he found them.

"Superstition on 'The Sword' says you don't have bananas aboard," said Kothe. "Sam decided they were the reason for our start line 'bingle' with *Nokia* – so he made us eat all the bananas. Then he discovered a banana cake! That was just as bad as having bananas, so he made us eat all the banana cake because we didn't need any more bad luck. There we were, all sitting around stuffing ourselves with bananas then banana cake. As it turned out it would be the last solid meal we'd eat for quite a while. We were all fuelled up."

As *Sword of Orion* sailed into a rugged grey dawn Kothe was listening on the radio to the Bass Strait oil rigs reporting their weather conditions. He started to hear 987hPa as a barometric pressure reading and called Eden Coastguard and asked them what was happening in their vicinity. As the winds increased in strength, the crew continued to reduce sail but still had no thoughts of retiring. The wind was then starting to top 40 knots. The fast-flowing east-coast current and wild waves coming in from the west were starting to collide. There was no doubt that the yachts in the middle to back of the fleet would be the ones that would feel the full force of the blow.

Sayonara and *Brindabella* were neck and neck having averaged 15 knots since the start and had entered Bass Strait before sun-up. At around dawn, ABC chopper pilot Gary Ticehurst and his television crew were in the air and heading away from Merimbula in search of the leaders. He was stunned by what he discovered.

"I've never in 16 years seen them so far south. We got to *Brindabella* first and she was in 40 to 50 knots from the south west. The seas were already around 30 feet with nasty breaking tops. I remember one shot that Pete got while we were hovering there alongside *Brindabella*. She came out of this wave and the front half just dropped down about 15 feet into the trough. The whole mast just vibrated and the boat shook."

Brindabella had already lost all communications. The crew had missed the morning sked and was anxious to have a message relayed back to *Young Endeavour* and to shore that they were progressing well. Ticehurst did the relay for them. He then turned east and found *Sayonara*, about five nautical miles directly abeam of *Brindabella*, faring somewhat better due to more favourable weather conditions. Ticehurst was amazed there could be such weather fluctuation in such a small area.

★

Sayonara's navigator, Mark Rudiger, was troubled by what he was seeing. The digital barograph was dropping alarmingly and the satellite imagery showed they were right in the middle of the system. After scanning weather faxes and forecasts with Rudiger, Larry Ellison was convinced they were tackling a storm of cyclonic proportions. His theory was correct. The weather was winding up towards a cyclone right where *Sayonara* and the other big boats were sailing. Fortunately for them, they would be far enough south to miss the worst of the wind and seas. It was those following them that were headed straight for the cauldron.

★

Team Jaguar Infinity III, owned by Sydney's Martin James, had covered 220 miles in the first 20 hours of the race. The 18 crewmembers were comfortable and becoming increasingly confident that they would achieve their goal of a top five place across the line. The 65-foot sloop was George Snow's previous *Brindabella*. It was built in 1989 and took line-honours in the 1991 Hobart. Since taking over ownership James had gone to great lengths to improve the performance, including having a carbon fibre mast fitted for the previous year's event. That very expensive piece of equipment sheered at deck level and tumbled over the side when *Team Jaguar* was about 200 miles down the course.

This year, with the reliable old aluminium mast in place, the crew aboard *Team "Jag"* were hoping for better fortunes. The crew included Melissa McCabe, a student at Eden Marine Technology High School, who had been chosen from a host of applicants by race sponsor, Telstra, to sail as part of a sporting youth promotion scheme in rural regions. The CYC organised offshore and inshore sailing training for her so she would be fully prepared.

In the early hours of December 27 *Team Jaguar* pushed on into Bass Strait, thinking they were prepared for what was ahead. At around 10.30am the yacht was seen to be sailing comfortably, travelling at around 13 knots with the sheets slightly eased and very little angle at heel. Principal helmsman Tim Messenger had the mainsail trimmer easing the mainsail at the time to cope with the gusts. The sleek green and white sloop began to rise over a 25-foot wave then crested it and lunged into the trough behind. The shockload of the landing was not severe but it was enough to send a shudder through the yacht. The trimmer, who was looking up at the mast, saw a diagonal piece of stainless steel rigging (the D2) break with a loud bang. The rig began to fold like a bird's broken wing.

The yacht had suffered considerable damage and the crew then had the onerous task of repairing what they could. Hacksaws were deployed and rigging was cut away, but as the mast went over the port side it took with it several stanchions and lifelines, the VHF radio antenna, the HF backstay antenna, the GPS unit, Satellite communications unit, as well as dan buoys and life rings from the stern! After waiting for 10 or so minutes to ensure the mast had sunk, Messenger went back to the helm and set *Team Jaguar* on a course of between 350 degrees and north. That way the seas came at the yacht from the port aft quarter, 45 degrees off the stern; a comfortable angle.

They motored steadily for around an hour and a half, all the time fearing a mammoth wave would topple them. Finally it came and it was like a watermelon seed being squeezed out from between two fingers. The wave caught the stern of *Team Jaguar* and the yacht nose-dived almost half its length before being tossed sideways. The mastless yacht rolled to more than 90 degrees. Two crewmembers – one sitting near the companionway stormboards and one on the starboard side of the cockpit – were caught by the broken crest of the wave and hurled over the side. As soon as the hull settled there was a scramble to grab their safety harnesses and haul them back into the cockpit. Messenger thought the engine had simply stalled, but unbeknown to him one of the crew that went over the side had grabbed a fabric bag fitted in the cockpit where many of the sheets and lines had been stored. The ropes had burst out of the bag and had snared around the propeller, effectively strangling the motor. It would later take a diver in Eden an hour to remove the tangle of ropes.

The 13 crew below deck – many of whom were chronically seasick – had been haphazardly hurled about the cabin. Hundreds of gallons of water had been forced below – through a gap in the stormboards; via the hole left where the instrument panel had been in the cockpit; through the mast gate in the deck; and through other control line exits. Incredibly, despite what must have been exorbitant pressure, the forward hatch had not imploded. The deck had compressed six inches and the deck frame above the galley had fractured. The compression on the saloon cabin grab post saw it sheered at the deckhead.

The 18 crewmembers were left with no propulsion, no known position and no communications. And they were aboard a yacht that had been badly damaged. The last remaining method of communicating with the outside world, the EPIRB, was activated. While some crewmembers began pumping and bailing, two others attempted to rig a whip aerial for the HF radio. They succeeded and soon Race Control aboard *Young Endeavour* was contacted and advised of the situation.

★

Locky Marshall, a professional fisherman out of Eden for some 15 years, had witnessed rotten Sydney to Hobart weather on numerous occasions. When he saw the police car arrive at his home mid-afternoon on December 27, he sensed that it was going to be a request for assistance. Local Sergeant Keith Tillman told him that there was a yacht, *Team Jaguar*, in trouble in Bass Strait. Marshall didn't hesitate and he and Tillman went straight down to his office on Eden's commercial fishing dock.

Moira Elizabeth, the rugged and robust 70-foot steel trawler that Marshall managed, was at the time heading for Gabo Island to shelter from the storm. She was on a passage to Portland, on Victoria's Bass Strait coast when the weather forced a retreat. Marshall called the skipper, Tom Biddy, on the radio and asked if he could go to the assistance of *Team Jaguar*. Biddy was initially reticent due to the severity of the storm and the time it would take to reach the yacht, but Marshall explained to him there were 18 people on board who desperately needed seaborne assistance.

Biddy turned the helm of *Moira Elizabeth* to starboard and the big boat began ploughing its way through the horrendous seas out into Bass Strait. The speed was down to a mere five knots. He plotted an approximate position for *Team Jaguar* then tried to calculate the drift in those conditions. An intercept position was then plotted and an ETA (estimated time of arrival) of 11pm advised.

Team Jaguar's drift was far greater than even its crew could anticipate – at times up to six knots, and what was originally planned as a perfect intercept soon became a dangerous downwind chase. It would be 4am the next day when *Moira Elizabeth*, its deck and searchlights ablaze, loomed high over a monstrous wave and finally cornered its quarry, and another nine hours after that before *Team Jaguar*, with the majority of its crew still in shock, would be towed into Eden.

★

In the early afternoon of the 27th, *Young Endeavour* was just south of Montague Island – around 200 miles from Sydney and carrying little more than steadying sails. The officers' wardroom had, as in previous years, been converted into the communications centre for Lew Carter and his fellow radio officers. It is a very comfortable rectangular cabin, around four metres by three metres, one deck down from the main deck and a few metres aft of the bridge.

The cream-coloured sidewalls and bulkheads were laden with memorabilia – primarily plaques and photographs, including a signed photo of Queen Elizabeth and the Duke of Edinburgh. These and other photos told of *Young Endeavour*'s many voyages, visits and visitors over the previous decade. Carter and Michael and Audrey Brown were seated on the long, dark, floral-patterned lounge in one corner of the cabin with the bank of radios on a table – HF for long range communications and VHF for the more localised links – immediately in front of them. They were preparing for the 14:05 sked. Carter would broadcast to the yachts the special race weather forecast that had been received from the Bureau of Meteorology in Sydney.

Three times a day, prior to each sked, the radio room received a weather forecast specially compiled for the Sydney to Hobart. It is broken up into sectors, depending on where the fleet is located. It may be from Sydney to Gabo Island, Gabo to Flinders Island on the other side of Bass Strait, or Flinders to Tasman Island. There is an additional report for Storm Bay and the Derwent River.

Carter and Michael Brown read the 1209hrs weather report received from the Sydney Bureau:

WIND: W/SW 25/35 knots, with stronger gusts, increasing to 40/50 knots offshore south

of Merimbula today. Wind decreasing to 15/25 knots north of Merimbula Monday and 25/35 knots south of Merimbula during Monday.
WAVES: 2 to 3 metres, rising to 4 to 5 metres offshore in the south today.
SWELL: 1 to 2 metres, rising to 3 metres in south.

There was a second race forecast issued from Hobart at 1240hrs:

FORECAST FOR NEXT 24 HOURS – 38S to 40S: West to south-west winds 30 to 40 knots – locally 40 to 50 knots near the Victorian coast – easing to be 25 to 35 knots by early Monday morning then 20 to 25 knots by midday. 5 to 6 metre seas slowly abating. South-west swell 3 metres. Showers. Visibility fair to good.

At around the same time, 1210hrs, the Victorian Office issued the following forecast:

EASTERN BASS STRAIT: West/south-west winds at 45/55 knots easing to 30/40 knots overnight and to 20/30 knots tomorrow. Seas/swell 5 to 7 metres abating to 3 to 5 metres overnight and to 2 to 4 tomorrow.

✵

In the minutes leading up to 1405hrs all navigators aboard the 90-plus yachts still at sea were tuning their radios into *Young Endeavour*. Many of the off-watch crews, prone in their narrow bunks, had their ears pricked, anxiously awaiting the forecast as well as news of what was happening elsewhere on the course. They also wanted to know how they were performing against their strongest opponents. Some crew, though, were already too seasick to care. The yachts were now beginning to climb swells, some 30- and 40-feet high and despite the helmsman's best intentions there was not always a soft landing on the other side. Often the yacht would spear into mid-air, all 10 or 20 tonnes of it, and plunge down into the trough that followed. It was like launching a truck off a 30-foot ramp and awaiting the crash – continuously.

What many competitors didn't know was that wind strengths and wave heights given in official forecasts were merely mean, or average, figures. For wind strengths, a plus-or-minus figure of 1.4 can be factored in; for wave heights the factor was 1.86.

After delivering the weather forecast, Carter began the process of calling all yachts in alphabetical order for their position on the race course. At that stage *Sword of Orion* was around 70 miles south of Gabo Island. Rob Kothe had wedged himself into the nav station. Every massive wave – some peaking at 40 feet – threatened to dislodge him from his seat and the resting crew from their bunks. On deck the two on-watch crew were all securely harnessed to strong points. They were in "storm-mode" and had been that way since early that morning and had thus far managed to evade seasickness. Kothe had continued to gather information and plot the weather into the afternoon, checking the barometric pressure constantly.

He was amazed that by the time the sked had reached the letter "F" for position reports no one had talked about the weather. He knew that to do so was in breach of race radio procedures and might be seen as providing outside assistance to other yachts, but he also knew the "thumbprint" of the swirling storm he had on the chart in front of him, and what was being experienced outside, should outweigh everything. His decision to say something and warn others came only moments later.

"They were calling yachts that were six or seven before us on the list when I saw our wind speed instrument read 78 knots," he recalls. "The boat was now laying over fairly well on its side. I considered it was a safety issue. So what I did was I gave my sked position and I said to Lew that during this sked we have had wind strengths regularly over 60 gusting to 78."

It was a statement that echoed in a frightening fashion around the fleet. For the first time every crew, every navigator and every skipper knew that this was becoming a storm of horrific proportions. The news hit like a hammer and confirmed their worst fears. Most yachts were then between 30 and 100 miles from shore.

"It's most important during the sked that we don't get any chatter on the air," said Carter. "We try to get through the position reports – otherwise you find that you block up the airwaves for way too long. But I consider that what Kothe did was wise. To alert myself and others of the pattern of wind that he was getting was a commendable move. On hearing that report I asked if any other yachts were in the area and could confirm what *Sword of Orion* was saying. *Yendys*, owned by Geoff Ross, came in. It was a little bit north and east of 'Sword' and confirmed the weather conditions. I spoke to 'Sword' again and they confirmed gusts of 80 knots, and that the seas had really built up. They were breaking over the boat, but they didn't show any concern at that stage.

"Considering the circumstances, and the fact that I was in charge of communications, I took it upon myself to broadcast to the fleet a suggestion to the skippers that they consider their situation. I suggested that with night approaching, the seas building and the knowledge that there were worse winds further down the track, they take a good look at their position. If there was any suggestion of motor trouble, rig trouble or seasickness my suggestion would have been to seek shelter. Not necessarily to retire, but to seek shelter for the evening until the weather improved and maybe continue on in the race after that. I repeated that a couple of times. At that stage quite a few yachts decided to either seek shelter or retire."

Fundamental Rule 4 of the Australian Yachting Federation's Racing Rules of Sailing reads: A boat is solely responsible for deciding whether or not to start or to continue racing.

In his 25 years of being part of the race, nine as radio officer, Lew Carter had never seen nor heard anything like it. And for the first time he and the Browns needed to reassess their options. They called the skipper down and discussed their own situation. It was decided not to proceed into Bass Strait but to monitor an area north of Eden down to Gabo Island and 20 miles out to sea.

★

Little more than an hour after the sked, the storm had begun to turn. The waves were now huge – some the height of six-storey buildings and many near vertical. They were breaking as though they were pounding onto an ocean beach. They weren't the usual rolling monsters. And they had no pattern to them. The waves were making a low, powerful roar and the wind was shrieking through the rigging. Yachts with their smallest of sails set were heeled over at precarious angles as they were raked by the wind and pummelled by the seas.

Most yachts just had one storm sail set – either a storm jib or trysail – so that they could maintain steerage and be guided over the raging waves. Sometimes the yacht would have to be slowed in order to avoid being overwhelmed by a cascading wall of broken white water. Even the maxis were being flogged mercilessly. On board *Sayonara* Larry Ellison had never seen anything like it, and was caught on deck at one stage without a harness. He was lucky not to have been swept away. For helmsman Chris Dickson there was another consideration beyond the storm that he had to contend with. His wife of less than one week, Sue, would be waiting for him in Hobart – and here he was in a life-threatening situation.

America's Cup winning tactician and Hobart race veteran Hugh Treharne was similarly stunned by the waves he was seeing – endless 20-foot monsters with broken white water stretching it seemed from horizon to horizon. Almost every crew discussed retiring or continuing. For most retiring meant the same set of conditions simply on the opposite tack. For those who were more to the east, it was an enormous upwind battle back to safety. The options were to continue, turn back, hove-to with a small storm sail set and the helm locked, or lie-a-hull and just drift.

✯

Tough little *Canon Maris* was coping admirably with the conditions and was pushing well into Bass Strait by mid-afternoon. While the yacht was handling it under a No. 4 headsail and reefed mizzen and was in second position on handicap, Ian Kiernan was annoyed with himself. If conditions worsened it might be safest to set a sea anchor and ride out the storm. A sea anchor was something that sailors could use to slow the yacht's progress. It took the form of a drogue – usually in the old days a large canvas tube that looked like a windsock – that could be set just below the water surface behind the yacht. Modern race yachts didn't carry such cumbersome equipment.

"I realised I had forgotten some of the good things that I'd learned about seamanship with this yacht over the years," Kiernan recalls. "I used to always carry an old car tyre for a sea anchor and 50 to 60 fathoms of heavy polypropylene line. I have a special bridle that drops over the primary winches in the cockpit. The bridle trails out over the stern of the boat. You attach the polypropylene line and sea anchor or the car tyre – even an anchor on a chain if you want – to the bridle and just ride it out. It allows the boat to be slowed down and to keep its transom to the approaching wave and it lets the transom rise. By having it attached at the cockpit and not the stern, the hull can 'hinge' with the waves – the stern can rise as the crest approaches. Jack Earl taught me this. As things got worse in Bass Strait, Dick said, 'We've got to slow this boat down'. With no sea anchor the only way I could slow it down was to go to a spitfire jib, and that's what we did. I didn't want to go to a trysail because we would be over-canvassed to buggery. The mizzen would have had to be taken down and we wouldn't have been balanced."

★

Life aboard an ocean racing yacht is cramped at the best of times – but in a vicious storm it's abominable. Seasickness incapacitates some crew – they almost become comatose and are unable to help themselves, let alone make any contribution towards sailing the yacht and surviving. Often stronger crewmembers have to care for them as well as the boat. Life below deck is miserable. Consider having 10 people inside a very narrow and extremely small caravan; there is barely any headroom and because there are insufficient bunks most people are prostrate on the floor atop wet sail bags. Everything is sodden, people are vomiting and moaning, and this whole scene is being buffeted, bashed and belted by mountainous waves. This is when those who are suffering agree that the joy of ocean racing is one of the world's best kept secrets.

Dave Haworth's experience aboard *Foxtel-Titan Ford* painted the grim picture with sobering clarity. For him the Hobart is an occupational hazard. He is a very talented television cameraman who just happens to love sailing. Not surprisingly he is one of the first to be called when it comes to racing aboard a Hobart yacht and gathering vision for the news and race reports. The 1998 race was his fifth and roughest, but he recalls even when they were in the thick of it they didn't consider turning back.

"Once the shit hit the fan – when we were hit by bombs – it just became chaos. It's just hell on board. For a start you can't stand up. The whole boat is subject to violent movement all the time. You're standing in the cabin one minute hanging on and next thing you know you've been hurled into your bunk or head first into the stove. That's how a lot of people were injured – including Stan Zemanek and another guy and girl on our boat. You might be hanging on but as far as I can see the only safe place is on the floor. You'll be hanging on – the boat will come up out of a wave and it will just drop, almost like a free fall. You're still standing where you were but the whole boat has all of a sudden moved around you. Then, when it thumps into the bottom of the wave and stops, you are still moving. You catch up with it. You think you're in a safe spot but there is no safe spot.

"Down below there's just people everywhere. It's a disaster scene and it's disgusting. A lot of people are just dead to the world. They're in the bunks and they're just quiet. They don't move. Everything is wet. If it's not wet, it's damp. There's water sloshing around over the floorboards. In our case we had diesel fuel sloshing everywhere because one of the tanks had ruptured which made the whole thing even more dangerous. It was like a skating rink. Everything was like ice, it was so slippery."

Those who were capable did what they could, when they could, to purge the bilge of its fetid cocktail. Dave Haworth paid a price.

"One of the guys, Tony, had been bucketing out the bilge for some time, so I thought I should do my bit and give him a hand," he recalls. "He passed me a bucket that was bloody full, just four or five inches from the top. I started to pass it up from the cabin through the hatchway to 'Johnno', who was standing on deck so he could pour it out over the side. Just as I passed it up the boat fell out of a wave. 'Johnno' didn't have hold of it properly and the whole thing tipped back down all over me, from my head down. I had my bib-and-brace wet weather trousers on and the bib at the front was loose, so it acted like a funnel. I could just feel it go all the way down the back and front of my trousers, down through the legs. There was vomit, piss, diesel, salt water and I'm thinking, this is pretty low. This is a low point in the race. All I did then was go up into the cockpit and sit there just wanting a couple of big green waves to wash over the top of me. I didn't care that my thermals and other clothing were soaking wet. I couldn't live with myself. I just wanted to go onto the rinse cycle."

★

By late afternoon crews were facing a new fear – darkness. The crew of *Sword of Orion*, like so many others, watched the barometer continue its descent. It was heading towards 982hPa. Weather faxes only confirmed everything they already knew. The cauldron was well and truly boiling.

Part Two

Six
Destined for disaster

When Lew Carter commenced the 14:05 sked on the 27th, the off-watch crew aboard the South Australian yacht *VC Offshore Stand Aside* were listening to their radio with avid interest. As well as wanting to report their position and in turn let everyone know they were safe, they needed the latest weather forecast. They also wanted to know how they were faring against other yachts from Adelaide. To keep radio airtime to a minimum Carter called the name of each yacht and waited for a response – the yacht would repeat its name then give a latitude and longitude. Michael and Audrey Brown would each note the positions so they could be cross-checked later.

"*VC Offshore Stand Aside*," called Carter.

There was no response.

"Nothing heard," he said before moving onto the next yacht. At the end of the sked he went back through the yachts that had failed to report their positions and called *Stand Aside* again.

Still nothing heard.

Stand Aside had just become the first casualty of the race.

✷

Sailed by Jim Hallion, the 41-foot fibreglass composite sloop was built in New Zealand. It was a Young 12 class – a plump, relatively lightweight design that was renowned for its downwind speed. Hallion, his brother Laurie, and a friend, had bought the yacht soon after it was launched in 1990. It had been raced with some success in St Vincent Gulf around Adelaide and across Spencer Gulf to Port Lincoln. The Sydney to Hobart was an inevitable goal for the yacht and 1998 was chosen as the debut.

The original plan was to sail it to Sydney and in early December it left from Adelaide with a crew comprising some of those who would be aboard for the Hobart and a couple of friends. Trevor Conyers, a Hobart race rookie but capable offshore sailor, was aboard the yacht for the delivery to Sydney. Conditions were reasonably smooth until the yacht reached Cape Jervis where they decided to pull into Wirrinya for the night and head for the local pub, expecting to set off the following morning when the weather had cleared.

It didn't improve, but they pushed on nonetheless the next day and reached Kangaroo Island about lunch time. They stopped there, right on the eastern end of the island, to eat a meal. Jim Hallion had caught a virus which refused to go away, and when they set sail again around 8pm, his condition quickly worsened. The rotten weather was soon taking its toll on most of the crewmembers and they decided to turn back to Wirrinya. Conyers had to sail the yacht back almost single-handed. Considering Hallion's condition, the fact that time was rapidly running out for the trip to Sydney and that bad weather might further delay them, they decided to sail back to Adelaide and put the yacht on a truck.

One week prior to the start of the Sydney to Hobart *Stand Aside* was docked at the CYC, rigged and ready to race. The crew was in good spirits and feeling confident. One of the crewmembers, 45-year-old father-of-three Mike Marshman, had taken up sailing only seven years earlier. This was to be his second Hobart. Before his first in 1997 aboard Gary Shanks' *Doctel Rager*, he'd proudly announced, "I don't get sick and I don't get scared."

☆

On the ride down the coast on the 26th the *Stand Aside* crew was "whooping and hollering" as the yacht notched up an average speed of around 18 knots on a tailor-made spinnaker run. With spinnaker and mainsail straining in the building sea breeze, *Stand Aside* was picked up by a sharp following sea and hurled forward down its face, surfing for hundreds of metres. It was exhilarating sailing. That evening, as they threaded their way between two spectacular thunderstorms, they regularly monitored their radio, but like so many competitors still weren't exactly sure what they were in for.

By the morning of the 27th, they were "nicely placed". As the wind strengthened and the seas grew, sail area was correspondingly reduced. *Stand Aside* was handling the conditions surprisingly well, spearing off the backs of waves only on the odd occasion. While the 12 crewmembers were far from comfortable, they were happy with the way the yacht was performing. They sailed under a storm jib until early afternoon, when the weather seemed to go from bad to horrific in just a few minutes. The gusts were strengthening – first 55 knots was registered, then 60 and soon 70.

Stand Aside was very pressed under the storm jib and they were getting flattened by the gusts as the yacht crested the waves, so they decided to lower the jib and run under bare poles until the weather improved. At this point there was no talk of retiring or returning to Eden. It was then 1pm and they were well into Bass Strait. They knew that if they could reset sail soon and get the boat back to speed they would be off the Tasmanian coast by around midnight.

As with most other yachts in such atrocious weather, a crewmember was always posted on "wave watch", as the helmsman could not look upwind into the near horizontal rain and spray. The man on wave watch shouted information on how best to angle the boat for the approaching wave. The one thing none of the crew liked hearing on deck was "This one's going to break!".

As the weather continued to worsen they were faced with two choices – 10 to 12 hours back to Eden or about eight hours forward to the other side of Bass Strait. They decided to continue. Because there was no sail set, *Stand Aside* was beginning to behave very erratically. It was difficult steering up and over the monster waves so the helmsman decided to "let her have her head" and let the yacht find its own way down the face. He would use the helm only when possible.

For much of the time *Stand Aside* chose a course more towards New Zealand than Tasmania. No one had a desire to finish up on the other side of the Tasman Sea and fly home so the storm jib was set once again. With the wind blowing at more than 70 knots and the yacht now being tossed by mighty seas, resetting the sail took 40 minutes. *Stand Aside* was back to a more desirable course as the 14:05 sked approached. Rod Hunter and Andy Marriette were wedged into the tiny navigation area on the starboard side, near the bottom of the companionway, waiting for the position reports to commence.

The forecast from *Young Endeavour* certainly didn't correlate with what the *Stand Aside* crew was experiencing. Hunter and Marriette discussed the seeming chasm between forecast and fact and agreed that their position meant that the yacht was right on the edge of the worst of the depression. They also agreed that, based on the forecast, things would get better sooner rather than later. They were aware numerous yachts had retired but weren't surprised to hear *Sword of Orion* come on air and warn the fleet that 78 knots of wind had been experienced.

"*Young Endeavour* was about three-quarters of the way through the sked when I heard one of the guys on deck shout with considerable alarm, 'A real bad wave, WATCH OUT!'" recalls Marriette. "The boat went up and up then we started to roll, and roll rapidly. The noise was sickening – first it was water just pouring in like a river through the companionway, then there was the cracking and tearing sound. The deck and cabin top were splitting open."

The cabin roof had imploded. The force of the water as the yacht rolled tore away a huge section of the cabin roof around the companionway slide. It hinged down like a giant trapdoor and pinned both Hunter and Marriette in the nav station. Much to Marriette's amazement, when the yacht came back upright he found himself in the same position as when it all started – still holding the radio microphone. The two set about smashing their way out of the nav station to save themselves and whoever else might still be on board.

Bob Briggs rushed up from the cabin and started calling out names like it was a roll call. He wanted to make sure everybody was still on the boat but much to his horror he saw John Culley swimming frantically towards what was now a wrecked yacht. Culley had been in the process of going on deck and attaching his safety harness to a strong point when *Stand Aside* rolled.

★

Mike Marshman was among the eight crewmembers on deck when the megalithic monster wave thundered out of nowhere. He remembers turning in time to see it coming but knew they were powerless. It broke at the top and with an almighty crunch threw him into the air. As quickly as it had rolled, the yacht righted itself, reefing him through the water by his harness and depositing him underneath the rigging. Instinctively Marshman felt across his chest, searching for the clip of his safety harness. Then he remembered an early lesson in the sport which said you should never let go of your boat. He sensed the rigging wound around his right arm was becoming loose, so he kept trying to wind his arm around it. The loops became larger and before he knew it the end of the thin and flexible wire that was trapping him had slipped free.

The crew on deck saw his head suddenly burst through the surface like a balloon released underwater. As he was surfacing Marshman realised that Simon Clarke was in the water right alongside him. He too had been trapped underwater by the rigging less than a metre away. Marshman saw the boom in front of him folded in half and he grabbed a stanchion with his right hand.

John Culley was in the water upwind of the yacht. A couple of big waves along with wildly flailing arms delivered him back to *Stand Aside* at a rapid rate. Crewmembers grabbed him and dragged him aboard. The remainder of the on-deck crew had been left dangling over the side at the end of their orange lifeline tethers after the capsize. They were hauled in one by one and lifted from the water and unceremoniously dumped on deck.

Marshman had made no effort at all to get back on deck. He just continued to hang onto the broken base of the stanchion and wallow, all the time reminding himself he was alive. Hayden Jones came across to help him up, and that was when Marshman noticed the blood pouring from one of his fingers. He had lost about half of the top joint of the ring finger on his right hand. Yet he could feel no pain. Andy Marriette, a registered operating theatre nurse, discovered others were wounded. Clarke had damaged the cartilage in his ankle; Bob Briggs had a severe laceration on his forehead between his eyes; Trevor Conyers had a large gash across the back of his head; and Marriette had a badly cut thumb.

Those still below deck were in waist-deep water. Bulkheads and much of the internal structure of the yacht had failed and the sides of the hull were panting in and out with each passing wave. There were pieces of cabin roof and deck floating around and razor sharp pieces of carbon fibre and fibreglass threatening to slice at hands, fingers and legs. The floorboards and food were floating, bunks had been ripped off the side of the hull, diesel fuel was spewing from the motor, the batteries were submerged, and crew clothing was bobbing around in the water.

There was little doubt *Stand Aside* was destined to sink at some stage and the decision was made to inflate the life rafts. The first six-man orange and black raft, which had been stowed below, was triggered and much to everyone's delight took only seconds to be inflated and deployed at the stern – attached by a rope tether. The second life raft, a brand new one, had been stowed on deck. It wouldn't inflate! The crew looked on in disbelief as increasingly desperate efforts were made to inflate it. Nothing worked. They tried to pull it back aboard so they could manually trigger the inflation mechanism.

Next, much to their horror, the painter line attached to the raft capsule snapped. The crew was now confronted with a sinking yacht, one six-man life raft, 12 crewmembers and mauling, relentless seas. Their yacht was now their one real hope for survival and keeping it afloat was crucial.

Massive bolt cutters were brought on deck and within seconds the giant jaws were snapping through solid metal rigging as though it were a carrot. The mast was cut free and jettisoned – the chance of the broken sections of aluminium punching a gaping hole in the hull had been eliminated. Two crewmembers below deck bucket-bailed continuously while two others were assigned to manual pumps. Everything possible was thrown overboard – it was imperative that the yacht be made as light as possible; and it was important to leave a debris trail so, should *Stand Aside* sink, rescue crews would have a distinct search area and a better chance of spotting survivors.

The grab bags – holding essential stores for the life raft – were put on deck. A hand-held VHF radio was located and it was Charles Alsop's sole task to continuously send out a mayday call. Amid the confusion, a waterproof camera popped to the surface between Hunter's legs in the cabin and he took some of the most harrowing and graphic photographs imaginable.

☆

Gary Ticehurst, at the controls of the ABC chopper covering the race, and his journalist and cameraman, had completed the day's filming and were heading back to Mallacoota for refuelling. It was late afternoon and Ticehurst was worried. He had been filming *Foxtel-Titan Ford* fighting 50-foot waves in 60 knots of wind and had been amazed to see *Helsal II* also grinding its way through the storm.

"We headed back to Mallacoota to refuel and let the journo jump on a small plane and fly back to Merimbula with his video tapes," Ticehurst recalls. "He was keen to get across Bass Strait to Flinders Island that night because the leading yachts were really sailing fast. I knew I had to convince him that we should stay where we were for the night. I was a little concerned about the winds we might encounter crossing the Strait, but more importantly my experience told me that most of the drama would be just off the coast where we were."

Five minutes later a police car was racing across the tarmac towards them. The police asked Ticehurst if he could scramble his helicopter and head out to sea. An EPIRB signal and mayday call had been received by AusSAR. Ticehurst shot out of Mallacoota like a rocket at about 3pm, hitting 180 knots of ground speed assisted by a 60-knot tailwind. As they neared the search area they were sure they were entering a small cyclone. The chopper was handling the conditions well and they were reassured by the presence of a fixed-wing aircraft also searching from above. They both spotted *Stand Aside* at the same time, about 40 miles east of Mallacoota.

As Ticehurst hovered down closer he established communications with the damaged yacht. He didn't have winching capabilities aboard his chopper, so he radioed AusSAR and told them *Stand Aside*'s condition and position and that there were injured crewmembers aboard. Ticehurst was told a rescue helicopter was on its way.

It wasn't the first time Ticehurst had been frustrated his helicopter wasn't fully equipped to conduct rescues. His concern had been such that he made his own, unofficial plans and had installed a homemade ladder. While the ABC chopper hovered like a guardian angel over *Stand Aside*, waiting for the rescue team to arrive, Ticehurst offered words of encouragement to the beleaguered crew below.

☆

The Northshore 38 fibreglass production yacht *Siena*, owned by Iain Moray, was 30 miles south east of Gabo Island when the 14:05 sked was broadcast. The crew was elated, having covered some 230 miles in 25 hours. They heard the forecast for winds of 45 to 55 knots, but they were already seeing 75 knots, so, as well as the euphoria there was a growing anxiety about what might be ahead. *Siena*'s navigator, 50-year-old Tim Evans, was struggling to keep himself jammed into the nav station on the high (starboard) side as the yacht was pounded by wind and waves.

Suddenly a mayday burst through the airwaves. It was *Stand Aside*. Moray and his crew waited deliberately for a few seconds to see if anybody else responded. That didn't happen. Evans then grabbed his radio microphone and acknowledged *Stand Aside*. They worked out the yacht was ahead of them and, after making contact with the ABC helicopter, proceeded to the location to lend what assistance, if any, they could.

"We found them right on the button," said Moray. "Initially, because of the size of the waves, we couldn't spot them. But we did see the helicopter and that gave us our goal. In fact we didn't see the yacht until we were about 100 metres away. We told the helicopter we were putting our engine on. Our plan was to stand by and help pick the guys off the yacht if the helicopters couldn't get some or all of them. We just had the storm jib up and for about the next hour we were tacking up and down around the yacht. We still weren't clear whether the helicopter could actually get to them. I was one of two guys on deck when this huge wave hit us and knocked us flat – with the mast in the water. Tim, who was still on the radio talking to the helicopter, didn't hear the call from the deck of 'Bad wave!'. The noise of the storm was too great."

The force of the sudden knock-down was such that Evans was hurled like a sack of potatoes across the cabin and into the stove in the galley. The pain was instant and excruciating; the result, it would later be learned, of three broken ribs and a punctured lung. He regained his feet and his composure and, despite being in agony, went straight back to his radio to continue monitoring the situation. On deck Moray made sure that the helmsman was still aboard. He then checked on the situation below. Evans' injuries soon proved too serious and he staggered to a bunk. Pain-killing drugs were administered in a bid to make him as comfortable as possible. Lifting him in a sling or harness would be out of the question. They decided to head for Eden.

The engine and storm jib were being used for propulsion – until the engine died – the consequence of seawater forcing its way into the fuel tank via the breather tube. Twenty hours later *Siena* made the best possible landfall, Bermagui. Evans was rushed to Moruya where he was stabilised and prepared for surgery. Doctors discovered that pneumonia had already set in and it was suggested he may not have lasted another 24 hours without medical attention.

✮

Above the mayhem, Gary Ticehurst was starting to have problems of his own. Because the cloud cover was so thick, darkness was descending more rapidly than usual. The fuel gauge on his chopper was also starting to remind him that the time to return to shore was fast approaching. But he didn't want to leave *Stand Aside* before the rescue chopper arrived.

✲

The Helimed chopper team had done a remarkable job in reaching their target little more than an hour after being directed to the rescue. They arrived to find the broken yacht taking on water at an alarming rate. The *Stand Aside* crew kept bailing to keep their yacht afloat, all the time watching as the big chopper moved around them like a jumbo-sized dragonfly. What the sailors didn't know was that their apparent saviours were actually discussing forsaking the mission because it was too dangerous. After much deliberation the Helimed team decided to make an attempt at a rescue and reassess the situation after that. Forty-year old Peter Davidson, father of two teenage children and a Helimed airwing crewmember for eight years, was to be the "live bait" – the man lowered from the chopper to make the rescue.

The *Stand Aside* crew was asked to put the first two men to be rescued – the worst injured – into the life raft and then let it drift a considerable distance away from the yacht on an extended line. That way the chance of Davidson being slammed into the side of the yacht was minimised. It was also easier for the pilot, Peter Leigh, to concentrate on the raft and not the yacht. Davidson clipped onto the wire winch cable and began the descent. Gary Ticehurst watched from the controls of the ABC chopper, fearing for Davidson's safety but lauding his courage.

"It was unbelievably difficult for the chopper to hold station with the yacht coming up at him in the 50-foot seas," Ticehurst said. "There were two survivors in the life raft which was tethered to the yacht. It was flicking around all over the place, being washed over and rolled.

The crewman on the wire had to be placed in a position near the raft. It was a nightmare trying to get him there. He was being rolled and dragged across the ocean surface by the wire from the chopper, sometimes on top of the water, sometimes under. At times he was just snatched out of the water because the trough was deeper than the cable was long. It took 10 minutes for the first survivor to be taken out of the life raft. The energy the crewman had to apply was amazing. That guy is a real hero. He went and did another seven rescues. I think it took forty minutes to get the rest of them."

Davidson was the next best thing to a human tea bag. After several unsuccessful attempts to get him into the raft he was winched back up to the helicopter for a re-think. He was placed into the water as close as possible to the raft so he could swim to it. It was a procedure that worked and once Davidson had his first rescue complete all the confidence that was needed was there. It was a perilous mission for both the chopper crew and Davidson – the chopper pilot was forever concentrating on the approaching waves because the cable on the winch was barely long enough. At times he would have to gain altitude rapidly to allow a rampaging wave to roll underneath. Mike Marshman and Simon Clarke, the two crewmembers with the most severe injuries, were sent to the chopper first. They were about 50 metres from the yacht when an enormous wave rumbled in towards them. As it curled at the top the lanyard securing them to the yacht went tight and flicked them through the top of the wave. They were shaken, stirred but had survived. Davidson's effort continued until he had his full bag of fish – eight of the *Stand Aside* crew in the chopper.

"There were two very bad moments for me," Davidson recalls. "One was when the helicopter was buffeted by a wind gust. I'd just managed to get the harness around a guy when suddenly it felt like we'd been caught in an explosion. It was as though we were standing on our feet one minute then the next second we were being picked up and hurled across the surface. We were both launched out of the raft and as we hit the water one of the monster waves – a 50- or 60-footer – broke over the top of us. I just didn't know what was going to happen. I thought I'd broken my back but then realised I could still feel my legs. The impact was incredible. I thought I'd lost the guy out of the harness – but he was still there. I managed to wrap my arms and legs around him and hang on." The next instant the helicopter suddenly climbed and Davidson and his man were launched from the water like a missile.

★

While the Helimed team was completing their part of the rescue the SouthCare rescue helicopter out of Canberra came into the circuit over *Stand Aside*. Its task was to rescue the four crewmen remaining aboard. The pilot was Ray Stone, the crewman was Mark "Delfie" Delf and the two paramedics were Kristy McAlister and Michelle Blewitt, both helicopter rescue rookies. A few hours earlier the SouthCare chopper was on a return flight from Sydney to Canberra when it was tasked to another emergency in the NSW country town of West Wyalong. As they prepared to head to West Wyalong the job was cancelled. The four crew joked that they would probably get a rescue job with the Sydney to Hobart race. Ten minutes later that's exactly what happened. AusSAR told them they were needed in Mallacoota.

The chopper returned to the SouthCare base at Canberra airport to refuel and be equipped with special rescue gear. It wasn't until they were in the air and heading for Mallacoota that they were re-routed to

Merimbula. They were to do a "hot refuel" – not shutdown – then head 60 nautical miles off the coast to back up Helimed on the *Stand Aside* rescue.

Thirty-year-old McAlister had been brought up on a sheep and wheat property near Quandialla in western NSW, and had joined the Ambulance Service in 1991. In 1994 she became a paramedic with SouthCare and was selected as one of 13 paramedics to work on the helicopter when it joined the ambulance service. McAlister had been airsick for the first time in her life on the way out to Merimbula. The worsening weather wasn't helping.

"I was feeling fine until we found the yacht and started doing tight circles waiting for Helimed to finish their winching. It was really turbulent and next thing both Michelle and I were sick. I was also feeling scared. It was my turn to go down the wire. I was watching what Peter was doing and how much he was getting tossed about. Delfie was just continually making little comments like, 'Oh … oh … oh … oh shit … oh no!'. In the end I said to him, 'Look, will you please stop it! I'm petrified already and you're making it worse for me'. Delfie just said, 'Oh, I'm sorry,' and he didn't say another word."

Once the Helimed chopper had completed its rescue the SouthCare machine moved into a hover situation just astern of *Stand Aside* and 100 feet above the water. McAlister, who was wearing her wetsuit, put on her swimming fins before Delf handed her the winch cable. She clipped it onto her harness and moved to the open door, and almost instantly the immediacy of the situation cured her of her airsickness. While she was looking down a large set of waves pummelled the life raft and one of the men was separated. McAlister signalled she was going to go for him. As if it was an initiation ceremony for someone making their first open ocean rescue, McAlister was pounded by a 50-foot breaking wave as soon as she hit the water. It pushed her under for 15 seconds and rolled the life raft. Before she had a chance to catch her breath, yet another wave dumped her. When she surfaced again she was miraculously only 10 metres away from the *Stand Aside* crewmember. She reached him, told him what needed to be done then both were winched to safety.

Andy Marriette and Bevan Thompson were in the life raft when it rolled while McAlister was descending. Thompson then drifted off but was picked up by McAlister. John Culley then jumped into the raft.

"I went down again and by this stage there were two guys hanging onto the life raft," recalls McAlister. "I didn't realise it had been capsized again. The waves were tossing the raft everywhere and the guys were getting thrown all over the place. I made my way over to one of the guys and had the strop half on him when the other guy started saying, 'No, don't take him, take me. I can't hang on any longer.' I could only say, 'Look mate, I'm sorry but I've already got this guy about ready to go. We're not going to leave you. You're just going to have to hang on.' What else could I do? The guy I was with then started saying, 'It's OK, you can take him.' I said, 'No, I'm taking you. You are it.'

"Just before we began to winch up we got hit by another set of waves and the life raft became tangled around our winch cable. I didn't realise this until we started to be winched up and the life raft was coming with us so we got plonked down into the water. As we hit the water the winch cable got caught on the side of my neck and carved a welt into it. At that moment another set of waves came through. It was just sheer luck that the waves untangled the life raft from around the winch cable. As soon as I realised we were clear I gave the thumbs up and we were gone."

She then handed over the winch wire to Michelle Blewitt, a mother of two, who had spent the last few minutes being sick. By the time Blewitt got to the water Marriette was understandably distressed. She had to struggle with him to get the rescue strop over his safety harness and inflatable life jacket. It was soon apparent Marriette would have to float on his back so Blewitt could put his legs through the ring and then move it up to the proper position around his chest.

"As soon as they started the lift I began saying to this wonderful woman, 'Will you hurry up and get us out of here. I hate heights, I'm the biggest chicken you could ever have on a rope'," Marriette recalls. The pair were lifted about 20 feet above the water with the life raft tether wrapped around the winch cable. The chopper crew lowered them back into the water so it could be untangled. As Blewitt tried to clear the rope, the life raft was caught by another savage gust of wind and flung into the air. The metal cylinders that supply the gas to inflate the raft when it is deployed, and which hang on a strap, flipped up and smashed Blewitt on the side of her head, knocking her out for a moment. When she regathered her senses Marriette suggested that they try again to untangle the rope. He was concerned because there was still one crewmember, Charles, on board the yacht and the raft would be needed for his rescue.

"I said to the paramedic, 'I'll try to untie the rope, so we can keep the life raft and get it untangled'. She said 'No, No, No,' and with that ripped out her knife and sliced through the 10mm Kevlar line as though it were butter," Marriette recalls. The life raft bolted like a wild horse freed from a tether. It immediately flipped up onto its edge and took off at around 80 knots, bouncing from wavetop to wavetop. Marriette could not believe what he had just seen. He arrived at the welcoming door of the helicopter "absolutely knackered". Blewitt then went down again and did a water rescue of the last sailor. He had to jump into the water with his life jacket on and clutching a safety line still attached to the yacht. That way, if something went wrong, he could haul himself back aboard. This rescue turned out to be relatively quick and simple.

With all four crew safely on board the door was closed on the SouthCare chopper and pilot Ray Stone turned towards the coast; destination Mallacoota. When the chopper landed the locals were on hand with blankets for the survivors. They went straight to McAlister and Blewitt first.

"They thought that we were the ones who had been rescued," said McAlister. "Michelle and I were saying, 'No, no, not for us. Give them to the guys we just rescued'. I couldn't describe the looks on their faces. They were just saying among themselves, 'Oh my God, these girls are the ones that did the rescue'." With the crew either hospitalised or released after a check-up by doctors, they each began to make their plans to head home to their loved-ones.

Mike Marshman, the crewmember who had been trapped under the rigging when the yacht rolled, returned home a changed man. "I've been a pretty selfish bastard – just ask my wife. But all the emotions I faced out there really stunned me. All my values in life have changed. My relationship with my wife is 10 times better. The house is fun again. I want to spend more time with my kids and I'm back to actually enjoying my work."

Andy Marriette didn't go straight home. Instead he stayed one more night in Mallacoota to celebrate the fact that he was still alive. That night he was arrested and charged with being drunk and disorderly. His "motel room" for the night was a cell at Lakes Entrance police station.

Seven
AMSA

Its full title is the Australian Maritime Safety Authority, but it is located a long way from the sea – in Airservices Australia's rather drab building in the heart of the national capital, Canberra. AMSA covers the regulatory aspects of maritime operations in Australian waters including the control and surveillance of shipping movements around the coastline. It is an all-encompassing group that includes the relatively new AusSAR – Australian Search and Rescue.

It was after the rescues of the round-the-world racers, Britain's Tony Bullimore and Frenchmen Thiery Dubois and Raphael Dinelli in late 1996/early 1997, that maritime authorities realised Australia's search and rescue system was both inefficient and inadequate. All three were rescued from their wrecked yachts at up to 1000 nautical miles south of the Australian continent in the largest exercise the AMSA had ever undertaken. Seven national rescue headquarters across the continent were then replaced by the centralised AusSAR.

AusSAR's Rescue Control Centre (RCC) is located in an open-plan room on the fourth floor of the Airservices Australia Building. It is alive 24 hours a day, with at least two officers on hand to monitor activities across a sizeable chunk of the world. It seems incongruous to many visitors that such a small facility oversees such a sizeable jurisdiction. The AMSA umbrella covers 47,000,000 square kilometres – one-ninth of the world's surface. It extends from 75 degrees east across to 163 degrees east and from the Indonesian archipelago down to the ice of Antarctica.

A bank of computer screens in the RCC incessantly digest information from three satellite tracking stations – Wellington in New Zealand, Bundaberg in Queensland and Caves Beach near Albany in Western Australia. They are searching for signals from EPIRBs; small devices which are activated either manually or automatically when a vessel, aircraft or individual is in distress. AusSAR's EPIRB detection region, which is part of a worldwide safety net, extends beyond its search and rescue domain, reaching all the way into the South Pacific as far as Tahiti.

When a satellite detects an EPIRB signal it delivers an approximate latitude and longitude position back to AMSA. That position is accurate to roughly 20 kilometres. To pinpoint it exactly, SAR (search and rescue) authorities need to either put an aircraft into the area or wait for the passing of another satellite – which can take up to three hours. The information from the second satellite gives what is called a merge – a far more accurate location for the beacon.

EPIRBs of 121.5/243mHz provide no indication of what the target might be. It could be anything from a type of vessel in mid-ocean to a four-wheel-drive vehicle lost in the middle of the continent. The latest 406mHz beacons, which are registered with SAR authorities at the time of purchase, emit both a position and an identification code. That code is cross-referenced to a database which immediately details the nature of the target.

✯

On the afternoon of December 27, Rupert Lamming was the Search Mission Coordinator in the RCC. There were four other officers working with him on what had been a quiet day, apart from an EPIRB that had activated after being lost accidentally from a ship in Bass Strait. The office was well-versed on the staging of the Sydney to Hobart race, so much so that Sam Hughes, an AusSAR search and rescue coordinator, had been assigned to brief competitors on procedures before the race.

This relationship between AMSA and the CYC had been established after incidents experienced in the rough 1993 race. With 371 yachts set to enter the 50th anniversary race in 1994, both the club and AMSA wanted to ensure that the best possible safety net was in place. It was decided that AMSA should always have a representative at race control, and it was Hughes who acted as a liaison officer between AusSAR and the club. As a result of this relationship, a contingency plan had been developed. Part of that plan was to have an Air Force aircraft stationed at Richmond, west of Sydney, dedicated to race SAR should it be needed.

Rupert Lamming and his team were well aware that the intense low developing in Bass Strait was going to generate atrocious conditions, but were comfortable in the knowledge there was an emergency strategic plan in place, right down to having Naval vessels, the Air Force and search and rescue aircraft readily accessible.

The yacht race was just one thing on their minds. An emergency that afternoon could involve a commercial ship, an ocean liner, an aircraft or a recreational vessel anywhere in their region. They had to be prepared for everything.

★

It began with a single blip on a computer screen in the RCC. An EPIRB had been activated at around 2.30pm in the north-east corner of Bass Strait. It was the first drop in what would become a rainstorm for AusSAR. Next, mayday distress calls were being monitored along the coast and details were being relayed to AusSAR. Then more EPIRBs started to appear on the screen. Within minutes Lamming and his team knew something was afoot. Their immediate questions were: How bad will the weather get? How many yachts are involved? What is the nature of the emergencies? How many more yachts will need assistance?

Lamming set about collating the beacon detections on the screen. The relevant charts started to appear on the large plotting table in the room. The aviation section was already working as fast as possible to find every available civilian fixed-wing aircraft and helicopter. The whiteboards on the wall were being filled out with aircraft availability and location. Extra staff would need to be called in. AMSA public relations officer Brian Hill, who was on call in case of an emergency, was summoned to handle the inevitable deluge of media inquiries. Hill arrived at the office at 3.30pm and, after being briefed by Lamming, called AMSA's public relations manager, David Gray, warning him what was ahead of them.

Gray waited for a while, all the time strongly suspecting a disaster was developing in Bass Strait. He didn't wait for Hill's next call but farewelled his family who had gathered for a post-Christmas celebration, and drove to the office. He arrived around 4.30pm and was astounded by the sheer scale of the calamity. Upon arrival, seven people were busy in the SAR room, but within an hour this number had swelled to more than 20. What started as a trickle of beacons soon turned into a torrent as more and more yachts in distress activated their EPIRBs.

AusSAR's disaster plan was running to capacity and reaching levels never previously experienced. It was soon realised the Royal Australian Navy's frigate HMAS

The Mooloolaba entry *Midnight Special* making good speed towards Hobart before a strengthening north-easterly breeze. This yacht was rolled twice and eventually sank during the storm.

Solo Globe Challenger heads away from the coast south of Sydney. This supposedly very seaworthy design was dismasted during the storm and went within an ace of being lost.

The Tasmanian entry, *Business Post Naiad*, surges south under spinnaker towards her home waters. Just a day later the crew were fighting for their lives and to save the badly damaged yacht.

The 42-footer *Miintinta* was entered in the race for the fun of it. Its lines came from one of Australia's most respected yacht designers of the 60s and 70s – Ron Swanson.

Sword of Orion was sailed by one of the most experienced crews in the race. At the height of the storm this Grand Prix level racer had to contend with waves considerably higher than its mast.

With a bone in her teeth the beautifully restored *Winston Churchill* makes an impressive sight under spinnaker. Her design is in direct contrast to *Sword of Orion* (above) which was badly damaged and also nearly lost.

The no-nonsense race yacht *Kingurra* has survived the worst that 13 previous Hobart races could deliver. This yacht became the centre of one of the most amazing man-overboard rescues in the history of offshore racing.

Wayne Millar's *B-52* was one of the favourites for top honours in the Channel Handicap division. Around the same time the next day this yacht was upside down for four minutes in mountainous seas with seven crew trapped inside and two crew outside clinging to the upturned hull.

Zeus II, the race's smallest entry, won the classic in 1981. Not even this tough little yacht could survive the wrath of the storm.

High speed running under spinnaker was a feature of *Team Jaguar's* effort early in the race. But for the second consecutive year this yacht would lose its mast – this time becoming the focus of a major search and rescue effort in the early stages of the storm.

Canon Maris, sailed by "Mr. Clean-up-the-World" Ian Kiernan, was originally owned by one of the race's founders, Jack Earl. One of the crew, Jonathan Gibson, was the son of John "Gibbo" Gibson, who survived 30 hours in a wrecked life raft after *Winston Churchill* sank.

VC Offshore Stand Aside was the first yacht to be claimed by the storm. It was a miracle that this crew survived.

Foxtel-Titan Ford enjoying the best part of the race – the stretch up the Derwent River to the finish. It was so far offshore when the storm struck that it had to keep going.

The start of the storm. *Brindabella* begins to smoke its way across Bass Strait under considerably reduced sail.

One of the best known names in the world of ocean racing, *Ragamuffin*, skippered by 30-year race veteran Syd Fischer. It was déjà-vu for Fischer who also survived the calamitous 1979 Fastnet Race in England.

Nowhere to hide. *Aspect Computing*, crewed by disabled sailors, probably provided the race's most remarkable result. They survived the storm and went on to win their division. This, and other remarkable photos in this section were taken by Richard Bennett and his daughter, Alice.

Going sideways as fast as forward, the pocket maxi *Bobsled* is trapped by the worst of the storm. The ferocious wind was blowing the seas flat, yet every so often a breaking wave more than 60 feet high would arrive on the scene.

Breaking waves play Russian roulette with *Aspect Computing*. If the yacht had been only a few metres ahead it would have been hammered by this breaking wave.

So little sail is almost too much. *Secret Men's Business* experiences the business end of the storm.

Winning form. The eventual race winner – the yacht that won on handicap –
was *Midnight Rambler*. Even when the storm was at its worst crew members
still perched on the windward side to help keep it upright.

The race's first major casualty, *Stand Aside* (**circled left**) is abandoned and the helicopter carrying its crew (**circled right**) heads for the coast. In the foreground is a wave calculated to be in excess of 80 feet high. It broke over the yacht and sent it surfing down its face at more than 20 knots. *Stand Aside* is believed to have sunk soon after.

Newcastle, which was on an eight-hour emergency stand-by, would need to be enlisted and brought into action. Navy Sea King and Sea Hawk helicopters out of Nowra and Air Force aircraft from Richmond in NSW and Edinburgh in South Australia would also be needed. There was an official procedure to follow before HMAS *Newcastle* could come into action and it involved first contacting AusSAR's Assistant Manager of Operations, Steve Francis.

"He [Lamming] explained the situation with the weather and detailed an increasing number of beacon alerts," said Francis. "He then requested permission to spin-up the *Newcastle* because, in his judgment, things were going to get worse. I then went through the challenge process with him. It's not an interrogation, just a procedure. To spin-up the *Newcastle* and send her out to sea is to spend a whole lot of money, so you'd better know why you're doing it. I agreed with Rupert and authorised that HMAS *Newcastle* be requested."

★

Steve Hamilton had enjoyed the Christmas break with his wife Susan and their five-year-old daughter, Amber and eight-year-old son, Owen. It was the first time in four years that they had been able to use their South Coogee home at that time of the year, and in particular they'd enjoyed lazing on the nearby surf beach. While he was feeling very relaxed Hamilton knew all the time that the next telephone call might mean that he would be heading to sea in a matter of hours. He was the recently-appointed Commander of HMAS *Newcastle* – or "warship" *Newcastle* as they say in the trade – and it was the Navy vessel on emergency stand-by. There was only one more day of stand-by remaining, then the task would belong to HMAS *Melbourne*.

Although the ship's complement was also on leave at least half had to remain close enough to the ship's berth at Sydney's Garden Island Naval base so they could depart within eight hours. Prior to them going on leave they had been briefed on what circumstances might see them brought back to the ship. In particular, they'd been told the possibility of further riots and general unrest in Indonesia and around East Timor might require them to "evacuate nationals". Hamilton, known to his mates as "Twister", would not have minded if the ship was called out. Although he had joined the Navy upon leaving school in 1973, HMAS *Newcastle* was his first command and there was an element of pride and excitement associated with that.

Just before 4pm on the 27th Hamilton received a call and was told the weather had turned nasty in Bass Strait and there were problems with the Sydney to Hobart fleet. He was also asked if he could revise down the ship preparation time from eight hours to four. Hamilton began recalling as many of the ship's crew as possible and told the crew of the ship's Sea Hawk helicopter that they would most likely be needed. Soon after, AusSAR confirmed they wanted the helicopter immediately and also advised that the decision to "spin-up" the ship was now on hold until further notice.

The Sea Hawk was at HMAS *Albatross* in Nowra. The flight crew had taken it there on December 3 to "put her to bed" while the ship was on stand-by. The helicopter needed to have enough hours left in reserve before its next scheduled service so it could be available for emergency work. The crew flew it only briefly mid-month so they complied with regulations which require them to fly at least once every three weeks.

Hamilton had watched the television news that evening with his family. They saw vision of the dramatic incidents taking place in the race. At eight o'clock he put his daughter to bed. "Daddy might not be here when you wake up in the morning," he told her as he kissed her goodnight.

"Oh, over Christmas?" Amber inquired.

"Yes darling. I think we're going to be involved in the rescue of the men you saw on television on the yachts."

"Oh, in that case it's alright then. You can do that."

★

Just before 6pm Lieutenant Commander Adrian Lister, flight commander of HMAS *Newcastle*'s $40 million Sea Hawk helicopter, alerted his crew that they were likely to be needed. Lister already had an interest in the Sydney to Hobart. He had taken his family to the Navy base HMAS Watson at South Head on Boxing Day to watch the start. Lister's co-pilot, 28-year-old Lieutenant Mick Curtis, and his wife Melissa were preparing for a barbecue with friends at their Bondi Junction home when Lister called and gave notice to stand-by. Twenty minutes later, just as their friends arrived, Curtis was waving good-bye. His bag was packed and he was on his way to meet Lister, whose wife would drive them to Nowra.

Their first task was to go to the ship and collect special equipment they might need – immersion suits, wetsuits and swimming fins for the diver. They would then pick up the chopper's sensor operator, Lieutenant Marc Pavillard, from Cronulla and finally another crewman, Leading Seaman David Oxley, from farther south at Albion Park. American-born Pavillard, his wife Jodi and two children, Kate and Alistair, had had a hectic Christmas with family from both sides crammed into their three-bedroom townhouse. After spending the day at the beach, Pavillard had "just started to crack a beer" when he was told he was needed. It was a case of putting the beer down, grabbing a small bag of clothes and farewelling the family.

Chief Petty Officer Henry Wakeford was in charge of the maintenance team for the Sea Hawk aboard HMAS *Newcastle*. On Boxing Day he too had watched the race start on television with his parents-in-law at their home at Shoal Harbour, near Nowra. They were surprised a few hours later when they looked from the house out to sea and saw the first of the race yachts charging south under spinnaker. Soon after, Wakeford received a call from Lister telling him that he was wanted. The entire team had then been called in. In a remarkable effort, the Sea Hawk was launched from Nowra and destined for Merimbula just four hours after being assigned the SAR task.

☆

AusSAR's effort was unprecedented. There was an ever-increasing number of EPIRBs and mayday calls being received, and while they were coming in, the problems associated with coordinating such a massive task were rapidly increasing. Fixed-wing aircraft and helicopters were descending on the airports at Merimbula and Mallacoota like bees to a hive. They were being refuelled as fast as possible and assigned to SAR targets. Mallacoota was chosen as the main airfield for SAR as it was the closest to the search area, but it did present a couple of problems. Firstly, it is a small airport and so there were constraints on flight movements, and secondly, it was running out of fuel. Search mission coordinators decided Merimbula provided a better logistics environment and had better communications so it was targeted as a base.

The speed with which calls were coming in was taking everyone by surprise. Steve Francis and his team were continually changing priorities as yachts in more serious circumstances called for help. It was obvious that with so many aircraft being based out of Merimbula a huge amount of fuel would be needed. AusSAR went to the NSW Southern Police Command and asked that they take care of that problem. In an exercise that involved the State Emergency Service and other community groups, fuel tankers were, within hours of the request, heading from Canberra and Nowra along highways towards Merimbula.

AusSAR soon realised they needed to be in closer proximity to the unfolding events. The decision was made to have one of their officers, Arthur Heather, establish a Forward Field Base at Merimbula so they had more of a hands-on feel for what was happening. That gave the RCC a direct communication link to facilitate the flow of intelligence from search aircraft and make for a better briefing process for SAR personnel. Initially, because the magnitude of the disaster was unknown and daylight was running out, helicopters were the desired SAR asset. The AusSAR people knew that they were tasking these chopper crews into an extremely dangerous situation.

"We were sending choppers 50, 70 and more miles offshore and when they were coming back they were bucking a hellish headwind," said Francis. "Some of them, I suspect, were probably coming back close to empty. We were very aware of that, so we had to make sure when we tasked the helicopters that we weren't putting them into an absolutely ridiculous situation. Of course once they got out there it went tactical on their part and there was nothing more we could do for them."

Dave Gray was thankful the emergency had happened in not too remote an area – further towards Tasmania would have spelled even greater disaster because of the limited search and rescue assets available.

Eight
HMAS *Newcastle*
spin-up

According to the Australian Constitution, a Naval ship cannot put to sea for a search and rescue mission before a due process of elimination is undertaken. The situation must be of sufficient severity and be beyond the scope of every available resource, starting with the local police force and ending with whatever facilities the State might be able to deliver. If it is deemed to be simply too treacherous for any of these authorities, then, and only then, are the armed forces called in.

After being warned in the late afternoon that his ship, HMAS *Newcastle*, might be needed for race search and rescue operations, Commander Steve Hamilton began planning ways to reduce the normal "spin-up" time from eight hours to around four. He strongly suspected his ship would be called out on the night of the 27th of December. Sure enough, at 11pm the telephone rang at his home. It was Maritime Headquarters saying it was time to go. The Commander was told it was uncertain what exactly the ship's task would be.

There was a scramble to contact crewmembers at that hour and the ship's car went and picked up the second officer and then collected Hamilton and the executive officer. After a quick brain-storm on the way to Garden Island, they organised responsibilities and as soon as they arrived at the dock, set about accomplishing their various tasks. Hamilton went to his cabin and met with senior officers before going to the operations room to initiate a review of search and rescue procedure. Lieutenant Mike Harris, the warfare officer and the navigator from HMAS *Melbourne*, was aboard in place of *Newcastle*'s usual navigator who was on leave interstate.

"It was hectic," said Hamilton. "There was a telephone network going on. People would be phoning five or six people and they'd in turn ring another five or six. We were waiting for answers to come back, all the time reviewing the people we didn't have. We got the doctor who was on stand-by at HMAS *Penguin*. We rang St Vincent's Hospital, which is nearby, and got some of the extra bits and pieces we decided we needed. The fact was we didn't know what to expect out there so we were going for the worst case scenario rather than the best."

At 3.30am, with the ship's powerful turbines rearing to go, the crew of HMAS *Newcastle* assembled on the flight deck at the stern. A head count was done – 75 of the usual complement of 200 were present. Checks were made – how many engine room watch-keepers, radar operators, helicopter controllers? It was a bare-bones crew but it was enough for this mission. They had the capacity to remain at sea for eight to 10 days if need be. At 4am, in the steely silence of a Sydney morning, the dock lines were dropped and *Newcastle* edged towards the main channel that would take it out to the Sydney heads and the open ocean. As the ship passed between the two towering cliffs that stand as bastions at the harbour entrance, the crew had a taste of what was to come.

"The first indication that it really was rough came

when we went through the heads and turned south,"
recalls Hamilton. "We took a big roll – like 35 or 40
degrees. When you're a captain you sit there, and you
hang on, and you listen for *clunk, clunk, clunk* which tells
you something's not been secured. We passed that test."

The ship's speed was increased to 25 knots as the
pursuit of the Hobart race fleet began. However it was
soon obvious such a speed could not be maintained in
the horrible head seas. *Newcastle* was taking a pounding.
Hamilton called for 19 knots and as the lights of Sydney
disappeared astern he went to the operations room to
discuss with the crew their plan of action.

★

Soon after 9am on December 27, just when the crew
of *Brindabella* was battening down for a battle across
Bass Strait against 50 knot winds, a twin-engine high-
winged aircraft, an Aero Commander, swooped out of
the sky and started circling the yacht. Experienced crew
knew immediately who it was – Richard Bennett, the
highly respected yachting photographer out of Hobart.

It was the start of what Bennett had hoped would be a
big day for his business. Forty-eight hours later he would
set up shop on the edge of Constitution Dock in Hobart
and sell to yacht owners and crews photos of their yachts
during the race. It was something he had done with
considerable success for the previous 23 years. The big
difference this year was the weather. While most of the
"yachties" thought otherwise, Bennett saw it as "fantastic"
– rough conditions invariably meant spectacular shots.

The TasAir aircraft was piloted by Ralph Schwertner
with John Townley as co-pilot. Bennett was wedged in
the back against an open door so he could capture the
widest possible angle. His daughter, Alice, also a
photographer, was sitting alongside her father and was

assisting him with the quick re-loading of film. Bennett photographed *Brindabella* then did the same with *Sayonara*, which was seven miles to the east. They then decided to return to Merimbula and refuel so there would be plenty of time to cover the bulk of the fleet in the same region in the early afternoon. They had no inkling from forecasts at that stage just how bad the weather would become.

"We flew back out to the same location expecting to see the yachts in 45 to 50 knots," said Bennett. "We knew the barometer was amazingly low at the time but we didn't expect what we saw. It was only when we went down low to look at the first yacht we spotted – *Bobsled* – that we realised how bad it was. I reckon there must have been 80 knots of bloody wind – not 40. In places the wind had blown the wave tops nearly flat and there were streams of spume coming off them. It was pouring with rain. You couldn't see where the sea ended and the bloody sky began. The air was full of salt. The scene with *Bobsled* was amazing – a pocket maxi just going sideways with a storm trysail up. Then we found *Aspect Computing* and it was in among the big waves, the real big waves where the top 30 feet was just breaking off and rolling like breakers you see surfboarders riding in Hawaii. They were sailing remarkably well. When we got to *Midnight Rambler* the wind was so hard it was blowing the surface off the water and into the air like smoke. It was an incredible sight."

It was not long before Schwertner knew that the pursuit of pictures was "getting to the silly stage". He had worked as Bennett's pilot for many years and was similarly enthusiastic about getting the best possible results, but this time, with low visibility and an intense buffeting from the wind, it was time to "pull the plug".

"We were all pretty depressed, even Ralph, because we

felt we had been cheated out of getting some of the ultimate sailing shots," said Bennett.

As Schwertner began preparing the Aero Commander for its final approach into Merimbula airport, AusSAR in Canberra alerted him to an EPIRB that had been activated on the race course. They were asked to investigate. Minutes later, after refuelling, the plane was back in the air and heading for the yacht *VC Offshore Stand Aside*. Richard and Alice Bennett were still in the back of the plane, but this time they were search and rescue observers aboard the first fixed-wing aircraft to enter the disaster area.

Radio communications were already proving problematic so the Aero Commander circled above *Stand Aside* at 1500 feet to relay information to helicopters and AusSAR. While they listened intently to the radio, the airwaves were pierced by another mayday. It was *Bilstex Ninety-Seven*, Graham Gibson's 47-footer that had stunned the world by taking line honours in the harrowing 1993 race. It was disabled with a steering failure and a huge container ship had emerged out of the murk just 400 metres away – on a collision course. The container ship was approaching from the east after having been forced to turn into the enormous waves. It too had limited manoeuvrability. The crew on the yacht fired off a collision flare while Schwertner tried to make radio contact with the ship. Seconds later the ship's crew advised that they had spotted the yacht. They altered course slightly and *Bilstex Ninety-Seven* got its reprieve by the narrowest of margins.

For the next four hours Bennett and his team remained as a communications post over the fleet, relaying to AusSAR in Canberra vital information on yachts in distress.

Nine
Winston Churchill –
Part I

After hovering as a sentinel for some considerable time over *VC Offshore Stand Aside*, the ABC helicopter was running low on fuel and would have to battle 65 to 70 knot headwinds to get back to Mallacoota. Gary Ticehurst had continually monitored his tanks, calculating how much he would need on the return journey. He also calculated a "worst case scenario" – how far it was to the coast should things go wrong. He could always land on a beach or headland somewhere if he had to, but that would put his machine out of action. It could take a day or more to get fuel to an isolated location, and there were plenty of them on the coast. He knew a limited supply of aviation fuel in drums was kept on Gabo Island so he telephoned them. He could not get an answer.

With an hour and 15 minutes worth of fuel left, Ticehurst made the decision that in five minutes he must leave *Stand Aside*. Just as that five minutes expired, another spine-chilling mayday penetrated his headset.

"Mayday, mayday, mayday. Here is *Winston Churchill, Winston Churchill!*"

"*Winston Churchill, Winston Churchill*, ABC chopper, go ahead with your position. Over."

"We are 20 miles south east of Twofold Bay. Over."

"Nature of your mayday. Over."

"Affirmative. We are getting the life rafts on deck. ABC chopper we are holed. We are taking water rapidly. We cannot get the motor started to start the pumps. Over."

Ticehurst reassured the nine *Winston Churchill* crewmembers that their mayday was covered and that he would relay the message to *Young Endeavour* and to shore. Ticehurst was faced with a burdensome dilemma. He could not initiate his own search even though the yacht was probably within 10 miles of the chopper – perhaps five to 10 minutes away. All he could do was relay the mayday back to AusSAR and then make the slow return trip to Mallacoota to refuel.

★

The mayday and Ticehurst's communications with *Winston Churchill* were also heard aboard *Young Endeavour*. The instant he had monitored the call, the ship's captain, Lieutenant Commander Neil Galletly, ran the 15 paces to where Lew Carter and his team were located in the race communications centre and explained the situation. For a very brief moment Carter was stunned into silence. He felt sick in the stomach. He knew most of the blokes aboard *Winston Churchill* and had sailed with many of them over the years. Carter shook himself free of his thoughts. They were already dealing with emergency situations involving *Stand Aside* and *Miintinta* and they were about to be bombarded with countless more distress calls. His conviction was reinforced by the fact that a few minutes earlier he had been up on deck and was horrified by what he saw.

Galletly and Carter agreed that the gravity of the situation meant it was best they combined forces. Galletly would take over the plotting situation while Carter and his team monitored the radios. The plot for *Winston Churchill's* position had it only about 11 miles from *Young Endeavour*. At that stage the *Young Endeavour* team did not know it was a "Dead Reckoning" (DR) position – an assumed-position but given that the *Winston Churchill* crew was preparing to take to their life rafts it was a definite priority. Yachts were struggling to stay afloat in those conditions, it would be living hell being in a raft. Darkness was still around three hours away. The decision was made to proceed immediately to *Winston Churchill*.

Despite the conditions there was an element of excitement building among the Navy crew and youthful sailors aboard *Young Endeavour*. The ship had executed an excellent rescue from an upturned yacht during the gale-ravaged 1993 race. They were hoping they could repeat that performance once more. Galletly was already developing a rescue plan. The scuba diver was briefed. It would be too dangerous to launch the ship's large, diesel-powered, rigid-bottom inflated boat. Probably the best and safest procedure would be to inflate a life raft, hold the ship directly to windward of the person or object, and let the raft drift down to them with the diver playing a pivotal role as a "direction control unit".

While they were proceeding towards *Winston Churchill*, they received another report directing them to a different position. Even though they felt their original course was correct, they duly changed direction as instructed. At that stage they had the seas on their starboard side and they had to turn completely around to head back north again, gybing the ship with only the storm sails up for stability. The new course saw them sailing dead downwind in 40- to 50-foot waves. It was a very dangerous situation.

The captain alerted all watches. It was all hands on deck for the gybe. Everyone was wearing their wet weather gear, life jacket and safety harness. After some 20 minutes, just as they were completing the gybe, a monster wave rumbled in out of nowhere and picked up the massive vessel as if it were a toy. *Young Endeavour* heeled over in a dramatic fashion – close to the point of capsize. Carter could only look on and cling to a safety rail in horror. Eventually, through good seamanship on Galletly's part and the pendulum effect of the ship's keel, it came upright. Chastened and shaken, *Young Endeavour* and its crew headed off to the new and considerably more distant location. Night was falling, the storm was worsening and visibility was down to 100 metres.

★

Winston Churchill was a classic yacht of powerful proportions and had been restored to perfection by its owner, Richard Winning. Winning had assembled an experienced and well-balanced crew which included Bruce Gould, John "Steamer" Stanley and Jim Lawler. Gould's impressive credentials included 32 Sydney to Hobarts; while Stanley had notched up 16. Like all the other yachts continuing in the race they were down to minimum sail by early afternoon on the 27th. At that stage clouds of spume were starting to burst from the tops of the waves as 50- to 55-knot winds whipped them into a frenzy. Occasionally the alarm on the wind instrument would activate – a signal that a wind gust had topped 60 knots.

Winning, Stanley and Gould were more than pleased with the way the "old girl" was handling the conditions. They could, however, only manage 30 minutes at a time on the helm. It was impossible to continue much longer than that because the rain and spray, propelled by the savage winds, ripped at the eyes and face. Gould was on the helm for half an hour in the early afternoon. They were down to a storm jib and were doing about five knots, sailing at about 50 to 60 degrees to the face of the waves. They debated what the next step would be but ruled out going to Eden. Steamer had some reservations about whether or not it would be safe to heave-to.

At around 3.30pm Winning was on the helm with John Dean sitting nearby, seeking what shelter he could from the coach-house – a box-like cabin near the stern. Stanley was in his bunk in the aft coach-house while Gould was trying to sleep on the cabin sole of the main saloon – the most comfortable spot available despite the annoying leaks. *Winston Churchill* continued to power impressively through the big seas – 25 tonnes and five knots seemed a great combination. Stanley was considering their options. Bare-poling it was one, but that would have the yacht completely at the mercy of the seas. *Winston Churchill* was a long keel yacht designed to heave-to.

"We had a sea that just came out of nowhere," said Stanley. "I could feel it from where I was in the aft coach-house. It just picked the boat up and then rolled it down its face – 25-tonne of boat – into the trough at a 45 degree angle. It was like hitting a brick wall when we got to the bottom." Stanley was pinned to the windward side of the coach-house and the three windows were smashed. He heard the other crewmembers calling for help up on deck and he rushed up to find Winning and Dean hanging in the backstay rigging and around the boom with their feet about two feet off the deck. Stanley quickly untangled them and got them down.

John Gibson was rummaging around in the main saloon with full gear on, including his harness, looking for the trysail and tidying up some of the sails that had been taken down below when the wave hit. Every now and then he'd stick his head up out of the companionway to observe the conditions. Although there was the odd bang, he didn't feel the situation was out of control and he certainly wasn't aware the lee rail was under. He was on the windward side of the saloon moving along when suddenly he was picked up and thrown about seven or eight feet across the saloon. He was upside down and had done a somersault, giving his head a nasty knock in the process. Within seconds he was covered in blood and gear which had fallen out of the lockers. He got up, saw some of the other crewmembers were stirring and then noticed that all the floorboards had been lifted up and thrown towards him. The boat was taking water from the bilge area, but the exact location was impossible to pin-point. The companionway ladder had been dislodged so he repositioned it and went up on deck.

Bruce Gould was also down below and had flown through the air, dislocating his thumb. He recalls vividly how he fixed it. "I said to Mike Bannister, who was in the lower leeward berth, 'Here, grab hold of my thumb will you, and pull it hard' and that's exactly what he did. The thumb went immediately back in place. I then went straight to the deck. The boys were still dangling like puppets on a string. Steamer was trying to sort them out. There was no one on the helm so I grabbed the wheel. I could feel straight away that there was a lot of water in the boat. I stayed on the helm because the others knew the boat better than me. Steamer was going around trying to sort out the extent of the shit fight – on deck and below. He told Richard to try to start the motor so we could operate the bilge pumps."

Winning turned the ignition key and the engine started. It ran for just five seconds and then spluttered to a halt. Gould was in no doubt the yacht was going to sink and suggested they send out a mayday. With the main radio out of action because of an influx of water, Winning went to his only source of communication – the short-range VHF radio. It was vitally important to give an accurate position, but the water that had wrecked the HF radio had destroyed that chance. The monster wave had taken the yacht's charts and GPS unit with it. Winning could only guess where they were – and give a DR position.

Stanley went forward to go down the companionway into the main cabin. As he did he saw there was six feet of the heavy timber bulwark amidships completely shattered. A large section of the bulwarks, about six to eight feet in the area of the leeward shrouds, had been carried away. The planking had been removed and the ribs were exposed. When Stanley got below he discovered there was already 15 inches of water over the floor. Debris was everywhere. Immediately he told the rest of the crew to get on deck and take the life rafts with them.

"We decided that we wouldn't put the life rafts in the water until the deck was awash," he recalls. "I had heard of people launching rafts too early and the boats going one way and the rafts going the other. Also, you should always step up into a life raft – not down." In the middle of all this Stanley added dryly, "Well fellas, this looks like the end of our Hobart."

Bruce Gould told the guys to put on their life jackets and prepare to abandon ship. Then they took down the storm jib because all the rigging on the port side was slack. Gould wanted the headsail off because they had enough troubles already without the added hassle of the mast falling down. He pulled the boat away and sailed downwind. The sheets for the storm jib were flailing perilously around like lethal steel bars while Mike Bannister worked on lowering it. Regardless of the danger, the crew did not panic and continued to work tirelessly and methodically. Dean and Lawler prepared the raft on the leeward deck. The question was raised as to whether the EPIRB had been activated and there was a reply to the affirmative. Gould steered the yacht dead downwind until the very end – some 20 minutes after impact.

"We were running in these huge seas with the wind over our quarter, getting lower and lower in the water," he recalls. "Next thing a massive wave, 40 feet plus, came over us and swamped us. It filled the boat. I said to Richard, 'Well mate, this is it. You'd better tell the boys we're abandoning ship'."

John Gibson followed Lawler into a raft and was one of the last to leave. "As the rafts were being launched I was just thinking to myself that I'd like to go in the same raft as Jimmy Lawler," Gibson recalls. "That was my confidence in him and that's exactly what I did. It just happened that there was a spot available anyway. I would have got into either raft but I just consciously felt very comfortable out there because I regarded Jim as my mate. We were from the same club and also John Stanley was in the same raft."

Winston Churchill was sinking quickly but the line securing the raft was still attached. There was a loud bang and the lanyard to the raft parted. Gould recalls being hit by another enormous wave before he left the helm. He ran forward and did a swan dive towards the open tent flap of the nearest raft and was dragged inside.

All nine crewmembers had managed to escape, and as they looked back from the relative security of the life rafts, the hull of the once mighty *Winston Churchill* sank gracefully below the surface.

Ten
Kingurra

The rapidly expanding team of coordinators at AusSAR, in the Australian Maritime Safety Authority headquarters in Canberra, had never seen anything quite like it. Their computer screens indicating the position of EPIRBs were lit up like Christmas trees. The coordinators were focusing their attentions on one particular zone – the north-eastern corner of Bass Strait, between 20 and 80 miles offshore. The sheer scale of the search and rescue, the inability to prioritise targets and the hellish conditions were presenting a mammoth challenge.

Peter Joubert's robust sloop *Kingurra* was regarded as one yacht which could handle rough weather. In the last horrible Hobart – in 1993 – not only had the boat and crew survived atrocious conditions over a tortuous 18-hour period, but they had also rescued another crew from a sinking yacht before powering on to Hobart and completing the course.

Despite circumstances in the 1998 event being considerably worse, late in the afternoon of the 27th the strong, laminated timber 43-footer was making good progress south under a spitfire jib set from the inner forestay. Like most of the other yachts in that locale – between 30 and 60 miles into Bass Strait – *Kingurra* was close to the centre of the weather bomb. Winds were beginning to strengthen and were gusting between 60 and 70 knots, and the breaking seas were popping up like pyramids more than 60 feet high. In some cases, despite the size of the waves, a mere six or seven seconds was all it took for the yacht to travel the 60 feet down into the trough and then up to the next crest.

Peter Joubert had been sailing for most of his 74 years, but had never seen a tempest quite like it. He was holding course at around 180 degrees but this was falling unpredictably down to 160 or 140 due to the ferocity of the storm. At that stage *Kingurra* had the waves slightly on its aft quarter. Around 4pm Peter Meikle came on deck for his watch and was similarly astonished at how bad things had become during the four hours he had been below. Meikle suspected what they were experiencing was only a taste of things to come. He had paid close attention to the skeds and in particular the report from *Sword of Orion* stating they had endured some 78 knot gusts.

Meikle went onto the helm and was surprised at how well *Kingurra* was coping. The wind instrument was consistently hitting the maximum 68-knot mark and the waves were breaking all around the yacht. The recipe of sea and storm was not exactly what Meikle envisaged when he convinced his American mate John Campbell to come to Sydney and try for the third time to successfully complete a Hobart race.

At 33 years of age, Meikle had been ocean racing for almost 20 years. In that time he had started in eight Hobarts; four with Joubert. In 1992 he was preparing a yacht at the CYC for that year's Sydney to Hobart and that's where he met John Campbell. Campbell was in Australia as part of a lengthy adventure trip around the world, and wandered down to the dock a few days before the big race. He saw Meikle on board and inquired, "Any chance of a spot on the boat?"

"Sorry mate, we're full," was the response. "But hey, if you haven't had any luck, come back tomorrow. You never know what might happen." By sheer chance one of the crew fell ill and Campbell got his ride. But the mainsail shredded off the NSW coast and they didn't go the distance.

Meikle offered Campbell a ride the following year on his family's race yacht, *Fast Forward*, and Campbell accepted. But the 1993 event was the most ferocious prior to the 1998, and *Fast Forward* suffered rudder problems and was forced to retire. Meikle was starting to feel somewhat obliged to get Campbell to Hobart and a ride on *Kingurra* seemed like a sure bet. When it became apparent that there was a crew spot available in the 1998 race, Meikle called Campbell, and promised to pay for his airfare if he didn't get him to Hobart.

★

On the afternoon of December 27 Campbell found himself sitting in the cockpit with Meikle, being lashed by spray, wind, waves and rain. He was uncomfortable, chilled, soaked to the bone and tethered by his safety harness, and seriously questioning his decision to sail.

"When I heard the warning from *Sword of Orion* it was kind of like, *whoa!*" said Campbell. "But I never really sensed danger because all I've ever known personally of this race is that it blows. Also, everyone had supreme confidence that the boat would be able to handle anything, so I don't think there was need for panic. The rest of the crew were just kind of hunkering down because there wasn't all that much to do. I did the same. About every 15 minutes or so we would get a great wave falling all over us. It would fill the cockpit almost to our knees. That reminded me that before we left Sydney I asked the guys how dry the cockpit was in rough weather and they replied, 'Oh no, you almost never get water here. Just a little bit of spray.'"

As though someone had flicked a switch, the wind velocity rapidly began to increase. "The wind just went from your typical howling wind to screeching. It was very high pitched – just like a police whistle. I sensed there and then that the conditions had just stepped up a notch." Communication on board was near impossible due to the howling gales and once again without warning, the seas dramatically rose to meet the gusts. Campbell was determinedly trying to clear the cockpit drains when he was hit. Within minutes he would be in the water, drifting away from the boat and lapsing in and out of consciousness.

★

The experienced crew had ensured *Kingurra* was well prepared for the worsening conditions. The boom had been lashed to the deck, as it was far too dangerous in those seas to lash it to the leeward rail, for the passing water would certainly rip it from the yacht. It had been secured slightly to windward, clear of the life raft. This position made it quite uncomfortable for the crew perched on the steeply-angled windward-side cockpit seat, but comfort came a distant second to safety on board. John Campbell was sitting hunched just forward of the wheel and compass binnacle, Peter Meikle was forward of him with his cheek pressed against the windward side of the boom and Damian Horrigan was at the front of the cockpit. Antony Snyders was on the helm. It was just before 7pm and although it was still quite light, visibility was down to little more than half a mile due to the driving wind and rain.

The crew had two options – head for Hobart or head for Eden. They decided to press on in a southerly direction, but it wouldn't have mattered which course they had chosen. The following harrowing seconds later blurred in the memories of those on board. An enormous wave thundered in, swamping the yacht and rolling it over. Meikle found himself trapped beneath the cockpit in a tiny air pocket. After about five seconds, the boat rapidly righted itself and Meikle was left sitting alone in the bottom of the cockpit. He had no idea where the other three crewmembers were. The boom had torn the mainsheet winch from the deck.

Horrigan appeared from around the side of the cabin down near the leeward rail having gone out through the lifelines and come back in again. Meikle then spotted two crewmembers hanging from the stern of the boat on their harnesses, one either side of the backstay. Snyders seemed to be suspended quite comfortably, albeit with a shattered knee, but Campbell was hanging under the stern of the boat with his strop around his neck. Meikle called for assistance, unaware there was another significant emergency below deck. A large volume of water had flooded the cabin and Peter Joubert was badly injured. He had blood coming from a gash in his head and was suffering severe shock.

Meikle knew he had to get Campbell back over the side of the yacht. He straddled the pushpit and tried to lift Campbell by his harness strop and managed to get his shoulders to the top of the lifeline, but Meikle was unable to pull him over the top. He lowered him down again, spun him around and was then able to release the strop from his neck. At that point Meikle realised Campbell was unconscious. It didn't occur to him that he might be dead.

Tony Vautin was dressed in a T-shirt and safety harness. He started to help lift Campbell, and that's when they got into trouble. Campbell was wearing a wet weather jacket which had his safety harness fitted inside between the jacket and the lining. The lining was slippery in order for it to be easily removed in an emergency. Campbell was soaking wet and heavy, and as they lifted him the jacket started coming off.

"To our horror – and I will never forget the feeling – the jacket started to turn inside out and he just slipped out the bottom of it," recalls Meikle. "His right arm came out first and I grabbed his hand and held on to him. He was totally unresponsive. Then his arm slipped out the other side of his jacket. I desperately tried to hang onto his right hand, but he was getting washed around. He was facing me with his eyes closed just making these gurgling sounds. It was as if he was aware that he was slipping out of his jacket. I won't forget the noises he made as he slipped out. Then another big wave came along and I could hold him no longer. He was torn away from my grasp."

Following the capsize all the life rings and man-overboard equipment had become knotted and next to useless. Meikle shouted "Man overboard!", called for someone to write down the yacht's position, and took a bearing of Campbell's approximate whereabouts. The storm jib had been torn by the force of the water and was flapping around, but it was still providing enough windage for the yacht to be quickly moving away from Campbell. They hurled a life ring into the water and attempted to engage the motor, which had been powering the bilge pumps, but as they were trying, the engine took a large slurp of water and died. To the horror of those on deck, Campbell drifted away face down. The yacht was headed into the wind as much as possible to slow its progress while the remnants of the jib were lowered to the deck.

☆

The crewmember charged with the vital task of keeping sight of Campbell, Antony Snyders, saw his new seaboots float to the surface as he crested a wave;

followed shortly after by his wet weather pants. Peter Joubert, who was injured when a crewman crashed across the cabin from a top bunk onto him during the roll, had staggered to the nav station and grabbed the HF radio microphone. He pressed the red button indicating the desired frequency and called Lew Carter at Telstra Race Control on board *Young Endeavour.*

"This is *Kingurra*. Mayday, mayday, mayday. We have a man overboard and we'd like a helicopter."

"Who's gone overboard? What's his name?" Carter asked.

"John Campbell."

"What's he wearing? Has he got a life jacket?"

"Negative. He's in blue thermal underwear."

"Have you activated your EPIRB?"

"Not yet." Joubert then collapsed. He had a ruptured spleen and countless broken ribs.

The EPIRB was activated while Campbell drifted farther and farther away. The decision was made to keep the EPIRB on as it was still not known whether or not *Kingurra* was sinking. The trysail was thrown up on deck but not set. At that point Campbell was about 100 metres away but was only visible when both the yacht and he were on the crests of the waves. *Kingurra* was turned up into the breeze at about 80 degrees, then gybed around, all the while keeping sight of Campbell. Minutes later Alistair Knox popped his head up the hatch from the cabin and announced there was a ship being redirected and a chopper on its way. It was then a waiting game.

★

Gary Ticehurst had made numerous futile attempts to establish radio contact with *Winston Churchill* while he headed his chopper back to Mallacoota for fuel. There was no response and he was becoming concerned. The mayday call he had monitored from the yacht kept replaying in his mind. With so many search and rescue helicopters and fixed-wings descending on Mallacoota for fuel, the airport's limited resource began to rapidly dry up. Ticehurst and the chopper, which had just arrived from Melbourne, had to share what fuel remained.

Police Air Wing had just finished refuelling and Ticehurst was almost done when the local police approached them with news of the *Kingurra* situation. One of the toughest yachts in the fleet had been hammered. Ticehurst held grave fears for the well-being of John Campbell. Police Air Wing was soon scrambled and lifted off, bound for *Kingurra* and Ticehurst and Sinclair followed five minutes later to join the search. Police Air Wing raced away from Mallacoota as though flung from a catapult, roared toward the stricken yacht with a tailwind of at least 70 knots and was in the thick of it within 10 minutes. It was then early evening, with no more than an hour and a half of daylight left.

✯

The giant waves were making keeping sight of Campbell increasingly difficult. They could only see him for about two seconds in every 30, even though he was only around 200 metres away. There were however, two miracles beginning to unfold. Two helicopters – one fitted with rescue equipment – were rapidly approaching the area; and the hands of fate seemed to be supporting Campbell.

"My first memory is of coming out of an unconscious state and seeing the boat in the distance," said Campbell. "I was completely disorientated. It seemed like the yacht was about half a mile away. I had no idea where I was, how I got there or why I was in the water. Then a realisation washed over me that this was not a dream. I'm in real trouble here. A couple of things were going on in my mind, one of which was that I wasn't really sure of my level of consciousness. The guys said they saw me within about 10 seconds of being lost, face down and apparently unconscious but then acknowledging the boat and waving madly towards them. I have no memory of that. Obviously I was conscious sooner than I remembered."

Campbell was hoping as soon as the yacht saw him they would sail across and pick him up, and he tried swimming towards it, stopping every so often to wave his arms. He had no idea how he had managed to shed all his wet weather gear but he did remember taking off his oversize seaboots. He was certain the yacht was his only hope. Being upwind of *Kingurra* and always wanting to keep the yacht in sight meant he was facing away from the waves. He couldn't see them coming. The biggest waves repeatedly picked him up, sent him tumbling down the face and submerged him.

Campbell was beginning to see the yacht far less frequently. He'd been in the churning ocean for 30 minutes, but to him it seemed like just 10. It was just then that he thought he heard the sound of a helicopter above the roar of the wild weather. He noticed a flare being lit on *Kingurra*'s deck and when he looked up to the heavens there was a helicopter hovering close by.

"Next thing they cruised away," Campbell recalls. "My heart sank. For the first time I was starting to think I was nearing the end of my endurance; that I might have just another 10 minutes of energy left."

✯

Soon after 4pm on December 27 the Victoria Police Air Wing departed Melbourne's Essendon airport in response to an AusSAR request to join the Sydney to Hobart search and rescue operation. Senior Constable Darryl Jones was the pilot, Senior Constable Barry Barclay the winch operator and Senior Constable David Key the rescue crewman. Jones guided the chopper into Mallacoota to refuel and once scrambled and back in the air, AusSAR advised them of the coordinates for *Kingurra* and accordingly, the location of the search area.

The 160km/h tailwinds pressing the twin-engine French-made Dauphin chopper were the strongest Darryl Jones had encountered in 12 years of flying with the Police Air Wing. It meant their speed across the ground was an amazing 205 knots (390km/h). As they neared the coordinates they were met by rain showers and continuous sea spray and a cloud base ranging from 600 feet to 2000 feet. They were 65 nautical miles (125 kilometres) to the south east of Mallacoota. Wave height, wind, rain, low cloud and a horribly confused ocean made it near impossible for the crew of Police Air Wing to locate *Kingurra* and positively establish a search area. Jones commenced an expanding circle search pattern, turning to the north first. Just as the turn began Barclay spotted a red flare slightly ahead and to the left.

Jones accelerated towards it and within seconds Barclay called out that they were about to overfly the yacht. The helicopter was slowed as much as possible, the desire being not to lose visual contact. Barclay then made radio contact and Police Air Wing was advised that Campbell was approximately 300 metres to the west of the yacht. They tracked to a position about 300 metres upwind of *Kingurra* and shortly after Barclay spotted an orange life ring which he thought contained the crewman. It was empty. While looking at the ring Key saw a man waving his arms about 400 metres east of the life ring and 600 metres upwind of the vessel.

They immediately prepared for a winch and reconfirmed their planned actions discussed during a briefing en route to the search area. Jones took up a 100-foot hover over the survivor and Barclay commenced winching Key down to him. Key noticed the man was floundering in the water and was submerged a number of times as he was being winched towards him.

"I was trying to tread water using one arm while waving frantically with the other," recalls Campbell. "I was screaming 'Hey, I'm over here!' Then I thought to myself, that's a bit stupid. They can't hear you. Just keep waving. They hovered over me and then I saw the guy coming down the wire. I was trying to swim towards where he was aimed the whole time. I remember the pilot did a phenomenal job by putting who I now know was David in the water very close to me. I swam hard for maybe 15 or 20 metres towards the harness he was holding out. It was a beautiful target."

Darryl Jones held the extremely tricky 100-foot hover above Campbell without a single reference point. Barclay, who was relaying Campbell's movements over the internal communications, confirmed that he would have to pay out a large amount of winch cable to ensure Key's safety in such a large swell. Jones then looked ahead towards the grey horizon and was horrified by what he saw – a mountain of water coming out of the murk straight for the chopper. He shouted to Barclay he was initiating an immediate climb to avoid being hit by the wave.

"Go ahead!" Barclay shouted back as Jones hauled his machine another 50 feet into the air. The chopper's radio altimeter, which displayed the height above the ground or water, confirmed that the crest of the wave passed just 10 feet underneath. Key, who was in the water, was confronted by the same monster.

"I hit the water, then when I managed to break the surface, I was in a trough and saw a solid vertical wall in front of me. It was a 90-foot wave. I was sucked up the front of it then the buoyancy of my wetsuit took over and I was tumbled back down its face. I was driven under the water for 10 or 15 seconds before coming out at the back section of the wave. I was completely disorientated and had swallowed a large amount of seawater. I felt like I was a rag doll. I was hit by another wave and driven under the water once more.

"Then, as I came to the surface, I was looking straight at Campbell. He was just a few metres away. He had a blank look about him and was ashen-faced. We started to swim toward each other. I grabbed him as we were hit by another wall of water and I held on to him as hard as I could as we were both pushed under. He was a dead weight; he had no buoyancy vest on and no strength. When we re-surfaced again I placed the rescue harness over his head then put his arms through the strap as he was unable to assist me."

Just then the pair were hit by yet another big wave. Key realised the winch cable to the chopper was wrapped around his leg. If the chopper moved or the wire went tight he might as well have his leg in a guillotine. He quickly wriggled his leg free then signalled to Barclay that they were ready to be pulled out of the water and winched to the helicopter. The rescue should then have been complete – but it wasn't. As they approached the helicopter the winch froze, leaving them stranded just outside the door. When he saw that Campbell was exhausted, Barclay placed him in a bear hug and dragged him into the helicopter. Key then made his own way inside.

Campbell had sustained a broken nose and jaw, facial cuts and lacerations and was suffering from severe hypothermia. Key and Barclay lay on each side of him to transfer body heat and to try and stop shock setting in.

Back in Mallacoota Campbell was transferred by air ambulance to hospital for treatment. His parents were roused from sleep at 2am by CYC General Manager Bruce Rowley. They looked at each other stunned. This was the second time one of their sons had defied the clutches of death. John Campbell's brother, Clarke, had survived a climbing accident in America a few years earlier where some of the party had perished.

Eleven
Midnight Special

Ian Griffiths had one-and-a-half Sydney to Hobarts to his credit prior to 1998. The "half" effort occurred in the brutal 1993 event. Griffiths' yacht *Devil Woman* was 50 miles east of Eden and punching its way into Bass Strait with 45 knots of wind on the nose when it came to an untimely demise. Yet again, the collision between the north-flowing current and a solid wind from the south had proven to be a treacherous combination. *Devil Woman* had been behaving itself despite the deteriorating conditions, and while providing an uncomfortable ride for the crew, it was ploughing on without any real dramas. That was until it went over a particularly short, sharp sea.

The yacht's bow launched into mid-air, and when it pounded into the trough on the other side, the crew felt two "bumps" instead of one. They had a sneaking suspicion that the keel may have come loose. The helmsman pushed the helm hard over and the yacht's bow responded immediately, heading up into the eye of the wind with the sails flapping. They were lowered in haste while the bow remained pointing into the oncoming seas so that there was little pressure on the yacht.

The ensuing quick assessment revealed that the keel had done a heck of a lot more than just come loose. It had fallen off. All the high-tensile strength bolts attaching it to the hull had broken. To everyone's amazement, *Devil Woman* did not capsize, but certainly would have had the helmsman not reacted as he did. The apprehensive crew donned life jackets and assembled in the cockpit for what was to become a long and slow passage back to Eden under motor.

☆

Ian Griffiths lives in the pretty coastal port of Mooloolaba, north of Brisbane. An offshore racing enthusiast without a yacht, he was becoming restless, so he formed a syndicate with four mates from Mooloolaba Yacht Club to purchase another yacht. Their choice was *Midnight Special*, a light displacement 40-footer built using the fibreglass/foam core sandwich technique. It weighed just 5.2 tonnes. The syndicate represented an interesting cross-section of the local community; Griffiths, a lawyer, was joined by skin specialist David Leslie, earth-moving contractor Peter Carter, flower farmer Bill Butler, and bus company proprietor Peter Baynes. They got together with the principal aim of having fun.

After campaigning along the east coast – Sydney to Mooloolaba, Brisbane to Gladstone and Race Week at Hamilton Island – the big one, the Hobart race, loomed on the agenda. The nine assembled crewmembers were all locals. At 49 years of age, sailmaker Neil Dickson was the youngest in the team. He was very experienced in offshore racing and had recently returned from a magical four-year, 33,000-mile cruise with his wife, sailing their yacht to almost every beautiful island destination in the Pacific.

Through sheer bad luck but by no means lack of ability, he had only finished one Sydney to Hobart out of six attempts. On two occasions he didn't even clear Sydney Harbour. A mast breakage and equipment failure saw to that. This time though he was confident "a solid bunch of guys and a good yacht" would see him get to Hobart.

★

Midnight Special was no specialist when it came to hard downwind sailing – its hull shape wasn't ideal for running under spinnaker – so the crew were pleased as punch to be 20th in the fleet as they began the tough slog across Bass Strait. Their tactic had been to hug the coast before the leap off into Bass Strait. They were confident, considering the forecast for fresh westerly winds, that this move would bring dividends.

At around 2.30pm the wind-reading instrument at the masthead was blown off in a gust that registered 56 knots, and at about the same time the radio message from *Sword of Orion* warning of the extreme weather came through. *Sword of Orion* was only a few miles ahead of *Midnight Special*. About an hour later, race control aboard *Young Endeavour* read the race disclaimer, reminding all crews that it was the skipper's responsibility whether to continue racing or not. *Midnight Special* had not at that stage hit the worst of the weather and was still sailing strongly under a storm jib, averaging between seven and nine knots.

With the waves growing in stature very quickly, the wind shrieking and the spume and rain pelting horizontally at the on-deck crew, things were becoming truly miserable. The crew noticed the waves were starting to break severely at times, but while it was daylight the helmsman had no trouble threading his way around the worst bits and finding a safe passage over the crests. There was no talk of retiring. It wasn't until an hour or so later that they were tempted to turn back. The yacht then leading the race on handicap, Bruce Taylor's new *Chutzpah*, became a retiree and was soon after followed by Lou Abrahams and several other highly experienced sailors. *Midnight Special* was approximately 38 miles from Gabo Island and 120 miles from Flinders and the decision was made to head towards shore and seek temporary shelter behind Gabo Island or even Eden.

That decision was made even easier seconds later when the yacht took two exceptionally heavy hits from huge waves. The second knock-down, far worse than the first, hurled Griffiths from the chart table, where he had been innocuously plotting their position, across the boat and into the galley, fracturing his leg along the way. He was put in his bunk and sedated by Dave Leslie, the doctor in the crew. The yacht was then turned around and set on a course to the north. It appeared that the wind was coming from the same angle to the bow on the new course, but the waves were more difficult to read and almost impossible to attack when it came to getting over them.

At times the force of a wave would send *Midnight Special* surfing down the face "at ridiculous speeds" of up to 20 knots. The crew's concerns regarding sailing into the night – it was going to be like going into a fight blindfolded – became justified as darkness closed in. As the yacht was negotiating yet another monstrous breaking wave it was knocked down again and came close to rolling. There were two crewmembers on deck and the others were resting below as best they could. Neil Dickson was lying on the cabin floor and remembers flying through the air and cracking his head on either a cabin window or a grab rail. The impact knocked him out for a couple of hours.

The roll-over was sufficiently violent to rip cabin doors from their hinges and send a number of the floorboards flying like scythes through the cabin. The interior of the yacht was a shambles. *Midnight Special* was being hurled every which way and there was nothing the crew felt they could do to improve their lot. The storm jib was still set and was allowing a minimal amount of control over the yacht's direction. Bill Butler recalls going down the face of a wave sideways. He was one of seven crew below deck when the seemingly inevitable "trouble" arrived and was aware of a massive crunch followed by a torrent of water in the cabin. "All I heard was the crunch of the wave smashing into the boat and a deluge of water coming through the cabin top as we rolled. The cabin top was actually breaking open. It sounded like, and felt like, we'd been hit by a ship. The wave just pushed in the perspex windows and split the cabin right along the port side where the cabin meets the deck. That side had been the windward side when we were upright," recalls Butler. *Midnight Special's* rig had been ripped out and there was a huge hole in the cabin top.

"The first thing we did was rush to get everyone a life jacket," Butler said. "The water was knee-deep so I immediately got a bucket and started bailing out through the companionway into the cockpit. We didn't know what the extent of the damage was but we knew we had a bloody lot of water in the boat and had to get rid of it. Some flares were sent to the crew in the cockpit and set off and the EPIRB was activated. The whole thing was an amazing sensation. I didn't think we would get bombed like that, but we did."

Peter Carter had been on deck with Trevor McDonagh, and was on the helm during the roll. As he sensed the yacht was about to go over he fought hard to regain control. It was no use. The wave was already the winner. Engulfed by white water, he clung resolutely to the aluminium tiller, his only form of security apart from his safety harness. As the yacht inverted, the tiller broke off in his hands. When *Midnight Special* came upright Carter was back-slammed onto the deck. He was in agony. Unknown to him, or the crew at the time, he had broken two vertebrae. Crewmembers rushed to his aid and moved him below as gently as they could, laying him on the floor.

After bailing and pumping for some considerable time the crew seemed to have the water situation under control and could properly assess the damage. There were holes in the deck the size of a human head and one split on the port side that went up over the cabin to about the centre of the yacht and another long one that went along the side of the cabin at the deck. The shock of the roll-over was enough to jolt Dickson from his semi-conscious daze and he raced up on deck and started stuffing sleeping bags and sails and then spinnakers into the yawning holes.

"Baynesy and I then went and got rid of the rig," Dickson recalls. "We undid the rigging and tossed it over the side. All the halyards were then cut and we ended up with the whole rig hanging off the bow by the forestay. That wasn't fun, sitting on the bow cutting through it with a hacksaw. All the rails had gone so I was only attached by the harness. I had cut only about halfway through the forestay when the yacht lifted on a big wave and it snapped. It just went off like a bomb."

The continuous roar of the waves – especially when they broke and sent two-metre-deep walls of foam cascading down their face like an avalanche – made for a harrowing experience. The crew could hear waves that were around 50-feet high breaking upwind of them and all they could do was hope they were not in their path. The injury toll was alarming. Carter was incapacitated with his injured back; Griffiths had added two damaged ribs to his fractured leg; Roger Barnett was chronically seasick; Dickson was still suffering from concussion and Butler had a broken nose. Almost every other crewman had some form of rib damage or broken fingers after being hurled around the cabin. If that wasn't enough, they were all soaked through and freezing, and thirsty and hungry. The catering had "fallen in a heap" when the weather turned sour and the lack of food and fluids was affecting everyone.

Initially reluctant to set off the EPIRB, a quick tally of equipment damage and crew injuries soon affirmed it as the correct thing to do. The radios were not working at that stage, they had no instruments, they had lost the hand-held GPS and all the charts had spewed out of the chart table and into the bilge. In addition, Peter Carter's injuries were more serious than anyone had first thought and Neil Dickson was lapsing in and out of consciousness.

The yacht had gel batteries so there was sufficient power to start the motor. It also meant that the crew didn't have to endure their night of fear in total darkness as some of the cabin lights still worked. They strapped the broken tiller to both of the main sheet winches so they could hold the rudder straight ahead. That way, with the motor running slowly and the yacht making some headway, they were able to hold the yacht up into the waves. One crewmember was up on deck for a fair bit of the time during the night, watching for aircraft and ready to set off flares if needed.

At about 3am an Air Force Orion flew by. The crewmembers aboard *Midnight Special* sent up a couple of flares to attract their attention and the aircraft circled to indicate the yacht had been spotted. Around daybreak another fixed-wing aircraft roared out of the skies acknowledging the yacht and then less than half an hour after that, the first of the helicopters arrived. This should have signalled the end of their ordeal. In fact it was far from over.

★

Unable to communicate directly with the yacht, the crew of the SouthCare helicopter circled low overhead, using a form of sign language to indicate how they planned to carry out the rescue. David Leslie, Bill Butler and Trevor McDonagh were on deck at the time and the motor had been stopped.

"The helicopter came down and the guy at the door beckoned to one of us to get in the water," Butler recalls. "David, being a doctor and knowing the injuries that we had on board, decided that it was best that he go and tell the crew of the situation. He jumped into the water – and you have to remember it was still blowing and really rough – and drifted about 150 metres away from the boat. They then dropped the flare beside him to gauge the wind direction and proceeded to get him up. The next thing I knew was that our whole world had exploded. A massive wave, which we didn't see coming, just picked the boat up and rolled it upside down. We were just flung around like rag dolls."

It happened so quickly that the first thing Butler knew he was under the boat without air, tethered in his harness. The harness was stretched to its limit because he'd been flung over the top of the boom, which had been on the deck. He was trapped but did not panic, just assessed his predicament as calmly as he could. *Midnight Special* had been upside down for around a minute when another mammoth wave thundered in, pounding the keel and inverting the yacht. Butler was pinned between the lifelines and the boom, and had blood running from a cut to his head. He had smashed his thumb and broken some ribs but at the time was just thankful he could see daylight and breathe again. One of the crew that had been trapped below heard Butler's shouts for help and rushed on deck and cut him free with a knife.

✵

Sixty-year-old Trevor McDonagh had been sitting in the cockpit and operating the manual bilge pump when the yacht was rolled. Like Butler, he had his safety harness tethered to a strong point at half length – he'd looped it through the strong point and back to his harness – because it reduced the risk of being thrown around by the violent motion of the yacht. He was watching the helicopter when the big wave hit and was taken completely unawares. He too ended up underwater, under the boat, with no air. He was facing the stern and could see light coming in under the hull. Fresh air wasn't very far away, but he couldn't get to it. He tried to free himself from his harness but there was too much tension on the tether and before he could even try and do anything else the yacht had flipped back upright. Like Butler and so many other crewmembers, McDonagh's ribs had taken a beating.

✵

Midnight Special had suffered further structural damage in the second roll-over, and the six crew trapped inside the upturned hull weren't surprised to feel the water surging in as the yacht settled. They could sense the water level creeping up their bodies. Their problem was they didn't know if, or when, it would stop rising.

Neil Dickson was below. "We just heard a crash and then we were rolling around and tumbling in heaps of water again," he recalls. "Then it stopped and we all popped up, standing in near darkness on what had been the cabin ceiling. I was closest to the companionway. Some light was filtering through and I figured we had to get out. There were two guys on deck, obviously tied on deck, and probably trapped. It was no good the rest of us being trapped in the hull. The yacht was certainly making no move to come upright. She had a lot of water in her – waist deep – and just seemed to be sitting there. She didn't seem to want to move. I didn't stop to think about whether or not we were going to sink. I just decided I was going to get out. The companionway hatch slide was gone and the bottom storm board was in place. The top board wasn't in and I guessed the gap was enough for me to get through, so I dived for that. I swam until I was about halfway through the hole and got stuck. I couldn't go any farther, forward or back. I had apparently tangled myself in Bill Butler's safety harness. I just got angry with myself then, *'Shit, this is how it happens. This is the way it goes, hey? I'm going to drown. That was a pretty stupid move. I've left a perfectly good piece of air inside the boat and put myself under here.'* I was still fighting pretty hard to get through the gap. I was trying to get out into the cockpit. I remember thinking to myself that even if I got through the companionway I wasn't going to be able to get out from under the boat because of all the associated garbage that was hanging around there. I didn't have time to think about it for long because next thing the boat went 'plop', back up on its feet again. I ended up lying with my back on the cockpit floor and my legs still inside the cabin. I could see Bill tangled up and pinned by the boom. He was outside the lifelines."

★

Gary Ticehurst and cameraman Peter Sinclair were just recovering from seeing a crewman – Phil Skeggs – lying dead in the cockpit of *Business Post Naiad* when they heard that *Midnight Special*, which was close by, was being abandoned. He plotted the position and headed the ABC helicopter towards that point. "I kept saying to myself, how many people are we going to lose in this race? That was the trauma. When we got to *Midnight Special* we saw some fantastic rescue work being done by the SouthCare helicopter from Canberra. It was still blowing around 50 knots. Each time the paramedic went into the water he had to fight with the winch wire getting caught around his legs, arms and throat. He was also being smashed around by the waves. I said to Peter, 'Somebody's going to die in the water just being rescued. This is crazy'. But they had to try to do it. It was the only way these people could be rescued."

★

When *Midnight Special* came upright it was closer to sinking than staying afloat. The water was just below galley bench height. With the cabin agape it would take only one more big wave over the top for it to submerge. It was reconfirmed that the life raft was in the cockpit and ready to go. The next priority was to get people off as quickly as possible.

After recovering five crewmembers, including Carter and Griffiths, the SouthCare helicopter turned and flew away, much to the amazement and consternation of the four remaining on deck. They guessed the chopper was running out of fuel and they were right. They turned the EPIRB back on again and gathered at the stern with the life raft between their legs. About 30 minutes after the first chopper left another arrived and circled *Midnight Special*. It was the Victoria Police Air Wing. The chopper had joined the search soon after 5am. Senior Constable Darryl Jones, Senior Constable Barry Barclay and Senior

Constable David Key were initially directed to search for *B-52*, but while en route were redirected to *Midnight Special*.

Their rescue technique was a little different to that adopted by SouthCare. In the first rescue the crew jumped into the water and the yacht was allowed to drift away before the paramedic moved in. The police technique was to position David Key in the water about 10 metres astern of the yacht then have a crewman jump into the water. They would then swim towards each other and hook up for the lift. It appeared to be a quick and efficient method. The entire operation went very smoothly. After each crewman stepped off the yacht it was little more than 30 seconds before he was secured in the rescue strop and lifted from the water.

After three rescues were completed Key was exhausted and vomiting sea water. He had been hammered by the 50-foot waves every time he went down the wire. He took a brief respite while the chopper did a circle around the yacht, then he collected the last crewman.

"As we were being lifted back to the helicopter I watched the yacht sink," said Key.

✹

Peter Carter's back injuries kept him in a spinal bed for two weeks while shock impacted heavily on the other crewmembers. Six weeks after the rescue Bill Butler was still feeling a high level of emotional trauma.

"My doctor says it's shock. If I knew what it was, and I could fix it, I would. I'm just not performing like I should be. I'm finding it very difficult to concentrate. I'm certainly more forgetful than I ever used to be."

The nine crewmembers got together for a reunion four weeks after the event. When it was learnt the SouthCare helicopter had carried out part of the rescue and that they had some female paramedics on board, a friend asked Neil Dickson whether he had had "one of those nice, pretty young girls" come down and rescue him.

"No," Dickson replied, "but a six-foot-four, 15-stone policeman looked bloody good to me."

Twelve
Sword of Orion

Despite being a relative newcomer to offshore sailing, Rob Kothe's extensive competitive gliding experience held him in good stead when it came to reading and reacting to adverse weather conditions. He understood the synergy between the two activities and loved the sense of freedom and adventure they offered.

"It's the same sport. You spend a lot of time looking at the sky and understanding meteorology. In a sailplane you work the sea breezes over the mountains while in ocean racing you work the sea breezes off the coast. Both sports are also similar in that they are non-contact – well, most of the time at least."

Family and business commitments kept him out of sailing immediately after he moved to Sydney from the bush in 1980, but in 1993 he began taking part in twilight regattas on Sydney Harbour aboard a yacht his sister was racing. He was soon hooked and after a few experiences on charter yachts went out in 1997 and bought his first offshore racing yacht, a 40-footer named *Witchcraft II*. He took it to Hamilton Island Race Week and although squarely trounced, he learnt a great deal about offshore racing. The next outing was the 1997 Sydney to Hobart in which *Witchcraft II* fared far better, coming a healthy divisional second to *Yendys*. Kothe had promised his crew that if he did well in that race he would "step up"; find a better boat and get serious about ocean racing. He honoured that promise.

At 5am on the morning after the bulk of the fleet had arrived in Hobart that year, Kothe began his search for a new yacht. He carefully inspected *Quest, Brighton Star* and numerous others, standing for up to half an hour on each vessel to get a feel for them. He returned to Sydney and after consulting with a yacht broker decided that the Melbourne-based 43-footer *Brighton Star*, owned by David Gotze, was the one. He bought the yacht and had it registered in its original name, *Sword of Orion*.

First launched in 1993, *Sword of Orion* was a sleek, state-of-the-art yacht designed by the American Reichel/Pugh group. Like so many offshore racers of this era, it incorporated a long open cockpit designed to maximise crew efficiency. The most outstanding feature in the cockpit was the large tubular aluminium steering wheel with a mass of spokes. Its diameter saw it stretch almost from one side of the cockpit to the other. It was a thoroughly modern and cleverly-designed yacht and Rob Kothe was certain it would be competitive.

The 1998 Hayman Island Big Boat Series and Hamilton Island Race Week, both in Queensland's tropical Whitsunday Islands region, were the first targets. On the way up to Queensland the boat suffered a broken rudder, which ruled out winning the Hayman Island event, but after repairs Kothe and his crew were in tip-top form again and had a resounding win at Hamilton. Darren "Dags" Senogles had joined the yacht as "full-time yachtmaster" prior to the series. Kothe admired him because in Kothe's words, "[Senogles] treats a boat like it's his own". Following the Whitsundays campaign, preparations began for the 1998 Sydney to Hobart.

⭐

Having warned the rest of the fleet about the horrendous conditions they were experiencing during the afternoon of the 27th, Kothe and the *Sword of Orion* crew began monitoring their own position even more closely. Kothe was busy listening to the radio and had a reading of 982 on the barometer from Wilsons Promontory. He was concerned a number of yachts hadn't responded to the skeds – *Brindabella* hadn't reported her position; *Ausmaid* had been missing for two skeds and *Team Jaguar* had not reported at all. The sailing conditions were quite extraordinary and the wind was behaving erratically, gusting from 60 knots at the bottom of a wave to 90 at the top. It would also drop without warning to a relatively meagre 50 knots, leaving the crew scratching their heads and thinking they were perhaps out of the worst of it. *Sword of Orion*'s report on conditions at the height of the storm said everything:

> **Average winds during the storm 65 knots at 250 degrees magnetic. Strongest wind 92 knots at 250 degrees magnetic. Average wave height 12 metres. Biggest wave we encountered 20 metres coming from 240–250. Current of about 3 knots running north.**

The last point meant this region of Bass Strait, where the storm had exploded, had become a massive whirlpool. The strong current that had been racing down the south coast of NSW had taken a giant lick into the Strait. *Sword of Orion* was down to a storm jib by this stage and certainly didn't need or want any sort of trysail. Adam Brown, one of the strongest young men in the crew, had valiantly steered the yacht for five hours during the middle of the day, before relinquishing the job to Steve Kulmar. Kothe described Brown's effort as nothing short of heroic. A short while after Kulmar took the helm Glyn Charles went on deck to discuss their situation. Charles remarked dourly that people die in these sorts of conditions.

The pair talked about retiring but Kulmar pointed out that eight or 10 miles in front it might be only blowing 50 knots or less and would be manageable. But of course they could only speculate what was ahead of them, and when the barometer flew across the cabin and smashed, they had no way of judging just how low the pressure system was. Kulmar suggested Charles take the wheel while he talked about the situation with Kothe. After some discussion Kulmar and Kothe decided they would in fact have to retire, so they called the *Young Endeavour* and Lew Carter immediately rebroadcast the message to the rest of the fleet.

"We'd worked out a course which had nothing to do with going towards Eden," recalls Rob Kothe. "It was more about going at sort of 320 degrees. We wanted to make sure for safety's sake that we were presenting the yacht to the waves at the right angle. It varied somewhere between 60 and 65 degrees, but the waves were coming through with a variation of about 30 degrees. That meant the rogue waves would come through about 30 degrees worse so that's when you tended to get beam on to them."

Glyn Charles was still at the helm when the decision was made to turn back. Also on deck were Darren Senogles and other crew. Because of the irregular and threatening shape of the waves it was agreed it would be fastest and safest to gybe the yacht – turn its stern through the wind – instead of tacking to the new course. It was a carefully planned manoeuvre, right down to having the engine running and engaged to ensure the yacht maintained momentum through the 180-degree turn. It worked brilliantly.

"We then got things tidy on deck before some of the guys went below," Senogles recalls. "At that stage we had the boom lashed to the deck on the port side of the cockpit because it was the leeward side of the boat when we were heading to Hobart. It was on the wrong side for the new course because it was to windward and it blocked the view of the waves coming at you. Glyn continued to steer while three of us manhandled the boom to the other side. Once that was done the other guys went downstairs while I lashed the boom to the deck. It was just Glyn and myself on deck. It was still daylight – probably around 3.30 in the afternoon. We started chatting. Glyn was a little disappointed with himself because he had been a bit seasick. He was saying – it was more like shouting so I could hear him over the noise of the wind and sea – how he felt he'd let the crew down. My reaction to that straight away was, 'No, you haven't mate. If you're not well you can't be doing your job properly, so why do it? Let someone do it who is well.'

"He accepted that and then we got talking about his wet weather gear. He had brand new gear and he was soaked. He said, 'I don't like where I am here in nature's test lab … and worse still, this shit's not working'. He wasn't enjoying it at all. Fortunately it wasn't cold but the waves were bloody big."

Twenty minutes after announcing retirement and turning back towards Sydney, Neptune once again unleashed his fury upon *Sword of Orion* and its hapless crew.

"All I can remember was a big roar and then an incredible bang when it hit the side of the boat. It was like being slammed in a car accident," recalls Senogles. "The boat began to roll. I remember being amazed at seeing the mast on the surface of the water, yet it was angled down below horizontal. We were way past 90 degrees. The yacht was on its side being slid down the face of the wave with the deck getting pushed through the water. It seemed we were underwater yet still in mid-air. It was a weird sensation. I don't know what was happening to Glyn at that stage. We crashed into the bottom of the wave and all hell broke loose. It just continued to roll the boat over. It didn't happen fast but the force was unbelievable. I was pinned against the deck and really not able to move."

The yacht was upside down for four or five seconds, during which time Senogles was tempted to unclip his safety harness, but a moment later and with an equally powerful force, the yacht righted itself. Had he managed to free himself he almost certainly would have drowned. He immediately began looking for Charles. Senogles' first inclination that Charles was overboard came when he noticed the bright orange webbing strap of his safety harness which was still fastened to the yacht at one end, snaking over the side. His concern turned to sickening fear when he grabbed the strap, yanked it and it came straight to him, weightless, with nothing attached.

"I looked back in the water where I thought we'd just come from and there he was ... about 30 metres away. I knew it was impossible to get anything to him because you couldn't throw anything, life rings or ropes, upwind in those conditions. It would just blow back in your face." Senogles then screamed at the top of his lungs, "Man overboard, man overboard!"

Below deck injuries had been sustained and the yacht itself was a wreck, mortally wounded with gaping holes in the deck. The mast was destroyed – it had wrapped itself around the boat, and the entire starboard side was damaged – every ring frame was broken. Distress flares were rushed to the cockpit. Some were fired. Kothe had been sitting strapped in at the nav station one second then crashing from the top of the boat right across to the other side the next. He was covered in sails and was tangled in the restraining strap. Kulmar had been strapped into the upper forward bunk and was lucky to escape serious injury.

The crew instinctively split into two groups – some worked on the man overboard situation on deck while others assessed the extent of the damage. Senogles was at the stern calling out to Charles.

"I screamed at Glyn to swim. I know he heard me, but he did all of six strokes and that was it. I guess he didn't realise at that stage that he was badly hurt, but when he moved his arms to swim you could see it on his face. I can only guess he had broken legs and ribs. He was in pain. After just a few strokes he realised that he couldn't swim anymore."

Senogles started shouting to those below for rope – a lifeline he could tie around himself and try and swim to Charles. There were only seconds available before another wave would surely wash *Sword of Orion* an insurmountable distance away. The man-overboard buoy had been deployed and a heaving line thrown into the water, but both actions were about as effective as blowing smoke into a fan. The wind was gusting at 80 knots and Charles was directly upwind. Everything was blowing back at the crew.

It was total chaos below deck. The only suitable length of line was the anchor warp. It needed to be unshackled from the anchor but the toolbox couldn't be found. It had broken free from its stowage point during the roll-over and had disappeared. The search revealed another frightening problem. The base of the mast had been torn away from its step and was now angled into the toilet compartment – the head. As the waves continued to violently rock the yacht the mast was hinging at the deck. The bottom of the aluminium section was only centimetres from being speared through the hull. It would only take one more bad wave.

On deck Senogles began to remove some of his clothing but then realised that it was far too time-consuming a process. He elected to swim wearing much of his heavy clothing and wet weather gear. "Just as I got some rope tied to me we had another huge wave come through. It was so big it surfed the boat probably 100 to 150 metres farther away from Glyn. Suddenly it was a hopeless task. I probably would never have got to him – but at that stage I was still thinking about it. Then someone grabbed me and stopped me from going."

Steve Kulmar knew the yacht was moving away from Charles at a rapid pace and he also knew Senogles would have run out of rope before he reached Charles. In all probability there would have been two men overboard and drifting away from the yacht. Kulmar was overcome with grief. He was the one who had invited his friend, Glyn Charles, to join the crew, and he was now faced with the most horrific situation of his entire life.

"You could see him and then you couldn't," said Senogles. "He was just bobbing on the surface, trying to keep his head above the waves. Then he just went face down and disappeared. He seemed to be gone less than five minutes after we rolled. Even if I had been able to get him back to the yacht I dare say he probably would have struggled to survive what I believe were terrible injuries."

The boom had been ripped away from its attachment on the deck, and had most probably taken Glyn Charles with it. The broken and buckled spokes in what had been a substantial aluminium steering wheel were further evidence of the force of the impact. The starboard side deck at the gunwale had opened up from the stern to the aft end of the cabin – almost half the length of the yacht. Part of the deck and cabin top had caved in. The boat was cracked in half at deck level at the mast. The well housing the steering wheel had split open like a crevasse.

Below deck the structural damage was equally as extensive. The cockpit had been compressed six inches into the hull and the companionway hatch had imploded, allowing a considerable amount of water into the cabin. Senogles realised they needed to get some form of sea anchor out and keep the boat head to wind then cut the rig away before it did more damage to the hull. He appointed himself in charge of running the deck and clearing the mess while Carl Watson attended to the problems below. The EPIRB was sent up on deck, lashed into the cockpit and activated. While Senogles believed the yacht was relatively safe, water was still pouring in. It was highly unlikely that this fractured hulk, which only minutes earlier had been one of the sleekest and most sophisticated ocean racing yachts in Australia, could take much more.

"We were calling mayday, mayday on our VHF radio from the moment it was realised that Glyn was overboard," said Kothe. "We had no HF radio because it had been under water. The GPS was still functioning. We knew our position quite accurately. The condition of the boat was another major concern. We knew we were taking water but we didn't know where from. The old 'frightened men with buckets' approach was our quickest route to staying afloat. Actually, we could only find one bucket so one guy was using a drawer as a bailer."

The ring frames that brought structural integrity to the hull, plus the bulkheads, were now little more than splintered pieces of carbon fibre and the composite structure forming the shell of the hull had suffered substantial delamination. The first priority was to bolster the hull and the deck to ensure they didn't separate or collapse further. The spare spinnaker pole was cut up and buttressed between the floor and the deck to stop the deck collapsing into the boat and braces and other forms of support were hammered into place in the most vulnerable areas of the hull in a bid to build strength.

The mast had wrapped itself around the hull and appeared to be broken in at least five places. There were sheets and lines everywhere – tangled around the hull and drifting in the water. Even if they had been able to start the engine, lines and rigging would have immediately fouled the propeller. The jagged and buckled section had to be jettisoned. The already waterlogged yacht could be submerged at any moment. Help was probably hours, possibly even half a day away. Flares were fired in a desperate bid to attract attention from any yacht, any vessel, that might be in close proximity.

The big bolt cutters carried on board to sever rigging in such a situation were frustratingly difficult to operate in the sodden and slippery conditions. Hacksaws seemed more effective. There was a constant call for new and sharper blades so rigging and the mast section could be cut. While some crewmembers, all wearing life jackets and safety harnesses, sliced away at the mast and rigging, others turned to bilge pumps that could be operated from deck. Tired arms found new energy and pumped and pumped. Around an hour after the disaster a blur blasted out of the horrible grey murk and rocketed overhead. It was a search and rescue aircraft – attracted by either the constant signal sent out by the EPIRB or the incessant mayday calls on the radio. Suddenly radio contact was established, but simultaneously it became all too obvious that the range of the VHF was extremely limited, possibly only a few kilometres.

Kulmar had plotted the drift of the yacht since Charles was lost overboard – 3.5 knots at 070 degrees. The location of the roll-over and the fact that a man had been lost overboard at that time was transmitted to the aircraft. The pilot acknowledged the information and the aircraft then disappeared as quickly as it had arrived. The crew was left uncertain as to what would happen next, but they hoped to hear and then see a rescue helicopter before dark. A search for Charles would be initiated. Nearly two hours after the roll a crewmember saw something. He squinted, sheltered his eyes. He couldn't believe what he was seeing. He looked harder through the spray and spume and driving rain. Yes, it was another yacht, around 150 metres away.

"Get the flares, get the flares!" was the frantic call. The first package was torn open and the flare fired – upwind as required for the best effect. It rocketed off overhead and to leeward at somewhere near 80 knots. The yacht the crew could now clearly see continued on its course. The second red flare was fired, then the third, fourth and fifth. No reaction. For five minutes the battered crew watched in vain as the yacht, sometimes in full view and at other times hidden by the mountainous swells, continued under storm sails on a course to the south. The *Sword of Orion* crew could only surmise that either their flares went unseen or that the yacht was, like themselves, very much in survival mode. They hoped if the yacht did see them but couldn't assist it would relay *Sword of Orion*'s position by radio to search and rescue authorities.

This incident; the loss of a crewmate; the likelihood of rescue; the constant threat of being overwhelmed by another rogue wave; plus the approach of darkness was creating emotional overload for everyone on board. Kothe was lying in his bunk and knew the excruciating pain coming from his knee meant that it was broken or at least very badly twisted. A crude splint had been attached using blue webbing sail ties but it was offering minimal relief. He called an emergency bunk-side crew meeting to both organise their plan of action and bolster their flagging spirits. They had to keep bailing but they were all exhausted and desperately needed nourishment to maintain their energy levels. The stove was ignited and, with all cooking utensils and most provisions lost overboard, water was boiled in an empty can so at least coffee could be made. There was a search for either of the two medical kits. One had been lost but the second was found under the engine box cover in the engine compartment. How it got there was anyone's guess.

Through sheer guts, skill and determination the yacht was stabilised, and an anxious wait began. Only two crewmembers remained on deck, the others went to rest and continue bailing when necessary. Those lying down were strapped into their bunks to prevent further injury. The approach of darkness was far from welcome, and it cloaked the predatory seas in a terrifying shroud; a thunderous roar was the only indication of the maelstrom surrounding the stricken yacht.

★

Having made the difficult decision that it was far too dangerous to execute a night rescue of the crew of the badly damaged 41-footer *B-52*, the crew of the Navy Sea King helicopter, *Shark 05*, turned their attentions to *Sword of Orion*. They were aware that the yacht had lost a man overboard and was in danger of sinking. *Shark 05* was set on a course to the south and a position that would see it about 100 miles from Merimbula. The crew, assessing weather conditions and endurance at all times, knew they would have to fly through some very rough stuff before they returned to shore. The big grey bird lumbered through the stormy night sky at around 200 feet, crabbing at up to 35 degrees at times to counter the leeway being generated by the fierce westerly winds.

The savaged sloop was located with relative ease and communications established immediately. The first unpleasant task was to confirm that a man had indeed been lost overboard. His name was relayed to "Wacka" Payne who in turn communicated details back to AusSAR. It was then 10.45pm and the chopper's fuel supply was running low. They had been flying for three hours and would be travelling through totally unpredictable conditions on the 100-mile return passage. Once they had determined *Sword of Orion* had been stabilised and was out of immediate danger, the decision was made not to execute a rescue but return to Merimbula and see *Shark 20* assigned.

The decision to turn for home was justified a few minutes later when the weather turned particularly nasty, but *Shark 05* powered on and was soon away from the clutches of the worst of the cyclone. The lights of Merimbula appeared on the horizon. When it landed there was between five and 10 minutes of fuel remaining in the tanks.

☆

Even though he had 7500 hours on his helicopter flight card, Lieutenant Commander Tanzi Lea, pilot of the Navy Sea King *Shark 20*, had never experienced flying conditions quite like those he encountered that night over Bass Strait.

"When we launched out of Merimbula the weather was OK," Lea recalls. "Minutes later we were in it. We hit a turbulent wind sheer section which was the start of the bad weather feature. We went from seeing the stars one minute to a cloud base of about 400 or 500 feet. The sea was getting very angry and building the further we went in. We weren't seeing much because it was pouring with rain as well. We were deployed to the position of *Sword of Orion* – a position that saw horrible weather. The tops of the seas were being ripped off by the winds so there was white water all around. Luckily we had some brave guys in a light fixed-wing up there somewhere and they were able to relay any messages for us. I thought they were marvellous. With visibility so poor and nothing on radar we decided to set a search pattern – an expanding spiral search just to keep it simple. The distance between the spirals could only be as far as you could see with the searchlight on. In fact you have to overlap. If you can only see 400 yards then the distance between the spiral is probably 600 yards so you have that bit of an overlap towards the outer edge.

"And you can't go too fast because you want to be able to see things in the water. We were flying at 60 knots air speed which meant sometimes I was probably getting 10 knots ground speed upwind, so I just sped up a little bit, then as soon as I would turn downwind I'd have to pull back. There was one humorous bit during the search. We kept coming across the same yacht while we spiralled. They saw us so often they finished up asking us if *we* were OK. We turned and within five or 10 minutes we spotted some lights. It was *Sword of Orion*. They'd drifted about 10 to 12 miles from their previous position. It turned out they could hear us all the time on Channel 16 but we couldn't hear them."

The yacht appeared to be wallowing and Lea could see no one on deck. The condition of the yacht left Lea and his helicopter crew in no doubt that the sailors would require immediate evacuation. He didn't know a lot about ocean racing yachts, but he knew this one was definitely in danger of sinking. The *Shark 20* crew had to contend with the wind, rainsqualls that could obliterate visibility in an instant, massively powerful and unpredictable seas, and a target that just wouldn't stay still. Also, salt spray and spume that was being whipped into the air from the peaks of the waves was lashing their machine – two things that helicopter jet engines definitely don't like.

Lea flew upwind from the yacht and threw out a smoke flare. But that drifted away fairly quickly. They then tried passing a line – a Hi-line – down. The Hi-line carries a weak link that is designed specifically to break should it become entangled on an object during a rescue. The link means that the helicopter will not be permanently attached to a target should the helicopter have to pull away in an emergency. The 90-foot Hi-line that was passed from *Shark 20* to *Sword of Orion* parted due to overload within a couple of minutes of being retrieved by the yacht crew.

They then decided to pass another 200-foot Hi-line minus the weak link down to the yacht on the understanding it would not be attached but simply held by hand. When the crewmember had hold of the line it would be hooked to the winch hook, then the strop and cable could be pulled down from the helicopter, and the crewmember would be pulled to safety.

☆

Once the rescue plan was established and the Hi-line was lowered, Darren Senogles jumped in the water and started to pull down the harness from the chopper. The helicopter was then downwind, towards the back of the boat on the port quarter. Sure enough, the boat began drifting away and the harness landed about 20 metres from Senogles. The line then became unclipped from the harness.

"I guess I was down about a metre when I decided the best thing to do was unclip from the weight," recalls Senogles. "I was straight up and down in the water and the life jacket by that stage had gone up around my ears. I then tried to get myself to relax. That actually made the life jacket more buoyant and it allowed me to put an arm in the air so they could see me even better. The searchlight they had on me hardly ever lost me, even in those seas.

"I can remember seeing an orange light in the water and I thought it was another boat because I knew there was a ship close. What it actually turned out to be was they'd dropped a flare in the water to act as a guide for the pilot. He would look at that while the guys in the back of the helicopter tried to get the rope or sling to the target. It was a bit like standing in the middle of a highway and having a Mack truck screaming head on to you and then at the last minute just veering away and dropping a rope."

Senogles managed to secure the harness and was lifted some 10 metres out of the water but was then dropped back into the drink. On the way up he had been hammered by an enormous wave. The retrieval rate on the helicopter winch – 500 feet per minute – would not have been fast enough for them to get him over the wave and into clear air for the lift. The helicopter crew, always alert for approaching waves, saw this one approach and feared the mass of white water on its crest would have possibly injured Senogles. Quick thinking saw him dunked back into the water and pulled through the bulk of the wave before being lifted out.

Once in the helicopter Senogles was given a headset so he could talk with Tanzi Lea and eventually rescue coordinators at AMSA in Canberra. They needed to know about Glyn Charles, the condition of the yacht and who on board was injured.

✭

Despite the appalling conditions, the first two recoveries went almost according to the book. The third man to be rescued was Steve Kulmar. He had injured his shoulder and was severely weakened and it was unlikely he would make it up unassisted. He tried in vain by himself but when it became clear his injuries were making this impossible, Crewman Dixie Lee went down to Kulmar without a moment's hesitation.

"When I swam out to this ring I found it was hard to get into the actual harness because of the life jacket I had on," recalls Kulmar. "They are those bulky old fashioned form of life jackets, bloody useless. The first time I tried to get into the ring I had one arm through when I think he thought I was waving to him that I was ready to be pulled up. I got about five feet out of the water and I dropped out of it. I'd then lost the rope as well. So I had to swim around in this terrible ocean for about 10 minutes while they tried to get the rope back to me and keep a spotlight on me. He lost me out of the spotlight once, which wasn't a good feeling. The boat by this time was maybe 200 metres away. So I was absolutely at the mercy of the helicopter.

"The same thing happened the second time; I got halfway into the harness and he lifted me off again. So I fell back into the water. The third time he sent a frogman down, and I think he then realised how bloody hard it was to get in the harness with the life jacket. When I finally got into that harness I did not have one ounce of energy left because I'd been swimming around in the ocean for 20 minutes. As I was being lifted from the water I just remember looking up and seeing this brilliant white light above me. I genuinely didn't know if I was alive or dead. That was the defining moment. I knew that if I were alive then I would never do another Sydney to

Hobart. My wife, my children, family and friends meant too much to me – nothing else."

★

With three out of nine crewmembers rescued in one hour Tanzi Lea then had no alternative but to head *Shark 20* for shore. Fuel was running low and it was a 100-mile slog back to base at Merimbula. Lea wanted to keep enough in reserve should another emergency develop unexpectedly. The conditions were extremely dangerous for any craft whether it be at sea or in the air. Lea had already heard another rescue chopper was leaving Merimbula to go to *Sword of Orion*. That was small consolation for the frustration he and his crew faced in having to leave six men on a crippled yacht.

"We were monitoring all our instruments and it soon became evident to me that the engines had salted up reasonably badly," recalls Lea. "The engine temperatures were going up. The salt spray had been coming at us so hard while we were doing the rescue it even got past a protection device on the front of the engine. It was a situation that could be dangerous if, for any reason, I had to apply power very quickly. The salting restricts the air flow that you need instantly for extra power. It could have surged the engines – that's when you get an incorrect relationship between air flow and the fuel going into the engine. It can actually get the air flow going the wrong way from the engine and then it becomes very hot. That means no power is produced at all so you've virtually lost the engine." While not a serious emergency, Lea nonetheless took precautions and piloted the chopper in a conservative fashion back to Merimbula. Upon arrival he executed a running landing instead of the usual hover landing.

★

As soon as it was known that someone had been lost from *Sword of Orion* and that the yacht was in danger of sinking, a state of shock overtook the wives, family and friends of those on board. Their fears and anxieties were exacerbated by the sketchy information available. Libby Kulmar sensed the weather must have been pretty tough late in the day because the position reports which usually flowed from the club at regular intervals were slow in coming that evening. She also knew that earlier in the day *Sword of Orion* was placed seventh in the fleet.

After going to the movies with her two daughters, her sister Pam and her children, Libby returned home for what she hoped would be a good night's sleep. She was still tired after all the Christmas activities. She put Madeline to bed and then took Pip to her bed upstairs. She tuned into the late news and was horrified at the report which came through. "It's now common knowledge that there's a man overboard from *Sword of Orion*," said the reporter.

"The phone was ringing within a minute," recalls Libby. "My closest friend said, 'Do you want me to come over?' and I said, 'No, it's OK. I'm fine.' I was desperately trying to get onto anyone – the race press centre, AMSA, anyone – to find out what was happening."

Libby Kulmar then rang the author less than a minute after he had walked away from the television broadcast set in Hobart. Her voice was tremulous with fear.

"Rob, it's Libby Kulmar, what's the story?"

"Libby, what do you mean?" asked the author.

"What do you know about *Sword of Orion*?"

For an instant the author had a horrible thought Libby might be telling him it was Steve who was missing. "What can you tell me?" he asked with concern.

"Only what you just told me on TV," she replied.

"Libby, I was told officially that all the families of those aboard *Sword of Orion* had been briefed on the situation. Are you telling me you know nothing?"

"Yes. Only what you just said on TV."

The author gave her a direct contact number for AMSA Her girlfriend Heidi was certain that moral support was vital and came immediately around. Details were still being finalised at that stage and aside from ringing AMSA there was little they could do but wait.

At 3.30am the phone rang. It was Steve.

"Darling, I've only got about 30 seconds on this phone. I just wanted to tell you I'm safe. I love you. I'll call you again as soon as I can." Kulmar was phoning from Merimbula airport not long after he had arrived. He had a shower at the airport and was handed a pile of new clothes donated by a local surf shop. He stripped down to his soaked T-shirt and as he took it off, he sensed something hanging around his neck. It was the plastic pink piglet's head "good luck charm" daughter Madeline had put there the morning of the race and told him not to remove.

★

The Sea Hawk *Tiger 70* launched out of Merimbula at 2.47am on December 28 with veteran flight commander Lieutenant Commander Adrian Lister at the controls. In the seat alongside him and acting as co-pilot was Lieutenant Michael Curtis, while in the back Lieutenant Marc Pavillard and Leading Seaman David Oxley sat and pondered the severity of the storm. Just 15 minutes later, 40 miles off the coast, circumstances began to degenerate and the grey chopper was hurled headlong into the tempest.

"The conditions were atrocious, the worst I've ever flown in," said Curtis, an airman with just four years under his belt. "The weather did concern me but at the same time it was good experience, because being a young pilot coming through, I had a trusted guy next to me. It was really good to be under his command. I didn't have to make the decisions. That was his job. We certainly knew what we were heading for. We were listening to the Sea Kings talking about 50-foot waves and wind up to 80 knots."

They had heard how the crew of the Sea King *Shark 20* had carried out their rescues and they discussed the techniques that would prove most effective. They had no direct signal from the yacht, an EPIRB for example, to give them a target, so once they arrived in the area the searchlight went on. The chopper's powerful light amply illuminated the enormous seas and the crew was astounded a successful rescue mission had already been performed in such conditions. It was an hour before sun-up when the remaining *Sword of Orion* crew first heard, then saw, the Sea Hawk emerge from a thick bank of cloud.

It came in and remained at a high station, circling the yacht every 15 minutes, confirming the yacht's position and the prevailing weather behaviour. The Sea Hawk crew asked those still aboard *Sword of Orion* if they wanted to be lifted straight away, but they replied they'd prefer to wait until daylight. The wind was still gusting at up to 80 knots and a rescue attempt in pitch darkness would have been at least unconscionably hazardous, if not downright foolhardy.

"When the guys decided to wait until first light everybody was happy," recalls Marc Pavillard. "The only problem was our fuel. I thought we would have 30 to 40 minutes to rescue all remaining six crew. It had taken the Sea King guys around an hour and a half to get three. We carry 3800 pounds of fuel and burn roughly 1000 pounds per hour. What we did do while we were waiting was pull back the engines and do it nice and slow. We waited for about an hour until just before first light to make our first rescue approach. We'd already made a decision that Dave Oxley wouldn't go into the water for a rescue unless it was absolutely necessary. We lowered the Hi-line and got it to the yacht first try. We dragged it across the yacht as it trailed out behind us at about a 60-degree angle."

As the Sea Hawk descended to the lowest possible altitude for the rescue, Lister would lose visual contact with the yacht. Pavillard became the guide, talking to Lister continually as he moved the chopper towards its target. With the side door open he would lean out and keep eye contact on the yacht – "left on line, right on line, 10 yards, five yards, four, three, two, one, stand-by, steady." As well as monitoring the approaching waves, making sure the chopper wasn't too low, Curtis' job was to concentrate on all engine instruments. He had to be certain everything was functioning perfectly.

The jet engines were working overtime as the chopper continually went between lift, descent and hover. Engine failure at such a low altitude in that weather would be catastrophic. The pilot would have to try and fly out of trouble by dipping the helicopter's nose and gaining airspeed. If they were in the middle of a winch, the call from the pilot would invariably be to cut the wire and drop the man back into the water. Each crewman on the helicopter had access to a button to activate the wire cutter.

The rescue process was going rapidly and smoothly. Each time the Hi-line got to the yacht a crewmember would attach himself to it, jump overboard, wait for the yacht to drift away and at the same time pull the rescue strop towards him. But again the bulky life jackets, which in one way were keeping them alive, were also making it near impossible to get the rescue strop around their bodies properly. Pavillard was working the winch, trying to ensure that there was enough slack in the cable so the man in the water would not lose his hold on the strop. He had to allow for the waves charging through and leaving a massive trough behind.

"The seas were falling so quickly I was basically just winching out, winching in, winching out to keep just enough slack in it but also have the control needed to stop them going too far away," he recalls. "At one stage it all got out of whack. A big wave came through and the guy slipped away from me. He fell down the back of one wave and the wire went taut. He got washed away from us at an angle which caused the cable to get caught on the right front wheel, metal to metal, which isn't good. When we winched him in we could feel a problem with the wire but we just had to keep going with lifting the other guys."

Rob Kothe was this fourth "guy" having difficulties. When he went up on deck he could see why the helicopter was having trouble holding station – the yacht was bobbing up and down violently. Kothe was helped across the cockpit to the starboard quarter and he jumped into the water only to realise he was on the leeward side. As the yacht swung around, Kothe went under and clipped his head on the hull. While underwater he noticed the impressive carbon fibre rudder, but then to his horror he saw the line that led to the helicopter was looped around it. Despite his injuries and the buoyancy of his life jacket he managed to dive down and untangle the line. On board the Sea Hawk, the crew saw Kothe go under and feared he had been knocked unconscious. Thankfully he surfaced after a few anxious seconds and was winched to safety.

"The very last guy to leave, Carl Watson, was really buggered when he got in the water," recalls Pavillard. "He got hit by some big waves. Time was ticking away and he couldn't get the strop on properly. He just had it underneath one arm. It was jammed somehow in his life jacket. He started to go down for the count, it wasn't looking good for him. In the end we made the call." Half in and half out of the strop and suffering from severe exhaustion, Watson was finally lifted away from the damaged yacht.

With six sailors safe in the chopper the door was closed and the Sea Hawk headed for Merimbula. Adrian Lister was an extremely tired but satisfied man. It had been very close. Like Tanzi Lea and the *Shark 20*, the Sea Hawk made it back with precious little fuel left in the tanks but plenty of sea salt around the engines. Once on the ground Pavillard reported the chafe on the winch wire to the maintenance crew. They began pulling the wire off the winch drum until they found the damage – three broken strands. One of the maintenance men gave the wire a sharp tug. The wire broke.

Thirteen
B-52

Wayne Millar is a giant of a man – about six-foot-six (195 centimetres) tall and powerfully built – and a likeable no-nonsense sort of bloke with a permanent grin on his face. He loves a challenge – both in his business as a coal mine maintenance contractor, and in his sport of ocean racing. Millar's home is in Townsville in tropical far north Queensland and he is one of a growing number of offshore sailors from that area making a name for themselves.

His yacht *B-52*, a 41-footer that was a sistership to Lou Abrahams' *Challenge Again* and former Hobart race winner *Raptor*, was crewed primarily by locals, including lanky Townsville lawyer and yachting administrator John "JB" Byrne. Having raced against many of the better boats from the south in the August 1998 Hayman Island and Hamilton Island regattas, Millar and the Townsville team decided they would go to Sydney for both the Telstra Cup and Hobart race in December. They expanded their crew to include Ray LaFontaine from Melbourne, and Sydney's Don "The Admiral" Buckley.

After enjoying some hefty competition in the Telstra Cup they were primed and ready for the Sydney to Hobart. They had pulled out their secret sail, the blooper, on a couple of occasions and certainly turned some heads. The hope was that the blooper would give them an edge in the early stages of the Hobart, but that wasn't to be. The wind was not coming from the right angle – from directly behind – for them to use the sail effectively. Still, they enjoyed the ride as they careered down the NSW coast on that first day and into the evening.

Byrne believes they were one of the few crews fully versed on what was happening weather-wise and he's confident the bureau was doing its job properly. He felt the information available was clearly indicative of what they might be in for, and it was up to each crew to interpret and analyse the data and plot the best course. The *B-52* team had paid particular attention to forecasting as part of their race preparation. They knew that being correctly positioned for any change in wind direction over such a long course could make the difference between winning and losing. Millar had employed the services of Roger Badham and also availed the yacht of weather reports from every relevant coastal station, and even some of the oil rigs in Bass Strait.

They sensed before they left Sydney they were in for a bit of a hiding, this inkling was bolstered during the first night and verified early the next day. As the morning unfolded they were receiving wind updates from the coastal stations in Victoria and the rigs out at sea. They were confident they knew from which direction the wind would blow and how strong it would be.

Will Oxley, *B-52*'s navigator, came on deck around mid-morning with the news that the wind was gusting 70 knots at Wilsons Promontory and that there were some "decent" seas at the oil rigs. As the morning progressed the crew peeled down the sails – No. 4 to the storm jib and the trysails and then continued to try various combinations as the wind strengthened. The waves were on the beam or a little forward of the beam, and they soon found the storm jib was better than the trysail because the trysail kept trying to round them up into the waves while the storm jib kept pulling the head away, rendering the yacht much easier to control.

They were reasonably pleased with the way things were going and at the time of the 14:05 sked they were the 11th boat on line-honours. Despite their guarded confidence, they were paying close attention to the news coming through. One by one they heard the reports of stricken or retiring yachts – then the reminder to all owners about "responsibility"; Lou Abrahams saying he was going to pull out, or at least temporarily seek shelter in Eden; then from Rob Ainsworth's *Loki* reporting that they had suffered a fairly major incident – a 180-degree knock-down.

The *B-52* crew agreed to continue south with caution, and in doing so keep the wind and the waves at the right angle. They still felt in control, but had no intention of endangering either the yacht or those on board. They bare-poled it for a spell but that achieved little – it reduced their speed to four or five knots but removed the steerage needed to get over the worst of the waves. At that stage it was blowing around 60 or 70 knots, the seas were around 10 to 12 metres and with the storm jib back up they tore along at a lively but manageable 10 or 11 knots. They'd made the decision to split each watch in half so two crewmembers were on deck and the other two were down below dressed and ready if needed. When darkness fell around 9.30pm they planned to pull the storm jib down and bob around for the night. It would be light again around 3am so they would only be losing around six hours.

★

By 4.30pm that afternoon the weather had begun to steadily worsen. Like so many other yachts in the race, *B-52* was battling unpredictable seas of epic proportions. Just when the crew thought they had worked out the wave pattern, an unreadable new set would roll in and leave them flummoxed. Millar was about to complete his watch and hand over the helm to Mark Vickers and Russell Kingston. Buckley had been on deck with him. Before they changed over, it was customary for the new team to sit on deck for a bit, have a chat with the retiring crewmembers and generally acclimatise themselves to the wave and weather conditions. Vickers had been paying keen attention to the reports from the oil rigs and wasn't overly surprised at the situation which greeted him on deck. He began steering and quickly settled in to slowing the boat down to let the big breakers that were right in front go through and then speeding up to get away from others.

"About 20 minutes after I started steering, a couple of waves – well they were a bit more than waves, they were white-capped mountains – came through ahead, so I slowed the boat down to miss them," he recalls. "The scene was amazing; there was a whole heap of white water just charging across our path. Clouds of spume were being ripped off the top of it. I got the boat back up to speed quickly and just looked up, sort of over my right shoulder, and immediately shouted, 'Russell, hang on. This one's going to hurt!'. It was just 10 feet away – four or five metres higher than any other wave and with a steep face. It was a huge curling wave just like you would see on a surf beach. The next thing I knew the boat was upside down.

"The wave hit the mast and the rig first then dumped on us. I thought I'd just gone overboard. I knew I'd gone through the spokes of the steering wheel and it felt as though I was being dragged along beside the boat; it was that washing machine effect of being tumbled by a wave. Then it stopped and I realised while I still had my eyes open I just couldn't see. I then knew I was under the upturned boat. I knew I was attached but I couldn't move so I traced my way back along the harness to the wheel which was only about eight inches away."

Vickers could not believe what he was feeling. His harness tether was wrapped *twice* around the spoke in the wheel, meaning that his body had been forced through the large gaps between the spokes *four times*! Astonished the yacht had not self-righted, he calmly put his hand to the metal safety harness plate on his chest and unclipped. He then pushed himself down as deep as he could and swam out to one side. As he popped to the surface, gasping for air, he was greeted by the sight of Russell Kingston clinging to the edge of the upturned hull near the stern. Kingston too had had a lucky escape. His first attempt to swim out from under the yacht failed so he stuck his head back up in the cockpit well and found a small pocket of air. He took a deep breath and went under again. That time he was successful. Both men were on the downwind side of the upturned hull.

Vickers was worried they might become entangled in the mess of rigging and be dragged under the stern, but before he could do anything about it a rogue wave lifted him and carried him a good 20 metres away from the yacht. He was wearing his full wet weather gear without a life jacket. Due to the weight and restrictive nature of the gear, he was forced to dog-paddle back to the yacht. As he was swimming he watched the hull begin to sink stern first and was certain it was going to right itself. He had the foresight to check the areas around the keel and rudder to see if there was any damage. When he reached the boat he banged on the hull twice but there was no response.

"I swam around to the stern of the boat and grabbed the backstay. I then just hung on and hoped the thing would come upright. Russell was somewhere up near the bow. We had both worked out that when, or possibly if, the yacht came upright, being near the ends would be safest. That way you wouldn't be hurled around as much."

✶

Prior to the yacht named after a bomber being bombed by the mammoth wave, the crew below deck could do little more than lie in their bunks. Moving around presented a serious hazard to health – it was akin to being on the world's worst rollercoaster. Although the crewmembers were lying down, sleep was near impossible. John Byrne was in the leeward aft quarter berth and the conversation rarely veered from the weather and what best could be done to preserve the boat.

When the wave with *B-52*'s name on it did arrive, the initial sensation in the cabin was that the motion of the boat was not out of the ordinary. It felt as though the yacht had been hit by a stronger gust of wind and had begun to round up into the wind. But this round up was suddenly accompanied by a thunderous crashing noise. Byrne thought the mast was breaking and that their race would surely be run. The next thing he knew the boat was upside down and he had been hinged in and pinned by his bunk against the side of the hull. Sails and other gear had fallen onto the bunk making it impossible to lift. The only way out was to come forward like a snake and climb out over the galley; or more specifically, under the galley and onto what had been the cabin roof.

"I waited there for a couple of seconds, thinking, it's going to come straight back up, but then when I saw water pouring in I thought, this is a bit inconvenient to have to get out of here but shit, we could sink. I bolted out of my bunk and found the other guys already there sort of standing around taking stock of each other."

Millar was already organising for the life raft to be readied and the EPIRB activated. There were eight crewmembers trapped inside. Byrne distinctly remembers the eerie emerald-green light filtering into the cabin and the deathly quiet despite the chaos outside. They were understandably disoriented, debris was floating all around and right and left, top and bottom had been inverted.

"Even simple things like the engine became confusing because it was upside down," recalls Byrne. "And I couldn't work out what had happened with the stove. I thought the round metho tank from the stove was the engine filter, but then I realised the engine was now actually above my head. Fortunately fuel and oil didn't pour out of the engine and also, the fact that we had gel batteries meant that we didn't have battery acid going everywhere."

Before the race Millar and Oxley had watched a video on how British yachtsman Tony Bullimore survived inside his upturned yacht in the Southern Ocean. This was fast becoming a reality for them because their yacht was showing no signs of righting. Millar moved into the bow area to check on the forward hatch. If the yacht sank by the stern then that would probably be their only way out. "It's amazing what you do in situations like that," recalls John Byrne. "Ray LaFontaine grabbed the microphone on the radio and said, 'what about a mayday?' Will turned to him and said something like, 'I'll attend to that when it's appropriate.' Ray then let out this textbook perfect mayday. We all just looked at him bemused, as if asking, 'Who are you calling, Flipper the dolphin? Mate, we're upside down!'." Then, without warning, the ghostly silence was broken by an almighty *whoosh!* and all hell broke loose in the cabin yet again. *B-52* was back upright. It had been inverted for an estimated four minutes.

As the yacht settled Byrne looked down and noticed a pair of seaboots protruding just above the surface of the water in the cabin. He recognised them immediately, grabbed them and pulled as hard as he could. Lindy Axe came to the surface coughing and spluttering. She had been trapped underwater, under the stove, when it had crashed back into place. She appeared to have a nasty gash on her head.

☆

The two men on the outside hung on the best they could when *B-52* self-righted. At the bow, Kingston grabbed the remnants of the storm jib and its sheets and, using the lifting momentum of one of the massive waves, managed to get himself onto the foredeck. Vickers grabbed a stanchion and just clung to it for dear life. Because the cabin had been damaged and pushed out of shape, the crew that had been trapped inside had trouble getting on deck. It was not until LaFontaine literally smashed his way out through the stormboards that anyone could go up and see if Vickers and Kingston were still there.

Kingston spotted LaFontaine closely followed by Steve Anderson as they emerged on deck. After ascertaining how much water was in the cabin he went straight to the bilge pump and started pumping. He then began removing the twisted and tangled rig. Millar and his vanguard began assessing the situation below deck. They were unsure of the structural condition of the yacht and whether or not they should abandon ship. The crew was split in half, one group on deck helping jettison the rig and the other below, working on saving the boat. With two men manning the pumps and others bucketing the water out it wasn't long before the level began going down. That could only mean that the yacht, although badly damaged, was not adversely leaking.

"Because [sailing] the boat is very much a team effort, everybody is encouraged to have their own input," recalls Byrne. "The input from some people was that we should get off because we didn't want to risk sinking and being trapped. But as things settled down and experience came to the fore, attitudes changed. The thought was that maybe we should put the rafts on deck and inflate them and have them ready to go. That way we wouldn't have to wait while they inflated if we had to get into them in a hurry. While all that was being discussed, and with the water level continuing to go down, everyone became more certain the boat was going to stay afloat. The comment then was that we didn't need to inflate the rafts but we should just keep them on deck and tied on. If they were inflated they were going to restrict movement too much and blow around everywhere. Then Lindy, who runs the bow, grabbed some gear bags and put into them things that we might need in a life raft – bottled water, warm clothes, flare container."

The EPIRB was located once more and a debate started as to whether or not it should be activated.

"Well, we've got no radios because they've been flooded; we don't know if the engine's going to work; we've got no mast; we don't know what the structural integrity of the yacht is, and we're halfway across Bass Strait in 50 knots of wind and bloody big seas," said Oxley the navigator. "Yep, this is severe and imminent danger. Yes we should let it off."

The EPIRB was activated.

The crew on deck assigned to getting rid of the rig were thankful for the solid pre-race preparation. Special effort had gone into ensuring the pins in the rigging screws could be easily removed in an emergency and consequently the mast was consigned to the ocean in a very short time. Not long after the EPIRB was activated a fixed-wing aircraft, working off *B-52*'s EPIRB signal, appeared overhead. Flares were fired and the plane "waggled its wings" in acknowledgment. It then disappeared as quickly as it had arrived.

At about the same time some crewmembers on deck thought that they saw another race yacht in the distance, but it was difficult to tell because the waves were higher than most yachts' rigs. It was always a case of "now you see it, now you don't". Regardless, flares were fired in the hope that something might be there. Nothing more happened. Millar and two other crewmembers then tried to start the engine. They turned the flywheel over to make sure the oil hadn't risen above the pistons when the yacht was upside down. They tested the electrics and then sprayed the terminals to displace any residual water. Just as the engine fired into action the crew on deck heard another noise. A massive grey Navy Sea King helicopter, emblazoned in numbers and with lights flashing, came charging towards them out of the storm clouds.

★

The Navy helicopters, with their night search and rescue capability, were an invaluable asset for AusSAR's operation on the night of December 27. It was highly commendable that the Sea King *Shark 05* had gone from a 12-hour stand-by notice at HMAS *Albatross* at Nowra to being in the air and fully operational in just two hours. When the machine launched out of the Nowra base at 7.45pm, Lieutenant Alan Moore was the aircraft captain; the second pilot was Lieutenant Commander George Sydney (then Commanding Officer the Sea King's HS817 Squadron); Lieutenant Philip "Wacka" Payne was observer and Petty Officer Kerwyn Ballico was the aircrewman. It was carrying its maximum 5000 pounds of fuel; burned at 1000 pounds an hour and regulations required it to land with 500 pounds in reserve. This represented a four-and-a-half hour limit.

The initial task was to assist *Business Post Naiad*, but AusSAR redirected them to *B-52* with orders to assess the situation, make contact and ask the crew to turn off the EPIRB if they were out of immediate danger. East of Merimbula the Sea King hit heavy rain, extremely strong winds (60-plus knots) and a low cloud base.

"The aircraft was just washing around everywhere, we were being buffeted all over the sky," said Payne. "Because the winds were so strong we were drifting left at around 35 degrees, so to stay on course we were crabbing our way south. After a brief search we found them. We established ourselves in a hover – or more specifically, attempted to establish ourselves in a hover – and put some lights on them. We saw the yacht was dismasted and were pleased to see so many crew mustered on deck. Just looking at the conditions I knew immediately there was no physical way we could get them off the yacht. It was way too dangerous. I knew the limitations of the aircraft and of the personnel.

"They had no communications at all so we tried to get a line to them – a Hi-line which had a monkey's fist at the end. We had written a note and put it into the monkey's fist then lowered it to them. That got swamped and the note couldn't be read. Then we created a waterproof one and as we lowered that the line parted. It was extremely difficult to get the line to them, remembering that it was also dark and raining. While we were hovering we saw our altitude go at one stage from 80 feet to 10 feet – that's how big the waves were. Obviously we were in our own danger. We could have hit the sea."

Eventually a waterproof note was lowered to the crew who in turn responded they were distressed but not in immediate danger. The conditions were so bad and the yacht was in such a precarious position that the rescue would be extremely tricky. It was decided sending a man down would be overly hazardous and even getting the crewmembers into the life rafts could prove disastrous. Given that the yacht appeared to be relatively stable, the difficult decision was made to leave *B-52* for the moment and go to *Sword of Orion*.

★

While the Sea King thrashed about overhead in the stormy night sky, the crew on board *B-52* had planned, if it was possible, to put Lindy Axe into a harness and send her up to the helicopter. She could explain to the chopper crew the situation and that there was hope that the motor would eventually be fully operational. Also, Axe could be flown to shore and receive medical treatment for the wound on her head. They knew that to have her lifted off the yacht was extremely dangerous but they felt it would have been suicidal to have put her in the water to be picked up.

But there would be no rescue for the time being. They were on their own. "Watching the helicopter fly off was like arriving at a cab rank late at night and seeing the last taxi leave," said Byrne.

★

After several attempts the motor started and it was decided the safest place was Eden. That course put the waves at about 45 degrees to the bow. Occasionally *B-52*, which was already suffering from considerable structural damage to the cabin, would be almost submerged under the weight of white water that continually pounded it.

With windows cracked, the companionway cover gone and fissures in the deck, water poured freely into the cabin each time a wave hit.

"It was then around 2am," recalls Byrne. "People were sleeping through exhaustion. They were lying on the cabin floor in wet weather gear with water leaking in through the roof, pouring on top of them. I'd been lucky enough to get a fair bit of rest during the day so I just figured it was time I stepped up to the plate and did some steering. We decided to leave the EPIRB on because we knew that being a satellite EPIRB then AusSAR in Canberra would have been tracking it and, we thought, they would see we were making some progress against the wind and towards land.

"When you were on deck you would have to stand up every few minutes and have a good look around. There were other racing yachts out there and the last thing you needed was to have a collision. At one stage I looked behind us and I saw the red and green masthead navigation lights just at the right angle to be a yacht. They appeared to be only a quarter of mile behind us. At that moment the masthead lights did about 200 knots straight over the top of us then banked and flew off into the night."

Although *B-52* had been stabilised, the cracks in the deck were getting bigger and all on board were acutely aware that another freak wave could easily roll them again. The yacht had been so badly damaged in the first roll-over it was twisting with every wave, and every time it twisted the cracks were expanding. Then a complete window popped out and fell into the cabin. It was obvious that if a big wave dumped on them the deck could well cave in. *B-52* would be swamped and more than likely sink.

Oxley took the timber locker covers from the bunk mouldings and fashioned crude stormboards. He put them on the cabin side where the broken windows were located and then lashed them together across the inside of the cabin using webbing sail ties. That, along with sleeping bags stuffed in some of the cracks, helped stem the water flow. While they continued to make progress towards the coast, the *B-52* crew were unaware that grave fears were still held for their safety. Their EPIRB was activated and the authorities believed they were still in serious trouble. It wasn't until the ABC helicopter located them and reported that they were heading for Eden that those fears were allayed.

At 8am the coast was sighted. In many ways it was a huge relief – a sign of sanctuary and safety. But, as Byrne explained, it was also a tease. "I actually wished that that part of the coast was really, really flat. Because it was so mountainous we seemed to take forever to get there. After what we'd been through we wanted to see land and be there that minute. It took another five hours to get to Eden. As we got closer to shore we started to feel pretty good about ourselves and what we'd survived. Everybody started to peel their wet weather gear off. That made a nice old smell in the cockpit. When we got into mobile phone range we called AusSAR and advised we were going to turn off the EPIRB. Straight after that, when it was realised we were within phone range, there were eight people on deck calling family and friends at the same time. It was a ridiculous sight."

★

The damage to *B-52* was so extensive that it was later written off by insurance assessors. Experienced sailors who saw the ruined yacht were awed that it had managed to limp back to shore at all, let alone in such horrendous conditions.

Fourteen
Miintinta

For most people a weekender is a cosy little cottage tucked away somewhere beyond the outskirts of town. For Dr Brian Emerson and his wife Pamela, their weekender came in the form of the 42-foot yacht *Miintinta*, which is Polynesian for turtle. It had many advantages over the average weekender. For a start it had 360 degree water views and, if you didn't like your surroundings at any particular time, you could move.

In reality it was more than that for the Emersons – it was their retirement project. At 60 years of age, Dr Emerson was looking forward to retirement. He was a former university lecturer and was currently providing expert opinion in engineering for court litigation. He and his wife had long harboured dreams of leaving the big smoke and spending their days leisurely sailing from port to port.

In 1998 Emerson decided to race "the weekender" to Hobart. He knew it could be a tough course, but he also knew the yacht had the pedigree to cope with just about anything. It was designed by Ron Swanson, a legend in yacht design in the sixties and seventies. *Miintinta* was a "Swanson 42" double-ender, built in 1976 and had since cruised to America and back and done two Hobarts, in 1976 and 1977. Swanson created the design as a go-anywhere world cruising yacht. It was constructed primarily of solid fibreglass and weighed in at more than 12 tonnes.

Emerson had owned the yacht for little more than 12 months. The 1998 event was to be the third Hobart for a highly experienced yachtsman who had been sailing everything from small boats to ocean racers for more than 30 years. He went to great lengths to ensure the yacht was race ready, taking time to install new pumps, do a thorough rigging and electrics check and purchase some new sails. He chose five crew to join him – Lisa McKenzie, Uli Thiel, Bill Vukoder, Peter Volkes and Robert Gordon. Thiel, a master mariner, navigator and radio operator, had sailed around the world. She had spent 13 years at sea as a professional and was part of that exclusive band of sailors who had rounded the notorious Cape Horn.

Emerson and his crew's main objective was to finish the 1998 event unscathed but they also fancied being the first cruising division yacht from the CYC over the line. *Miintinta* was definitely a cruising type of yacht, and from the start, sailed more like a tortoise than anything else. Emerson's calculations had them second last out of Sydney Harbour. But once outside, and with the big multi-coloured spinnaker set, it began to gain ground. In fact, as the wind strengthened, *Miintinta* was running faster than it ever had before.

☆

As they neared Eden on the 27th, Emerson was pleased with the yacht's placement – 21st out of 38 in its division. And *Miintinta* was revelling in the rough going. The only problem was that McKenzie, an experienced harbour sailor, was not enjoying the rugged ride at all. Seasickness had hounded her from soon after the start and things were only getting rougher. When they heard the radio call from *Sword of Orion* during the 14:05 sked, alarm bells started ringing. Those bells got louder as the afternoon progressed when distress calls and announcements of decisions to retire started crackling across the airwaves.

Emerson had decided some hours earlier to prepare the yacht for the worst possible weather. The mainsail was lowered completely and secured and the storm jib and trysail set. Emerson decided it was too dangerous to press on across Bass Strait. The yacht would be tacked and head for the coast near Eden where they would shelter.

"I didn't expect a cyclonic bomb and I didn't expect waves of those proportions," Emerson said. "As we started to head towards shore – it was around 5 o'clock – there was just mayhem on the radio. There were distress calls seemingly coming from everywhere. We pushed on towards the coast for a while then I decided that with conditions deteriorating so much we would start the diesel and motor towards shore. That meant we were out of the race, but it also meant to me that we were probably safer. Soon we were dropping off backless waves; waves of ridiculous proportions. They were 10 metres at least and there were probably some bigger than that. Twice we experienced monumental crashes off waves. The yacht just shuddered when it landed.

"We had the trysail set but still we didn't seem to have enough power. Sometimes, when the worst waves hit us, we did complete 360 degree turns. One minute you would be heading on 270 degrees towards the coast and then the next minute you're heading on the reciprocal back out to sea. I reckon we got to within 20 miles of Eden when the damn diesel 'carked it'. It just stopped. Why? I don't know. All I know is that steam was coming out of the engine compartment and filling the cabin. It was just like blowing up the radiator on a car. I went straight to the engine and as soon as I took the rear compartment cover off I shouted, 'God, there's a lot of water in here'. It was stinking hot so I couldn't do much but I did check all the hoses."

It was the amount of water in the yacht and not the failed engine that was the focus for Emerson. First he thought a skin fitting – a through-hull fitting – might have ruptured. He rummaged through the yacht checking every one. They were all secure. Crewmembers manned buckets and pumps but buckets soon broke and pumps either clogged or simply busted. Emerson could not believe that a new heavy duty pump he installed specially for the race had fallen apart. Soon cut-down plastic milk containers became bailers and only one pump remained functional.

All this time Emerson was trying to find the source of the leak. It seemed that the water was coming in fast at times then, a few minutes later, more slowly. He surmised that the greatest volume of water entered the hull when the starboard side of the yacht was taking a pounding. His conclusion was that the hull was badly fractured, probably in an area behind a fixed settee berth near the mast. It appeared that when the yacht heeled over with the wind, and waves were on the starboard side, the weight of the keel led to the crack opening up. It was possible that the hull had fractured at the point where a steel frame was built to take the loads of the mast. Because of the way the yacht was constructed however, he could not get into the area to confirm that.

Thiel was at the wheel and was having difficulty holding the yacht on course. *Miintinta* kept being blown back out to sea. Some time between 11pm and midnight Emerson radioed Eden Coastal Patrol and stated although their bilge pumps had failed and they were taking on a substantial amount of water, they were still in control. He refrained from calling a mayday and instead requested a tow. Emerson followed the Coastal Patrol's directions to fire flares. These were sighted by Don Mickleborough aboard *Southerly* and the yacht's approximate position was confirmed with the coast station. Emerson was then advised that the container ship *Union Roetigen* had been diverted to stand by *Miintinta*.

The crew were glad to see the big ship appear in the background and were even happier when they were told the trawler *Josephine Jean* was heading toward them as well. Emerson felt there were most probably other yachts in more dire circumstances and radioed in that *Miintinta* was stable and would not require immediate assistance.

Just 45 minutes later he was back on the radio. "We're now taking too much water. We can't control it. Are you able to stand by us again?" To their delight, *Union Roetigen* soon returned to keep watch. About an hour after that, the *Miintinta* crew saw the trawler crest a wave. Their tow had arrived but time was running out for the now badly breached hull.

★

Lockie Marshall was still in his office with Eden police sergeant Keith Tillman late that night coordinating the rescue of *Team Jaguar* by the trawler *Moira Elizabeth*. The two-way radio in the office was almost jammed as search and rescue operations for so many of the Hobart race yachts went on incessantly. The pair heard the request from *Miintinta* for a tow. Deep down both knew that if any vessel was to leave Eden in answer to the call it would have to be one of Marshall's trawlers. Most were tied up at the dock – secured by double ropes and anchors to cope with the surge that the storm was sending into the small harbour.

Few trawlers worked that time of the year, but those that did usually reaped sizeable financial rewards. It was the summer high season, and prices were up to three times above their norm. Marshall did have one trawler out that night, the 70-foot wooden-hulled *Josephine Jean*. The rough weather had forced it into trawling close to the coast.

When the call came in, Marshall assessed the situation and realised that with the yacht sinking the quickest response would come via the diversion of *Josephine Jean*. Marshall also knew that if anyone could cope with the weather that was devastating the race fleet then it was the trawler's skipper, Ollie Hreinisson. He was a native of Iceland, and an extremely good seaman who had worked the big North Sea trawlers before coming to Australia.

"We could tell by the way the *Miintinta* crew were talking on the radio that they were physically and mentally exhausted. They seemed to be losing their ability to rationalise the situation, and that led us to believe the position they had given to the Coastal Patrol was wrong," said Marshall. "I calculated that they weren't quite as far out as they thought they were. I proved that to them when the ship went to stand by them. We then knew exactly where they were. We plotted that and worked out it would take between two and three hours to get there."

Just over two hours later the crew on *Josephine Jean* had *Miintinta* in their sights. Manoeuvring the lumbering trawler over and around massive breaking seas in the dark and getting it close enough to *Miintinta* so that a towline could be thrown took great courage and skill. Hreinisson made it look easy.

"It was brilliant seamanship on his part," recalls Emerson. "He circled us about three times with his big searchlight on us and then he moved in. It was the most amazing situation to be in. One minute the trawler was 50 feet above us and the next thing it was 50 feet below us."

After considerable effort Emerson and Gordon secured and lashed the towline to the bollard on the foredeck, but not before *Miintinta* stuck its bow into one big wave and a three-metre wall of water picked up Emerson and hurled him over the side. His safety harness saved him. The next wave washed him back over the lifelines and onto the deck. Through it all his main worry was losing his seaboots.

Emerson knew that they would have to continue bailing to keep the yacht afloat, but he was quite confident they would be able to save it. Volkes, a man in his fifties, ate and drank while he bailed.

"He cut off this blooming great slab of salami and then, while chewing on it, he drank a beer and kept bailing," recalls Emerson. "It was all too much for McKenzie. Her seasickness went from bad to horrible."

The crew didn't know *Josephine Jean* was making less than one knot headway back towards the coast. It was going to be an exhausting effort to keep the yacht afloat during the time it would take to reach Eden. An hour into the tow the last of the bilge pumps broke and both crews were faced with the frightening possibility that the yacht might still be lost. As *Miintinta* became heavier with rising water, the load on the metal bollard at the bow increased dramatically until it simply disintegrated. The towline went with it. Hreinisson did a phenomenal job getting the towline back to the yacht but even then, Emerson knew that his yacht was destined to sink.

At 3am Emerson radioed Coastal Patrol in Eden and advised that the only alternative for the crew was to abandon the yacht. "For God's sake don't fool around. If you have to get off then get off," was the response from the radio operator. Emerson then spoke with Hreinisson who suggested the crew jump onto the trawler, but the state of the seas and the thrashing propeller blades ruled that out. The life raft was thrown into the ocean and inflated at the stern of the yacht. The crew scrambled into it then Emerson followed – just. The umbilical cord between the raft and the yacht broke as a big wave washed through. Emerson threw a line from the yacht and it was grabbed by crew in the raft. They struggled to hang on, the line all the time cutting into their hands.

There was only one thing to do – take a flying leap. He did just that, crashing on top of those in the raft. They then watched patiently – for 45 minutes – as *Josephine Jean* began a long and slow loop back to the raft, all the time with *Miintinta* wallowing along behind like a half-submerged duck. The trawler was easy to see, its decks brightly illuminated by large lights. After circling so that he was positioned directly downwind of the raft, Hreinisson once again showed his skill by edging the trawler close. He recalls that the second the big boat was within reach, the Miintinta crew scrambled up the side "like drowned rats".

✭

The first light of day was appearing to the east when the six exhausted sailors, still soaked and in their wet weather gear, collapsed in a bedraggled heap on the aft deck of the trawler. Soon after they heard Hreinisson shout, "The tow's broken off!" As *Josephine Jean* continued on its slow passage towards Eden the crew watched in vain as their yacht, then very low in the water, began to list to one side. It hadn't sunk when they lost sight of it on the eastern horizon, but it would have gone under soon after that.

✭

When they reached Eden later in the day, Emerson went straight to Marshall and thanked him profoundly and profusely for what he and the crew of the trawler had done to rescue the *Miintinta* sailors.

"Look, I'm a professional fisherman," replied Marshall. "We make our livelihood from the sea. If I ever get caught in the way that you were, I just hope to God that someone would do the same thing and come and get me."

HMAS *Newcastle* on Sydney Harbour. "Warship" *Newcastle* is a guided missile frigate and the most modern in the fleet. Commissioned in 1993, it travels at around 30 knots, has a crew complement of 192 and can carry two helicopters.

A Sea Hawk helicopter being launched. The Sea Hawk is an anti-submarine chopper; carries three crew; travels at around 333km/h and has a range of 700 nautical miles.

Young Endeavour, radio relay vessel for the race

Aboard *Nokia* at the height of the storm in Bass Strait. At one stage a wave went close to sending 16 crew over the side. Marty Malka is at the wheel.

A savage sea sends water cascading towards the companionway aboard *Nokia*. Most crews experienced these conditions for more than 30 hours.

Fear and exhaustion are etched on the faces of two crew aboard *Stand Aside* while they await rescue. The photograph, taken by a fellow crewmember, shows how the cabin top was ripped apart when the yacht was rolled over by a mountainous wave.

Stand Aside lies at the mercy of the seas while its life raft trails behind. This yacht is 40 feet long, a fact that gives some indication as to the state of the seas.

Trapped by 80-knot winds and mauling seas that at times were more than 80 feet high, the 12 crew of *VC Offshore Stand Aside* await rescue. The yacht went close to being rolled yet again by this very wave.

Salvation for the crew of *Midnight Special* as their waterlogged yacht lies low in the water. Two female paramedics rescued four men from this yacht.

Heaven sent. In an unprecedented search and rescue effort paramedics winched 55 sailors to safety.

Covered in engine oil, Jim Rogers leads other *Business Post Naiad* crew away from a rescue helicopter knowing the bodies of two friends were still aboard the yacht.

A NSW water police launch located *Business Post Naiad* when the storm abated and towed it into Eden. The bodies of Bruce Guy and Phil Skeggs were still aboard.

One of the most miraculous rescues came when American John Campbell was plucked from the water 40 minutes after being knocked unconscious and lost overboard from *Kingurra*. An 80-knot tailwind got the Victoria Police Air Wing helicopter to him at a ground speed of near 200 knots. Campbell's rescuers were David Key (left), Barry Barclay (centre) and Darryl Jones (right).

Mike Bannister
Winston Churchill

John Dean
Winston Churchill

Jim Lawler
Winston Churchill

Glyn Charles
Sword of Orion

Bruce Guy
Business Post Naiad

Phil Skeggs
Business Post Naiad

The six sailors who perished

Fifteen
Business Post Naiad

Bruce Guy and his crew considered Bass Strait to be their home ground when it came to offshore racing and they were convinced they had seen about the worst it could dish up. Only weeks before the 1998 Sydney to Hobart, *Business Post Naiad* had powered through a bitterly cold and arduous storm to register a surprise win in a 120-mile race across the Strait from Melbourne to Stanley, Tasmania.

"We weren't bad for what some people might have called a bunch of weekend sailors," said Rob Matthews. "The Stanley race was on the nose all the way, and it blew. It reminded us again that you have to treat Bass Strait with respect. If you don't it can jump up and bite you." Matthews was probably the most experienced crewmember on board and had been offshore sailing for 33 of his 46 years, clocking up a monumental 50,000 sea miles along the way. They included nine Hobarts and a race around Australia.

Business Post Naiad was originally the successful New Zealand Admiral's Cup team yacht, *Swuzzlebubble*. Built in 1984 using the latest high strength/low weight composite construction technology and material, it came into Bruce Guy's hands after he purchased it from its Sydney owner in 1994. In 1998 Guy and a number of his

Hobart race crew sailed into prominence when they won Tasmania's highest-profile race, the Three Peaks. The Three Peaks is a gruelling ironman-style event requiring each yacht to race to three ports selected due to their proximity to a mountain. Upon arrival, two of the crew must scale the peak before returning to the yacht and setting sail for the next port. It is painful pleasure.

Guy was renowned for his meticulous race preparation. "The mast had been out of the yacht to be painted and re-rigged," explained Matthews. "Every track worked – everything worked as it should. Nothing was left to chance, not even with the safety gear. It was an attitude that led to us having no concern about the Hobart race, no matter what the weather. We believed the yacht had seen everything when it came to the weather and could handle it."

★

Twenty-four hours into the race *Business Post Naiad* was 40 miles off shore, having covered 230 nautical miles with the assistance of the southerly current. The crew was justifiably ecstatic. Just after midday the wind was blowing a steady 20 to 30 knots and the sky was a beautiful deep blue. The yacht was sailing nicely under a No. 4 headsail and a double-reefed mainsail.

"We'd heard the forecast, 45 to 55 knots, and we all knew what a storm warning meant," said Matthews. "There was no concern. We'd also heard the warning put out by Telstra Control on *Young Endeavour*, reminding every skipper it was their responsibility when it came to continuing to race or retiring. Bruce, Keatsy, Steve Walker and I were the sort of brains-trust, but we hadn't sat down and discussed it. We just thought, righty-oh, 45 to 55 knots. We've all been here before. If it gets to 55 we might have to take things very carefully, perhaps even run off, maybe even go bare poles. We'll just hang around and wait for it to go and then start racing again. We were also talking about the guys racing who hadn't seen Bass Strait in those conditions. There were some guys we'd spoken to in Sydney who were saying it was their first Hobart and that they were a little bit nervous. We'd all been there before, or thought we'd been there before."

At around 12.30pm on December 27, the crew tucked the third reef into the mainsail. Thirty minutes later the rain arrived and conditions began to deteriorate with alacrity. By 2pm the winds were blowing 35 to 45 knots and were showing every sign of getting stronger. The seas were worse than anything Matthews had ever seen. *Business Post Naiad* would soon be in the wrong place at the wrong time.

"The waves weren't all that high at that stage but they had a very sharp face and an almost equally sharp back," said Matthews. "We were still able to sail OK; we'd sail up the face and drop the nose of the boat off over the back. The boat was handling it reasonably well but it was starting to get a bit uncomfortable. When the wind got to about 45 we took the No. 4 off and just went under the main with three reefs. It was then that the wind and the seas got worse and worse. The wind went up to about 55 but the boat still seemed OK. We could see out to the west, there was a break in the cloud and we thought, well, you know, maybe this is it. It will all be over soon. Keatsy then came on deck from the nav station and said, 'We're going to get 24 hours of this shit now'."

At around 3.30 that afternoon the top batten in the mainsail popped out. The crew flaked the mainsail and tied it down as neatly as they could then put the storm jib on. The seas were getting rougher and the enormous waves were breaking in rapid succession. Matthews was steering and was having considerable difficulty getting the bow to head up the crests of the waves. He was concerned that if the yacht went down the face of an especially large one they might pitch-pole; stick the bow in and go end-over-end.

"Every now and then the boat would get raked by one of these big breaking crests and would lie on its side and surf along, the bow being pressed down by the storm jib. The rain was driving in. It made your face feel as though it was going to bleed. I had a couple of rain drops hit me in the eye a few times and they blinded me. It was at least half a minute until I got some sort of sight back. And the spume! It was even coming off the water out of the troughs of the waves – not just off the crests. It was being driven up and out of the troughs to become what was a horizontal white-out. It was hitting your face so hard that there's just no way in the world you could look into it. We obviously knew we had to do something to slow the boat and hopefully make it a little bit more comfortable. I wouldn't say that we were concerned, just cautious. We just wanted to let the storm blow itself out. There was no panic on deck. Everybody knew exactly what everyone else was capable of doing.

"The storm jib blew out of the plastic foil on the forestay at one stage when we got knocked off by a big wave. Steve went up and put it back in. About ten minutes later it did it again. After the third time Steve and Phil went up on the fore deck and spent an hour tying loops from the sail around the forestay. It was an amazing effort in those conditions."

In just a few short hours the *Business Post Naiad* crew had gone from a fast, satisfying race into a gut-wrenching fight for survival. Steve Walker remembers looking up and seeing waves towering well above the 17-metre-high mast. At times visibility was down to 20 metres. Still, there was no talk of retiring. By late afternoon though, as the winds peaked at 75 knots, the smallest of sails, the storm jib, was deemed to be too much. *Business Post Naiad* was being belted so hard and tossed around so violently that even the crew below deck were in danger of injury as they were indiscriminately thrown from their bunks. They realised to run off down the face of the waves in those conditions would be calamitous – the yacht would sooner or later have been pitch-poled. Thought was given to setting a parachute anchor or drogue off the bow. Walker, being the on-board sailmaker, was trying to work out how he could fashion something suitable from what was available. They decided to go under bare poles and let the yacht be picked up and accelerated forward by waves approaching from the aft starboard quarter then, once moving forward, be poked up into the crests before they arrived.

Business Post Naiad was travelling fast that afternoon and hit more than 25 knots, but still appeared to be quite stable, even when beam on to the sea. The crew was far from happy having to "bare pole it" in a race but they understood it was their only option. Amid the chaos, Tony Guy – who had just handed over the helm to Matthews – decided he'd sit on deck and have a cigarette. To everyone's astonishment his persistence was rewarded. He managed to light the cigarette in 70 knots of wind and bullet-like rain.

"Hang on, here's another one!" Matthews shouted as a towering wave appeared out of nowhere. The crew sensed it was bad by the alarm in his voice. A wave the height of a five-storey building was beginning to break some 40 feet above them and they were completely at its mercy. In an instant the gargantuan curling crest extended over the eight-tonne yacht, picked it up, tipped it on its side and hurled it into the trough. Instinctively the five crew on deck grabbed whatever they could in a futile effort to save themselves.

"The yacht landed on its roof and rolled very quickly, almost instantly," recalls Matthews. "The tiller extension was ripped out of my hand and I thought there was no point in steering when we're upside down anyway. The next thing I knew I was in the water alongside the yacht, on the windward side. There was a deathly calm because the wave had disappeared and the next wave hadn't arrived. My first reaction was to look straight up to see whether the rig had survived. It wasn't there. It was buckled and bent over the windward side. I looked around to see who was in the water with me and discovered there were five of us, all with our harnesses on just bobbing around. Keatsy had rushed up on deck, really worried about us because of what he had seen happen below. He helped get us back on deck then we all set about getting rid of the rig before it could push a hole in the hull. It was broken into three pieces. Phil Skeggs just said, 'This wasn't in the brochure'."

★

Steve Walker was below deck during the roll and remembers the stove and oven breaking away from its mount and hurtling across the cabin. The ice chest disgorged its 50 pre-packed frozen meals, and plates, cups, and saucers leapt out of lockers and went everywhere. Some of the floorboards flew out and the anchor chain and anchor ropes tumbled from the lockers that were unceremoniously transformed into upturned bunks. The two aluminium framed pilot berths were also broken.

"One of the windows – they were quite small – had broken and another was cracked," recalls Walker. "The bulkheads around the companionway had sprung away from the hull and the underside of the deck had delaminated. Water continued to pour in through the broken window when we were upright so we just stuffed a couple of pillows in the gaps. Thank God we had pillows. So much for the people who laughed when they saw us taking pillows on board."

"I heard this roar – this tremendous roar – and next thing we were upside down," recalls Peter Keats. "It all went black in the cabin, absolutely pitch black. I thought, oh well, that's it – she's all over. We're finished. At the same time you didn't have time to panic. It just happened and then the boat came upright. I ended up on the floor with a whole heap of sails over the top of me. I heard the guys call for help so I flew up and found them all over the side. I can still remember the noise of the storm while I was on deck. It sounded like an express train coming at you, or you could have been standing behind a jumbo jet as it was taking off. It was just this amazing roar."

★

Twenty minutes after the roll, at around 6.50pm, most of the crumpled mast had been dumped and the deck cleared. What was now little more than a hulk was being pounded regularly by the powerful broken crests of 60-foot waves. Each time one approached, those on deck would hang on, pinning faith in their safety harnesses but at the same time knowing this might be it. It seemed unlikely the weather had any intention of easing in a hurry, in fact it appeared to be worsening.

The EPIRB was activated and Keats grappled for the radio and issued a mayday. Fortunately the backstay, which was the yacht's radio aerial, was lying on the deck and functioning, albeit with a considerably weaker signal. Geoff Ross' Beneteau 53, *Yendys*, acknowledged the mayday and relayed the message onto Lew Carter aboard *Young Endeavour*. *Business Post Naiad*'s position was 42 miles into Bass Strait south of Gabo Island. Keats turned his attention to the engine and after a few frustrating minutes managed to bring it to life. The crew had now at least some control over the vessel, and they quickly turned towards Gabo Island. All the while water continued to pour in and the crew took turns with the bailing buckets.

"We were doing about five or six knots through the water but it was only about two knots over the bottom according to the GPS, partly due to the current and certainly because of the waves," recalls Matthews. "The motor would scream its head off every time it went through the white water and tops of the waves because the propeller would just cavitate. We were still getting knocked sideways by breaking waves and at times we actually surfed on our side for probably 200 metres. It was scary; really scary. We could hear Telstra Control on *Young Endeavour* dealing with *Team Jaguar* but they couldn't hear us. We called for further assistance through *Yendys*, asking for a boat to stand by. Keatsy also requested a chopper to take three off – me apparently being one of them because, for some reason, I couldn't move my arms."

After working on the *Team Jaguar* situation for some considerable time, Telstra Control came back to *Business Post Naiad*. Matt Sherriff was violently ill, and while the crew was concerned for him they didn't miss the opportunity to blame Keats' cooking. It hurt Keats to laugh at their humour. He had suffered two broken ribs when a sudden jolt sent him crashing from the companionway stairs down into the cabin.

"I didn't cancel the mayday," said Keats. "I was asked whether the mayday was still in existence and I said, 'Yes, the situation has stabilised. We are attempting to motor back to wherever we can get to; Gabo or Eden. At best, you may reduce it to a Pan Pan but certainly no more than that – and I would request that if there are any boats in the vicinity we would like someone to stand by.' The request for the boat to stand by us was in case we were rolled again. I didn't really get a reply. I turned to Bruce soon after and said, 'I'm not looking forward to us trying to go through the night like we are – I'm concerned'. He agreed. I again tried to contact Telstra Control to see if we could get a chopper but couldn't get a reply. They may not have heard us." At that point Telstra Control well and truly had their hands full. The crew discussed what should be done with the life rafts and it was decided they should leave them where they were for the time being.

★

Later that night, somewhere between 10 and 11pm, a light plane roared out of the night sky and circled low overhead. The plane, apparently homing in on the EPIRB, is said to have reported back to AusSAR that "Breakfast Toast Naiad" had been located.

Rob Matthews steered for some time that evening in perpetual awe of the ferocity of the storm. He had been sailing for 37 years and had never seen anything like it. He took over the helm and instantly tried to familiarise himself with the conditions and the motion of the yacht and found the only way to judge the course was to read the angle of the wind on his face. The boom with the mainsail wrapped around it was lashed on the windward side of the cockpit behind him, providing a modicum of protection. He was also trying to keep an eye on the dimly-lit compass that was just four feet away, squinting all the time in a bid to keep the stinging salt spray out of his eyes. Phil Skeggs went on deck, intending to relieve

Matthews of the compass watch. The noise of the storm was so great that he had to scream out the heading.

Business Post Naiad had motored some 20 miles, but was no nearer the coast. The course was due north. For a brief moment the clouds parted and the moon shed an eerie light on the mayhem. The moon disappeared as quickly as it had arrived, leaving the crew wishing it had taken with it the constant roar of the storm. Matthews was repeatedly calling out to Skeggs to hold on as each wave approached, but no amount of holding could prepare them for the monster wave which suddenly appeared. It all happened so quickly that Matthews' first recollection was being trapped underwater at the aft end of the cockpit, unable to move. The colossal wave had lumbered out of the night and had rolled the 40-foot yacht forward and upside down like a pebble on the road.

"It was very surreal, deathly quiet, because you could feel the yacht still surfing sideways," said Matthews. "All the time I was being slammed up under the side of the boat and my head was banging on the cockpit floor. My life jacket and float coat were holding me up there. I knew exactly where I was because I could reach aft and feel the stern of the yacht. I was underwater and outside the aft lifelines which are about a metre forward of the transom. Initially I didn't make any attempt to unhook my harness or try to swim out. I immediately struck trouble when I eventually did go to release my harness clip. The boat was still being surfed sideways and all the time my head was being slammed on the cockpit floor – above me. My harness strop was almost fully extended. There was just enough play in it to unclip. But each time I tried to unclip, the notch in the clip slotted over the stainless steel plate on the front of my harness. It just jammed and I couldn't free it."

Matthews was almost out of oxygen and would most probably have drowned but for another freak wave which swept through and lifted the stern just enough to let a puff of air dart under the cockpit floor. He pressed his nose against the floor and filled his lungs with the biggest gulp of air he could muster. Exhausted but breathing, he managed to free himself finally from the harness strop and pull himself to the back of the boat and up to the surface. His main concern was that Skeggs might be similarly trapped in his harness and he desperately wanted to dive back under the boat and search. But it was dark, he was fatigued from his own ordeal, and, apart from the time it would take to remove his buoyancy aids, there was the distinct chance he'd lose them altogether. Also, he didn't know where to start looking, and he could well have become trapped himself.

He remembered hearing of a single-handed round-the-world race competitor who had survived by climbing onto his upturned yacht and attaching himself to the rudder. Matthews devised a plan. He would swim around to the side, hopefully stand on one of the wire lifelines – or side rails – and somehow launch himself towards his target. The odds were against him being successful, but he had to try. As he swam to the side of the yacht he stayed as close to it as possible so he wouldn't be washed away. He felt something brush against his leg – something underwater. It was a section of the broken mast that had been lashed to the deck. Matthews sat on it initially to rest then tried to stand on it and prepare for the leap but he was too exhausted and all he could do was sit, hang on the best he could and pray.

The sea was unrelenting, and an agonising four to five minutes after the yacht overturned yet another behemoth of a wave came crashing towards *Business Post Naiad*. Matthews first heard it rumbling out of the gloom, then saw its churning white collar descending from above.

It engulfed the boat, but in doing so exerted sufficient force on the upturned keel for the yacht to be first tipped onto its side and, when the full pendulum effect of the keel took over, whipped back upright.

"I don't know what I was hanging onto, possibly a stanchion, but suddenly I ended up on my feet in a squatting position from where I'd taken off; on the piece of cockpit floor that had been above my head when I was trapped. I can only assume that I was flicked through the air, did a backflip of sorts and ended up back on the deck. My lifeline harness that I'd unclipped was there in front of me, draped over the lifeline. I clipped myself on and stepped back inside the rail."

As Matthews regathered his senses he was confronted with the sight of Phil Skeggs, face down in the cockpit. His legs hung limply over the broken boom and protruded over the lifelines. As well as being held by his harness, Skeggs' body was wrapped in ropes. Matthews yelled for assistance from below. Crewmembers scrambled on deck and frantically cut away the harness and the stray ropes and performed CPR and mouth to mouth resuscitation.

It was to no avail. Phil Skeggs was dead.

★

The massive wave had also wreaked havoc below deck. Half asleep, Steve Walker heard a loud swoosh then an enormous roar, audible even above the noise of the diesel motor. With the aid of the faint light from their miners' headlamps, he and Bruce Guy had kicked out the stormboards in the companionway. This allowed more water in but only to the point where the air pressure equalised. Thankfully a quick inspection of the keel revealed minimal damage. In the ghostly dim light a black figure seemed to appear out of nowhere. It was Jim

Rogers, saturated in oil. He had been dozing alongside the motor for warmth and when the yacht rolled it deposited its contents all over him.

The water was nearly knee-height in the cabin and was strewn with floating detritus – food, clothing, bottles, diesel, oil and sails. The seven crewmembers trapped inside could hear Matthews' frantic calls for Skeggs above the roar of the storm. Bruce Guy suggested kicking a life raft out through the companionway so that it was at least there if the yacht sank, but that idea was soon vetoed for it was likely the raft would become stuck either in the companionway or the cockpit.

"The thought entered my mind that the yacht would not come back upright," recalls Keats. "She was floating so comfortably upside down due to the wide flat deck. I was concerned because I couldn't see how we were going to get out. If the boat went down we were going to go to the grave with it."

When *Business Post Naiad* eventually came upright, a metre of water remained in the cabin.

"As the yacht righted, Bruce just seemed to slip in the water and almost went under," recalls Walker. "He struggled to get up and I went to help him. As I grabbed him I could see he was in terrible pain, mainly from the left side of his chest. His eyes just rolled back and he died immediately, there and then in my arms, a massive heart attack. There was nowhere I could lay him because he would be underwater. All I could do was sit on a bunk edge and hold him in my lap – hold his head above the water and try to keep his air passage clear. I felt for his pulse and his breath but there was nothing. I sort of knew instinctively that he was dead but I didn't want to give up on him. Jim and I held him and did what we could. At the same time we didn't realise that the other guys were trying to revive Phil up on deck."

The water in the hull surged towards the bow with every wave and threatened to submerge it. *Business Post Naiad* was within centimetres of sinking and water was still flooding into the hull, sloshing into the cabin out of the cockpit. A stormboard was finally located and put in place – a makeshift and temporary measure in a dire situation.

☆

Amid the confusion a life raft was passed up from the cabin to the cockpit. As it went it was accidentally inflated and crewmembers wrestled with it until it was eventually pushed over the side and tethered to the yacht. Flares also arrived on deck but no one immediately available was experienced in firing them. Peter Keats was frantically trying to read the instructions through his salt-encrusted glasses, but his hands were covered in oil and even when he did manage to get one out of the pack he was unable to get the cap off.

"Eventually one of the guys got the first one going – an orange smoke flare – and gave it to me to hold," Keats recalls. "I then got hold of three parachute flares and let them go. I may as well have saved my energy. They went up fine and ignited, then disappeared to the east at an unbelievable speed because of the wind. They seemed to come back over us at a hundred miles an hour."

The batteries had been underwater and had short circuited so the radios no longer worked. Hansen put some sails over the bow on a rope to act as a crude sea anchor. The second life raft, which was then on deck in its pack, was pushed back down below so it would be better protected, but on the way it too was accidentally triggered. Four crewmembers struggled with the rapidly-expanding rubber monster and ultimately got it on deck and deployed over the side with the other one.

Rob Matthews remembered the bow ventilation port between the anchor locker and the forward cabin was open and he waded forward, smashed open the toilet door and put the vent cover in place. That done, he rushed back to the raft. "We had thrown everything we thought we might need into one of the rafts – extra water, thermal rugs, some food, flares and things like that," he recalls. "When I went back on deck the raft was upside down and everything was lost."

With both bilge pumps clogged or broken, the bucket brigade started what was to be a three-hour battle against the incessantly rising water. Two crewmembers handled the buckets below while two others on deck tipped the contents over the side. Peter Keats was on deck furiously bailing, soaking wet and freezing. He called for a jacket, but the only one they could find had belonged to Bruce Guy. Once it was apparent that the buckets were stemming the tide some of the crew moved Guy's body into an aft quarter berth. Neither Rob Matthews nor Peter Keats knew at that stage that Guy was dead.

The water level inside the cabin was brought down to a manageable level of around one metre thus stabilising the yacht. There was still the distinct possibility of another roll but the weighted boat seemed to be handling the slamming waves a little better. The wind had lulled to 50 or 55 knots which felt like a pleasant afternoon breeze after what they had just been through. The sails over the bow were tending to hold *Business Post Naiad* up into the seas most of the time. There was no need for anyone to be on deck so crew that weren't bailing tried to rest. At around 3am another big wave swept across the yacht and submerged it, but this time it stayed upright. At one stage, well before daylight, one of the crew poked his head out of the companionway to check on the weather and saw something far more frightening. Both life rafts had gone. Their tether lines had either chafed through or parted.

"Some of the guys, particularly Keatsy, became pretty emotional about the loss of the rafts," recalls Rob Matthews, "but there was nothing we could do about it. We all knew that the only time you get into a life raft is when you step up to it. Our yacht had become our raft and it was floating quite well. At dawn Steve and I got up and went on deck to rig a red sail cover over the cabin top to make us more conspicuous because we had a white boat, with a grey deck, on a grey sea and white waves so we couldn't be seen too easily. We wanted to use the V-sheet, the orange distress sheet, but it had been washed out of its locker and lost. It was still blowing. There was still spume coming off the water so I figure it was probably about 45 knots. I went back in time and rigged an oil can over the side then punched a hole in it, it actually helped the situation. The oil drifting upwind on the surface of the sea did, to some extent, help smooth the seas as they came at us. It worked but it wasn't enough.

"Steve went back down below and I sat up there looking around for aircraft or something. At about 6am Matt came up on deck and I said to him, 'I haven't seen Bruce up and about'. I'd asked Steve during the night 'Where's Bruce?' and he said, 'Oh, we've put him in a bunk'. I said 'Oh right' and thought no more about it. Matt looked at me a little surprised and said, 'Oh shit, mate, didn't you know? Bruce died last night.' That brought me totally unstuck because I'd assumed he was down there in his bunk whacked and tired. It was seven hours after he died that I found out. I got really angry then, swearing and cursing and shouting about God knows what."

★

Around 7.30am on December 28 a light aircraft was spotted to the north west of *Business Post Naiad*. A red parachute flare was sent arcing through the sky while an orange smoke flare was ignited on deck to give a specific target for the course of the parachute flare. The plane turned and began circling the battered yacht and stayed there for an hour, acting as a beacon for a rescue helicopter the crew prayed was on the way.

The NRMA Careflight helicopter out of Sydney arrived shortly after. At the controls was veteran pilot Dan Tyler, Graeme Fromberg was crewman and Murray Traynor was the SCAT (Special Casualty Access Team) paramedic. They had been in Canberra on a medical mission late the previous day when they were "commandeered" by AusSAR and requested to join the Sydney to Hobart rescue effort as early as possible the next day. The only accommodation they could find at such a late hour was in the SouthCare headquarters at Canberra airport. The four grabbed two fitful hours of sleep; two of them on the floor and two in beds before a 4.30am launch for Merimbula. In Merimbula the Careflight team was initially asked to attend the Jarkan 40 *Midnight Special* and assist with a rescue there.

"On the way out we heard a top cover plane flying around saying they'd just spotted a flare coming from one of the boats," recalls Murray Traynor. "They didn't know who it was but gave coordinates. We also heard that the Victorian Police Air had completed the *Midnight Special* job. We were then only seven to 10 minutes away from where the flare had gone off and so we diverted and came across *Business Post Naiad*. They were waving at us from the deck. Right from the start I didn't like the look of what I saw. The yacht was just flipped up onto its side by a massive wave. I'd never seen a wave that big in my life.

"Graeme and I spent some time just looking out the door, looking at different ways we could extricate them out of the situation. The first thing we decided was that we were not going to be able to pull them off the boat because it was being thrown everywhere. We couldn't tell which way the boat was going to go from one second to another. One of us suggested we see if we could get them to jump off the back of the boat and swim away from it, then I'd go down and we'd winch them straight out of the water. We went into a hover near the yacht and acted out what we wanted them to do; I'd come down the wire and I'd have this strop. I then put it over Graeme's head and showed them what they were supposed to do. They seemed to acknowledge it."

Murray Traynor then clipped onto the winch wire and began what was only his second, and certainly most dangerous, sea rescue. He knew that one mistake could result in the wire wrapping around a limb or even his neck. It required an exceptional team effort between pilot, winchman and paramedic.

"We decided it would be safer if we looped one of the spinnaker sheets through my safety harness so that it could be double ended back to the boat," recalls Rob Matthews. "I figured that the guys would be able to winch me back to the yacht if the chopper guys didn't get me. Anyway, I jumped off the back of the boat and this frogman came down and swam towards me. I unclipped my harness, put my arms up and the strop went over my head then *whammo!* Next thing I'm being launched out of the water at a hundred miles an hour and up into this helicopter.

"They whacked a headset on me and started firing questions, obviously wanting to see whether I was able to tell them what they needed to know. Making me do mental arithmetic about how many guys were on the boat and how many were dead. They could see Phil in the cockpit. They were asking 'Is the guy in the bottom of the cockpit deceased?' I said, 'Yes, and there's another downstairs'. They wanted to make sure they got everyone accounted for. I also heard the pilot say, 'I think I'm only going to have enough fuel to get four on. We'll have to leave the rest until later'. The waves were still enormous and that boat still felt like it could roll at any time.

"The other guys started arriving in the chopper. I have to say that the one guy in the team who doesn't get enough recognition is the winchman. You've got the pilot, who's just unbelievable and the frogman who is outright mad, and then there's the winchman who is the integral part of the whole situation. He's the eyes and the ears of the chopper pilot. Things were obviously going well because after there were four of us on the chopper I heard the pilot say, 'These guys are good. Everything's going well. We're going to get them all'. There was a big surge of relief for me. It was a fantastic feeling."

Although the rescue mission was progressing satisfactorily, it was still a hellish experience for the chopper crew. Tyler had the unenviable task holding the machine in hover against 45 to 50 knots of headwind. Traynor was dicing with death each time he winched down, and was caught by two big waves. He had one crewmember in the strop ready to go when a mammoth wave appeared out of nowhere and broke directly over them. Two metres under, he paddled furiously back to the surface, blew the water out of his snorkel but before he could take a breath another wave pushed him under. He tried to relax and within a second he and the crewmember were hurtling skyward.

"During the first few winches I wasn't aware that there were two people dead on board the boat so I didn't have that thought pressuring me," recalls Traynor. "The realisation that someone might be dead didn't come until probably the fourth winch because I could see one person lying flat on the boat. I said to Graeme a couple of times when I was back in the chopper, 'What's happening with that bloke on the deck?' and he said, 'It doesn't matter, just keep going down'. He just thought I knew he was dead. I think it was the fourth winch when I just stopped halfway down and looked at this bloke on the deck, I looked up at Graeme, shut my eyes and crossed my arms across my chest. I signalled, asking if he wanted me to go and get him. He signalled 'Don't worry about it'. That's when I realised he was gone. I still didn't know there was a second person deceased on board.

"My biggest fear then was that I was going to have to go on board to get that person off. If I went aboard the boat I would have had to come off the hook, which means that my lifeline is gone. If the helicopter had to fly away I'd be stuck out there, and I'm no boating person whatsoever. That was my biggest fear during the entire exercise."

Some 35 minutes after the rescue had begun there were seven depressed and badly beaten men aboard the Careflight helicopter. Dan Tyler turned it towards the coast and at 9am on December 28 all seven had their feet on dry land. A police launch left the next day, located *Business Post Naiad* and towed it back into port with the bodies of Bruce Guy and Phil Skeggs on board.

Sixteen
Solo Globe Challenger

During the night of December 26, Tony Mowbray, owner of *Solo Globe Challenger*, was phoned by a television reporter from his hometown of Newcastle. A story was being prepared on the progress of the region's highest profile race entry. The reporter commented during the conversation that Mowbray appeared to be "pretty relaxed" about the forecast for 50-knot sou'westerly winds the next day. Mowbray, having covered thousands of sea miles offshore in small yachts, replied: "Oh well, you know, I've seen 50 knots plenty of times. I've been down to Bass Strait, probably crossed Bass Strait maybe 30 times." Twenty hours later Mowbray was shaking his head in disbelief and was having difficulty comprehending what was confronting him and his Cole 43.

Solo Globe Challenger is a comparatively slim yacht but Mowbray saw it as a strong and very seaworthy design that would hold him in good stead on his proposed solo around-the-world voyage in 1999. He had seven crew with him and they held a similar faith. Up until midday on the 27th they felt they were still competitive. They had been changing sails as required and were down to a storm jib. They were then about 30 miles into Bass Strait, not far from *Winston Churchill*, and encountering conditions Mowbray considered to be "fairly dangerous".

"We had probably 60 knots of wind and it was starting to get vicious. The seas were fairly short and sharp and close together; probably in the 20 to 30 foot range. Already the noise from the wind and the seas was amazing, just shrieking and roaring. You had to shout at the top of your voice to be heard by someone who was just a bodywidth away. At that point we pulled the storm jib off her completely and then we just proceeded to sail under bare poles. Ours is one of those boats where you can actually maintain a course under bare poles. We were getting up and over the waves, it was certainly the safer option at that time. We had no desire to run away square with the waves."

Mowbray had not slept since the start of the race some 24 hours earlier, so when the 14:05 sked came on he went below, climbed into the port quarter berth and tuned into the airwaves while veteran Bob Snape reported the yacht's position and monitored developments. He listened keenly as *Sword of Orion* detailed the conditions they were experiencing but he still felt confident that he had a solid boat and an excellent crew. Glen "Cyril" Picasso, a competent helmsman, was left at the wheel. Three other crew were on deck with him.

The fresh on-deck watch was amazed at the speed with which the weather was going downhill. In just 90 minutes, conditions had gone from what some sailors might call "fresh", to "frightening", to something that was nothing short of horrific. The wind seemingly rose in increments of five knots every 15 minutes and the waves more than doubled in height. At around 4pm a 60-foot monster came roaring towards the yacht, picked it up and threw it down on its port side. When the wave broke it dumped, and forced the yacht over to about 145 to 150 degrees before sweeping it down the face for about 20 seconds.

Mowbray was in his bunk below deck and was taken

completely unawares. "It was a surreal sort of thing. I was saying to myself, what the fuck is happening here? It's a situation where you are totally out of control, you're in a washing machine and someone's put it on bloody fast agitate and that's it, it's all over." The mast broke almost immediately just above the boom and the force of water engulfed the yacht, imploding the PVC skylight that was protected by a cockpit coaming and located just above his bunk. Water poured into the nav station at the for'ard end of the quarter berth and swamped everything – GPS, radios, Satcom C, mobile telephone. Bob Snape was sitting there and ended up a sodden and bewildered tangle of arms and legs.

"I managed to struggle to the hatch and open it," recalls Mowbray. "I had four guys up on deck. One guy had been knocked unconscious but was coming around. The mast had come down over the port quarter and was hanging out over the port aft side of the cockpit. His legs were pinned by the mast so as the boat was riding up and down over the waves the rig was sawing at his legs. Suddenly he was screaming like you wouldn't believe."

Mowbray's attention then flashed to the water behind the yacht. Picasso, still attached by his safety harness, was being dragged along under the water. He said later that his life was flashing through his mind. He was saying to himself "for Christ's sake this harness better not break". His harness suddenly went limp and he stopped dead in the water. He put his hand up, touched the boat's stern and grabbed the pushpit. In the pressure of the moment Mowbray uttered "one of the silliest things I've ever said: 'Cyril, for Christ's sake stop fucking around and get back on board'. I just turned around and went to help the other guys. As I did Cyril looked at me and said, 'Right oh?' So that's what he did, climbed back on board, busted ribs and all."

Meanwhile, Keir Enderby was trapped by the rig and Tony Purkiss was also lying there with a broken leg and a terrible gash on his head. The able crewmembers did what they could to make the injured comfortable in the cockpit but the yacht also needed attention. It had skewed off course and the smashed mast was now lying upwind. Each wave was slamming the broken and jagged aluminium spar into the side of the hull. The yacht was taking on a lot of water and was showing signs that it might be sinking by the stern. Cutting the rig away was paramount. Mowbray and three other crewmembers went up to the mast area and began working on the rig and within 15 minutes it had been removed. Fortunately none of it had snagged on the rudder.

Snape had triggered both on-board EPIRBs and had started bailing. Two others manned the manual pumps and after about 45 minutes the tide of water inside the hull was well down. Efforts were made to start the engine but its response was spasmodic. It would run and then die, apparently because water had found its way into the fuel system via the fuel tank breather and sediment from the fuel filters had been stirred up. With the situation reasonably stabilised, some of the injured were transferred to bunks below. It was found however that the crewman with the broken leg could not be moved without causing him excruciating pain. He chose to remain in the cockpit.

Mowbray was the only heavy-weather helmsman fit for action and went onto the helm to guide the yacht down the waves. It was then about 5pm and, with all communications lost, the crew were isolated in their little cocoon. Only their EPIRBs would be bouncing information back to AusSAR in Canberra. As yet the life rafts had not been prepared, a move which Mowbray felt should be a last alternative. During the night mammoth waves continued to pound the yacht, tossing the 43-foot, nine-tonne vessel like a cork. They were caught on the northern side of the low and running downwind, and were moving with the worst of the storm but they were destined to remain in foul weather for the next 15 hours.

"We went into the night thinking the next wave could be the one that took us out," Mowbray recalls. "It was a very, very fearful situation. As far as I was concerned, death was just there in the water alongside us. You could sense it was there. I was thinking if I get out of this I'm going to be a lucky bloke. We hadn't done anything special about preparing the life raft. It was still in place on deck near the mast. Actually I've never been a great believer about getting into rafts; it's a bit like slashing your wrists before you go. It's the absolute last alternative. As we charged off into the night we had a number of waves that really tossed us on our beam end. In fact the waves did all sorts of things to us that night. One monster just reared up behind and broke all over the four of us who were in the cockpit. We sensed it was coming and the others just dropped to the floor to protect themselves. I was steering and the white water just threw me forward into the wheel. It was just an unbelievable wave.

"The whole boat was completely engulfed in white water, completely submerged. I was standing and the water was at chest level. I was looking out across all this white water while the boat's just careering down the face of this wave completely under the white water. All I could make out was the top of the pulpit at the bow. I was yelling at the top of my voice, 'This is it! This is the one. We're gone'. I was thinking, as we hit the bottom of this bloody trough, the nose is just going to keep going down and we're going to pitch pole. Somehow, when we got to the bottom the yacht stopped and we bobbed back up onto the surface. There was one other wave that I will never forget. It was huge and the moment it hit us it skewed us 90 degrees to our course. It picked us up and the boat took off across the face of the wave like it was a surfboard. We were absolutely charging across the face of this wave, like I'm talking about literally thumping across the water like you do in a high performance sailing dinghy.

"But we're in a 43-foot, nine-tonne yacht. It's going whack, whack, whack across the wave, doing 15 maybe 20 knots, and I'm hanging onto the wheel, crouched down, waiting for the wave to break all over us. I'm thinking in a split second, what do I do? Do I try and pull the boat away? Do I let it go straight ahead and try to steady it? Do I try and pull up through the back of it or what? Then I realised the yacht was just hanging in there. I decided I'd just steer her straight and let her go the way she wanted. This is all happening in a split second. I'm crouched down waiting for the water to literally engulf us – that's how big this bastard was – and then suddenly I'm thinking, God I've got no water around. I've got my eyes and my mouth closed and there's no water. What's going on?

"I opened my eyes and I looked up and could see the water curling over us. We were literally in the tube of the wave. It was just a phenomenal, unbelievable situation. You could see it breaking over us, and we were just staying out of the break. Next thing, of course, it all caught up with us and *whumphh*, it broke all over us. Equally quickly it was all gone. I looked back upwind and could see white water for 400 metres. After that I made a few promises to myself. I decided that if I survived I was going to give away the plan to sail around the world. I'd imposed on my wife and children and my family and friends too much. You have to follow your passion but there also comes a point when you have to back off."

At one stage they considered setting a sea anchor to slow the boat, but Mowbray's experience in fighting a

50- to 60-knot Southern Ocean gale some years earlier assured him what they were doing was safer.

"Throughout the night I kept telling myself I wanted to see stars. We started seeing little patches of stars up there and I thought, OK, please stay open, open up. They'd close over again. We just had to be patient. I steered the boat from 5 o'clock that Sunday afternoon throughout the whole night. By the early hours of Monday morning I was absolutely ratshit. With my good helmsman injured I could do nothing else. I started hallucinating at one stage and saw a monkey sitting on the broken stump of the mast. When I knew that it wasn't real, I told the guys I could see it. I said, 'I can see a monkey on the mast.' They just said, 'Can you? Oh yeah, there he is.'"

The two EPIRBs were still operating but the crew did not know if their signal was being registered at AusSAR. They discussed how they might get off the yacht. The conclusion was that they probably couldn't get off – it was dark, the seas were unforgiving and the yacht was being hurled around like a bucking bronco. Someone would almost certainly be killed. Mowbray had never contemplated abandoning his prized yacht, but that night admitted to himself that if his life could be assured by leaving the yacht he'd do it.

"By 1am I was shattered; unbelievably tired. I said to the guys, 'have you got anything that can keep me awake' and they came up with the idea of giving me a cup of coffee. So Bob Snape made me three cups of coffee between 1am until about 4.30am. They were so strong you could have stood the spoon up in them. They were like drinking bitumen. I hadn't drunk coffee for six years but I did then. Each time I took a sip I'd just go 'Whoa, whoa', and my mouth would take on the shape of a cat's bum. But I drank them – straight black. Anyhow it kept me going."

When dawn broke, a glimmer of black slowly turning to grey in the east, Mowbray noticed signs of the wind abating. It was down to around 45 knots, and the 50- to 60-foot seas that had hounded them all night had quelled to around 40 foot.

As the light improved, tired eyes again scanned the skies for any form of assistance and around 7am the blissful sound of the Helimed helicopter filled their ears. Flares were fired and the big red and white Bell 412 turned their way. With no communications, the chopper crew indicated by hand they intended to take everyone from the yacht. But Mowbray thought otherwise. He was convinced *Solo Globe Challenger* could be nursed back to the coast and into port. He did, however, insist that the most seriously injured crew be lifted off.

Cam Robertson was the paramedic on the flight. They had been dispatched from Mallacoota at 6am and sent to investigate the *Solo Globe Challenger* EPIRB signal that AusSAR was registering. Despite the huge seas and high winds, Robertson saw all three rescues as "pretty straightforward". He would be lowered into the water near the yacht, the crewmembers would jump from the yacht, he would swim to them, place the rescue strop around them, give the thumbs up and head for the heavens. Amid the confusion and noise and the uncertainty about how much fuel the helicopter was carrying, one crewmember jumped into the water in haste and without a life jacket.

"It was Tony Purkiss, the guy with the broken leg," recalls Mowbray. "He believed that if you really seal up your wet weather gear tightly at the ankles and wrists and tie your hood down tight then there's enough air trapped inside your wet weather gear to float you for five minutes. So he put it to the test and it worked. When he was about to jump I saw he still had his seaboots on so I shouted, 'Get your seaboots off!'. But he couldn't because of his broken leg. We all thought he'd go straight to the bottom, but he didn't. While they were getting lined up for one of the lifts I saw the chopper just rear up into the air like a rocket. The next minute this huge wave just came through. It would probably have wiped him out. That convinced me even more that those guys were absolute heroes. The guys in the choppers and the plane guys, and in particular the people who went into the drink from the choppers to rescue others; they're all superheroes."

Two crew with broken ribs remained on board, reluctant to be lifted lest they suffer further injury. Glen Picasso was prepared to go, but then "mateship" took over. "Glen actually appeared with his life jacket and started to walk towards the stern," said Mowbray. "He was ready to jump overboard and be lifted out. Then he stopped, looked at me, shook his head and said, 'I can't do it. I can't leave you guys'. He turned, went down below again and closed the hatch."

With three rescued crew in its belly the chopper headed for the coast some 60 miles away. *Solo Globe Challenger* then continued on its drift, the remaining crew determined to get it back to shore. Mowbray was severely fatigued but somehow mustered the energy to organise the building of a jury rig. Picasso took the helm so that Mowbray, Keith Molloy and 66-year-old Snape could go about the task. Enderby remained below because of the extent of his injuries.

The spinnaker pole became a makeshift mast, while the storm jib and trysail were hoisted to create a crude sail plan. The seas, rolling from the south west, were still too big and dangerous to take beam-on so the course was slightly east of north. The two EPIRBs remained operating, indicating the yacht was still afloat.

★

Conditions eased dramatically during the Monday afternoon and *Solo Globe Challenger* came onto a more favourable course towards the coast. Picasso and Enderby, despite their injuries, worked tirelessly below deck to spur life from the motor. The engine had so many problems with fuel and sediments and water that the two crewmembers slowly pulled it apart, piece by piece, examining, cleaning and repairing where necessary. Unbeknown to them, the EPIRB they believed was transmitting overnight had actually stopped, apparently because the aerial was damaged. That led SAR authorities in Canberra to fear the yacht may have sunk. A new search was established. Even local news reports in Newcastle suggested they might have joined the race's list of fatalities.

Soon after sun-up an Air Force Orion roared overhead and circled low, the flight crew trying to identify the yacht. They then despatched smoke flares to check the wind speed and direction before dropping an emergency container into the ocean just ahead of them. It contained satchels of fresh water and a hand-held VHF. The remaining crewmembers aboard *Solo Globe Challenger* made contact with the 26-year-old captain, Paul Carpenter, who informed them HMAS *Newcastle* was about 36 miles away and heading their way.

★

HMAS *Newcastle* had spent most of the night searching for *Solo Globe Challenger* and the crew were extremely concerned because they knew that the yacht's EPIRB had stopped transmitting. Commander Steve Hamilton called on a special effort from all available on his undermanned ship to scan the ocean as they went into a search pattern 100 miles off the coast.

"We knew that the satellites had lost contact with the EPIRB on their passes so we were becoming more and more determined to find the yacht," recalls Hamilton. "We were frustrated by the fact that the seas were still around 25 foot; big enough to hide the yacht from our eyes and our radar. We based the search around their last known position, not realising that they had set a jury rig and were making ground north. Soon after daylight an Orion flew overhead and told us they had spotted the yacht 30 miles to the north."

★

Surmising the Navy would want to take him and Enderby off, Picasso doubled his efforts to start the motor and give Mowbray and the two remaining crew a better chance of reaching the coast. Only minutes before HMAS *Newcastle* appeared on the horizon to the south the motor roared back to life.

"We had the hand-held VHF radio turned on," Mowbray recalls. "The next thing words burst from it that I'll never forget. '*Solo Globe Challenger*, this is the warship *Newcastle*'. I thought, you beauty, if these bastards can't save us, who will? The ship came close to us and slowed. Then they sent two people – a male and a female – over to us in an inflatable boat. They came alongside and the young guy who was controlling the inflatable said, 'Good morning Sir' and I said, 'Good morning to you too'."

"'I'm instructed to remove all personnel from the vessel.'

"Look old mate, thanks very much for coming but I really don't want to leave my boat."

'Oh, hang on a minute.'

"He had a bit of a chat into his mouthpiece, obviously talking to the skipper, then came back and asked 'What would you like to do?'

"Well, we've got two injured people here. We'd like to remove them if we may."

"That's fine."

Picasso and Enderby stepped gingerly into the inflatable and were whisked back to the ship. They were helped aboard and taken to the ship's small but impressive medical centre where the doctor went about treating them. As HMAS *Newcastle* moved away and turned towards Sydney, *Solo Globe Challenger* was making about five knots – using its jury rig and motor – towards Ulladulla. As it disappeared, *Newcastle* advised that a fishing trawler had been sent out by an insurance company to tow the yacht into Eden.

✫

At 4.30am the next morning *Solo Globe Challenger* arrived in Eden at the end of a towline. Tony Mowbray still had his yacht and, possibly, his dream to sail non-stop around the world.

"I think it's a bit like childbirth for a woman. You tend to forget the hard parts and want to go again. There is one thing though I certainly won't forget after going from heaven to hell and back. I'm not the sort of person who goes to sea undercooked – I'm always prepared for the worst – or at least I thought I was. Before this I thought I knew where the top rung of the ladder was; now I know it's about 50 per cent higher."

Seventeen
Winston Churchill –
Part II

For a six-hour period on December 27 the north-east corner of Bass Strait was a hellish place to be. Many of the 115 yachts had been forced to retire through damage, injury to crew or seasickness. Some crews chose to apply "prudent seamanship" and withdraw from the race while others sought shelter in safe havens until the storm had passed. A tiny minority, through desire or circumstance, continued racing towards Hobart.

Two yachts that the *Winston Churchill* crew were most keen to beat, Don Mickleborough's *Southerly* and Ian Kiernan's *Canon Maris*, were among the retirees late that afternoon. Two other very seaworthy racers, Hugh Treharne's *Bright Morning Star* and Stephen Ainsworth's *Loki*, soon joined them. *Southerly* retired because of what, in hindsight, might have been a fortunate mistake. Mickleborough and his crew were unaware they were around 48 miles from Eden when they decided their race was run. Had they known they were that far south they may have continued deeper into the mayhem in Bass Strait.

Hugh Treharne had been aboard the Australian yacht *Impetuous* in the tragic 1979 Fastnet Race and ruefully remembers the conditions back then. "The Fastnet was like being in the fridge compared to this one. When a big wave poured over the top of *Bright Morning Star* [in the Sydney to Hobart] it was like being in a warm bath. The exposure to hypothermia over in England was much worse and that's why they lost so many people. The conditions – the wind and waves – were very similar though. The only real difference was that in Bass Strait the seas were a lot more confused. My technique was to sail fast enough so I could poke the bow up into the waves and then through them. We were sailing with a deep reef in the main and no jib. The options were to run away with it and set either the trysail or storm jib or retire and go back to Eden under motor.

"While I was trying to make up my mind this huge wave arrived. I was looking a long way up at its crest, like I had to stretch my neck. There was a lot of white water, a real lot of white water coming at me, and the wave just kept getting steeper and steeper. I braced myself by grabbing the wheel and leaning over it. There was nothing I could do to try to beat it. The moment it hit the yacht was knocked over to 90 degrees with the mast in the water. I couldn't see for quite a few seconds. I was under green water. It wasn't just spray or a splash, it was hugely green. The water filled the mainsail and held the yacht down; it could have been 40-feet deep for all I know."

By the time *Bright Morning Star* righted, three crew in the cabin had suffered broken ribs. Treharne's brother, Ian, rushed on deck and worked with him to lower the mainsail. The engine was started. Eden would be *Bright Morning Star*'s new destination.

★

Michael "Zapper" Bell was one of three crewmembers on deck on Stephen Ainsworth's Swan 44, *Loki*. They were about 70 miles offshore and sailing under a storm jib when the wind instrument hit a staggering 74 knots. A rogue wave of titanic proportions loomed out of nowhere and began to break above *Loki*. The yacht headed up the vertical wall of water and was then tossed back, landing upside down.

"What followed was the most amazing experience I've ever had at sea. There I was, underneath this upturned yacht in the most incredibly serene situation. I could have been swimming in the fishpond at home. In fact it was like swimming in the Caribbean – clear and warm. Everything was still and beautiful," he recalls. "I saw my glasses get washed off my face and had time to simply reach out and grab them. I remember all the coloured halyard tails and lines just wafting through the water like sea snakes. I was amazed that I felt no panic. I knew I had to release my safety harness at my chest to get out. There was no gasping for breath or panic, just deliberate movements to escape. Then, all of a sudden, the yacht righted itself with the rig and everything intact. All hell broke loose again. We were back into the real world. Not surprisingly we decided that that was enough. We set a sea anchor and ran under bare poles still doing seven knots. Some of the crew wanted us to head towards Eden – 70 miles upwind. 'Bugger that,' I said. 'We're heading for New Zealand. It might be 1200 miles away but I know I can catch a jet back to Australia from there. We are not going upwind in this'."

Eventually, when the wind died and sea conditions improved, *Loki* made it back to port at Narooma, south of Sydney.

★

Initially, there was a bit of father-and-son rivalry adding spice to the battle between *Canon Maris* and *Winston Churchill*. John Gibson, 65, was aboard *Winston*

Churchill, while his son, Jonathan, 31, was with Ian Kiernan. By the time the two yachts had entered Bass Strait and were being pounded by the storm all competitive rivalries began to dissolve.

Kiernan was reluctant to retire at first and was confident the yacht was performing well. The wind direction was causing him some consternation however – it was going to the west while the southern ocean was trying to squeeze through Bass Strait against a very strong current racing south. It was a deadly combination. Kiernan was standing in the companionway when a huge 30-foot plus wave came over and swept the spray dodger right off the boat. He wasn't prepared to sit still and watch his yacht be demolished nor risk the safety of his crewmates so he made the difficult decision to retire. They were then approximately 60 miles from Eden but thought they'd head for a port farther to the north – Ulladulla or even Sydney. It was around 6.10pm and they set the spitfire jib, selected the new course and began to extricate themselves from the worst of the storm.

They had heard *Winston Churchill*'s mayday but did not know the details. "When I heard Lew Carter mention over the radio that a search was underway and that there was no EPIRB signal I started to think the yacht had gone down and taken the raft and all the crew with it," recalls Kiernan. "I couldn't say that though. We had to keep a very positive attitude – a very stiff upper lip – for Gibbo's sake. He was hearing the reports come through and while he appeared stoic about it all he was very, very concerned. We were saying to him, 'Your Dad will be alright mate. They'll be OK. They'll be OK'. But in my heart of hearts I was already thinking they were all dead."

★

While race yachts continued to battle their way across Bass Strait and on towards Hobart the nine sailors crammed into the two *Winston Churchill* life rafts began their own battle to survive what would be a traumatic night. In the four-man raft with Richard Winning and Bruce Gould were 19-year-old Hobart race novice Michael Rynan and Paul Lumtin. In the other raft with Stanley, Lawler and Gibson were Mike Bannister and John Dean. Winning's raft carried the one EPIRB the yacht was required to have for the race. There was a small lifeline between the two rafts which soon broke. Stanley's raft possessed a drogue which was set to slow the rate of drift but as it was let out it became tangled. Suddenly it took up and John Gibson tried valiantly to hang on to it but the thin line tore through his fingers, cutting them to the bone.

"I felt an immediate numbing effect," he recalls. "I knew straight away I'd done some severe damage. The fingers were bleeding but I wasn't concerned that I was losing a significant amount of blood. There wasn't anything that we had to wrap them so I just left the wounds open and reckoned that salt water was the way to go."

The drogue was eventually set but lasted only 15 minutes; the acceleration of the raft down the waves was too much for it and it broke free. "Suddenly a big wave hit us and lifted my side of the raft," recalls Stanley. "The problem was that my body went up but my feet were still pinned under the other guy's legs. That was when I broke my ankle. I could do nothing more than say, 'Oh my God, my ankle's broken. That's not very good'. That then meant both Gibbo and I were out of play."

Unknown to Stanley, he had also torn tendons around both his artificial hips.

✯

As with the other raft, the drogue attached to Winning's raft parted only minutes after they had abandoned *Winston Churchill*. The four crewmembers decided their first job was to repair the "tent flap" on the canopy so they would be better protected from the elements. It was still pouring with rain and the 70-knot westerly showed no signs of easing. With the flap fixed they then rummaged through the raft's ration pack. It was like a show bag at a fair and contained a small amount of very basic food, water, medical supplies and other rescue and survival support equipment – an emergency pump for the raft, a knife, flares and a reflector mirror to attract attention.

Young Endeavour was on its way to the rescue area. It had been a nightmarish passage dead downwind. On no less than three occasions the massive brigantine skipped uncontrollably down the waves like a dinghy, and at one stage the pressure of water coming across the port side of the ship cracked the plate glass – an inch thick – in a steel-encased porthole. Most of the crewmembers were sick and Audrey Brown had been hit by a flying object. Visibility on deck was down to a measly 100 metres. They reported back to AMSA that there was no sign of *Winston Churchill*.

✯

Back on Bruce Gould's raft the seas were providing little relief. Around dusk they were flipped upside down. They tried to undo the tent flap but couldn't because it was tied up with some nylon rope. The only choice was to cut their way out. After doing this, Winning took off his life jacket and swam to the surface. There was nothing to tether him with so he just dived out and hung on. He grabbed onto a righting line and, with the help of the wind, managed to flick the raft back upright. He was quickly pulled back in. During the capsize, the aerial on the EPIRB had broken in half, but despite the conditions and the constant setbacks, morale remained high.

Around midnight yet another massive wave broke around the raft, capsizing it again. The raft was righted but towards dawn the lower of the two chambers began to deflate. They were worried that once the bottom chamber deflated, the canopy would start collapsing as well. They consulted the instructions on how to inflate the raft manually but the adaptor they needed had been lost during one of the roll-overs. They had to improvise and pulled a nylon piece out of the end of the pump hose and managed to jam that into the valve and tape it up. It worked. The raft continued to be hurled, tossed and tumbled, but fortunately for the four tightly-packed occupants it remained upright. As if they hadn't been through enough already, a five-centimetre slit had appeared in the floor. They were soon sitting in something akin to a toddler's wading pool.

"We don't know what caused the hole," recalls Gould, "it might have been the gas inflation bottle that was hanging off the raft or the broken aerial of the EPIRB. We couldn't find a bailer so we decided it was best to jam a sponge in the hole. We had no bailer and 16 sponges. Fat lot of good they were – we ended up having between six inches (15 centimetres) and two feet (60 centimetres) of water in with us for the rest of the time. The level depended on how big the wave was that broke over us. After a while someone said, 'Hey, here's the bloody raft repair kit'. We ripped it open and read the instructions – 'rough the rubber surface; make sure it's clean and dry and apply the patch'. We chucked the repair kit out of the raft."

They worked out the best bailing method involved using their seaboots and a plastic bag. One of the crewmembers had grabbed a *Winston Churchill* T-shirt as they were abandoning ship. The presence of the T-shirt brought another form of relief for the survivors – a hint of humour. All four debated whether the shirt from a yacht that was now sunk was bringing good luck or bad. It was decided, in a bid to appease the weather Gods, that the shirt should be consigned to the deep. It too was thrown from the raft.

★

The five crewmembers in the other raft were in even graver danger. They were lying across the floor of the square raft in sardine-like formation, all the time being hurled about by the violent seas. "No one seemed worried," recalls Gibson. "The spirit in the raft was excellent. We were very concerned about John's obvious distress; not that he was complaining. Every now and then, when we were thrown around, there were significant exclamations – totally involuntary moans like 'Oh Christ'. We were trying to make him as comfortable as we could and keep away from his legs. We went through the bag of goodies we found and discussed some of the stuff that was in there. We found some fishing hooks and I recall there were some jokes about what we were going to use for bait. Deanie and I were also saying how nice it would be to have some Scotch to mix with the water that was in the little plastic vials." With nightfall came the realisation that rescue was highly unlikely before the next day. The waves continued to buffet the raft relentlessly, and then the inevitable happened – a monster wave flipped it upside down. They finished up standing on the inflated arch that was built into the raft to support the canopy. What was previously the raft floor was now the roof.

"We felt surprisingly comfortable but we knew we were going to run out of oxygen," recalls Stanley. "You could just feel the air starting to get a bit tighter. Jim Lawler was next to the opening. He wanted to take his vest off to get out and do something about getting us upright. But it was just raging outside. We all decided it was too dangerous to get out one by one to turn the thing up. It would have taken just one bad sea when someone was getting out for us to lose them."

"It was a very calm discussion for about 20 minutes," recalls Gibson. "Certainly the comment was, 'Well, the damn thing's a lot more stable this way up than it is the other way'. It was certainly a lot quieter. Michael said words to the effect, 'We've got to get out and right this thing otherwise we're going to be in terrible trouble'. I recall saying to him, and my words are indelibly etched in my mind, 'Michael, it's death out there'. When I said it I thought to myself, 'Christ that's a very dramatic thing to say; that's overstating the issue a bit.' But I really was very concerned about it because it was pitch black and there were very, very large waves coming through. Anyone outside would struggle to hang on to anything."

The five were standing in waist-deep water in pitch-blackness. Torches were produced and an inspection of their upside-down world began.

"It was definitely safer being the way we were so we decided to cut a small hole in the raft floor – which was now our roof – so we could breath," explained Stanley. "There was a handle on the floor that had reinforcing either side of it. We slit it longitudinally, four inches (10 centimetres). To do it the other way would have been better, but it would have been only two inches, and that wouldn't have let in enough air. When we made the cut the raft submerged about another inch in the water. That didn't matter. At least we had enough air to breathe."

They were "comfortable and quite happy" being upside down while their new "roof" was pushed up and down like a giant rubber bellow to circulate air into the raft. They drifted along for what they believed were a few hours until another rogue wave could be heard roaring towards them. It was like being trapped in a railway tunnel with a locomotive coming at you without a light. The wave thundered in, picked up the raft like a beach ball and threw it back upright. Bodies spilled everywhere and crashed on top of each other, then the wave was gone. A headcount was done immediately. Everyone was present.

Throughout the night the raft was rolled, tumbled and turned some 30 times by the marauding waves. The floor had started to split where the cut had been made and was widening as they watched. On top of this, the canopy was shredding. They finished up hanging onto the inside rails of the raft and when the top canopy became fully shredded they put their hands on the outside and hung onto the rails. Gibson had been in full sailing gear when he left the yacht (including his seaboots and complete harness) and had attached his safety harness to the roof arch. Others were wearing cumbersome life vests around their necks. Seasickness had thus far spared all five crewmembers.

Some time in the very early hours of December 28 the mother of all waves arrived.

"Normally we had some warning, we could hear them coming like breaking surf," recalls Stanley. "But this almighty wave gave no warning. Suddenly the five of us were just crashing. The raft was hurled from its crest and was tumbling down its foaming face, 40, 50, 60 feet. I could only think about hanging on. I wrapped my arms around the roof frame and just hung on and held my breath until the wave went away. I knew that if I didn't hang on I was going to die. God knows how long it went on for, but it was for some time. When we finally stopped and I came up for air I was still hanging onto the roof frame but was on the outside of the raft. I yelled out 'Who's here?' The only reply came from Gibbo."

Stanley looked back to see a wide white veil of water that stretched for some 350 metres. Amid the turbulence, a considerable distance away, he could see two people.

"I'm not sure who they were," he said, his voice loaded with emotion. "All I could do then was dive underneath the raft and get back up inside so I could grab the roof frame again and hang on. I said to Gibbo, 'Mate, we're by ourselves here. We can't do anything for those boys. The wind is going to blow us faster than they can swim and we can't go back'. We can only hope that they can hang on till daybreak and be spotted by a search plane."

John Gibson has vivid memories of his experiences that night. "What talk there had been during the night was very positive but at that stage everybody was semi snoozing," he recalls. "We were just floating around and hanging on. My next recollection was my harness being taken up sharply, then all hell broke loose. I went on what I can only describe as the most extraordinary ride of my life. I was obviously in white water and travelling at great speed with a huge sensation of sound. I was just being dragged by my harness at terrific speed through white water and being hurled all over the place. Whatever handhold I had had gone and my body was being spun in all directions. I don't recall that I was scared. I just recall thinking, this is the most extraordinary experience. I don't recall that I had a problem with breathing. I don't recall panicking. I just recall this experience went on and on and on and on and on and I just couldn't believe it.

"I just went with it. I didn't fight it. It went on for a long time, a remarkably long time. There was also a sense of falling, I knew I was falling. I knew I was in fast water. I knew I was in white water yet I didn't feel I was going to drown. I just didn't know what was going to happen. I was just trying to somehow or other go with it, not fight it and at the same time just try and work out what the hell was going to happen next, but at no stage did I have the thought that I was going to die. Then it all stopped. It just stopped. It just stopped and it was dark. There was white water all around me and the raft was still. There wasn't a sound. I looked around and there was no one there. I heard a voice. It was from outside the raft. It was John. He said, 'Who's here?'. I said, 'It's Gibbo'. He popped up inside the raft. He'd obviously been flicked outside the raft but had obviously hung on. How he did it I don't know.

"We turned around and tried to see what was happening. I thought I'd lost both my contact lenses at that stage and my visibility was restricted. I was aware of white water but on recollection I still must have had my right lens in because I was able to see a strobe light come on. I knew exactly who it was – Jim Lawler – because he was the only person that had one. I had one as well so I activated mine and held it up. I thought, well, he can see that I'm still alive, but he was a long way back. Then I heard voices. I couldn't tell you what they were saying but I assume I might have heard words to the effect of 'Where are you?' or 'Who's there?' ... something like that. I'm sure I heard 'Who's there?' or 'Where are you Mike?' I don't recall exactly. They were human voices in the dark, in the white water further back."

Through a miracle, divine intervention, or sheer guts and determination, Stanley and Gibson somehow continued to defy the odds that night and hang on. Stanley said they were rolled at least five more times before daybreak.

★

The conditions the two rafts were experiencing by mid-morning on December 28 were horrifying. But, after having battled through such meteorological malevolence overnight, the scene was starting to improve for the *Winston Churchill* survivors. Bruce Gould remembers the winds easing to around 30 knots and moving around to the sou'west, and while the waves were still huge, and breaking regularly, they too had decreased in size. Inflating the raft and bailing out the water kept them amused during a fairly uneventful day. Most of the time it was Winning who was sitting at the small entrance to the raft canopy scouring the skies for any sign of a search aircraft. "I kept seeing ships and submarines and hearing aircraft all day. I wasn't hallucinating. I think it was just wishful thinking."

At around 3pm they heard, then spotted, a plane. By the time a flare was found, unwrapped and lit, the plane had gone. The already frustrated raft occupants could only watch as the plane disappeared towards the horizon. Then, about 20 minutes later, it reappeared. It was flying a planned search grid. The red phosphorescent flare, Gould and Winning's last, rocketed towards the grey sky. Anxious seconds passed as eyes desperately watched for any sign that it had been seen. The twin-engine plane, an AusSAR civilian search aircraft, began a gentle turn that gradually became more and more positive. It was turning back. But it didn't come to them. It kept circling, going around their position twice.

Unbeknown to the survivors in the water the plane spotters were frantically trying to locate the source of the flare. It was a small black spot with a tinge of orange somewhere on the surface of the wild ocean a few hundred feet below. Eyes strained in the aircraft, then there it was. A life raft. Thumbs went up and the aircraft was turned for an approach. It radioed AusSAR with a message that wives, families, fellow sailors, and the media across Australia had hoped to hear for nearly 24 hours. A life raft with occupants had been sighted some 80 miles off the coast. About 20 minutes after the plane spotted them the four survivors heard "the sweetest sound you could ever want to hear – a bloody big chopper coming at us."

☆

If rescuing people equalled a good day at the office, paramedic Cam Robertson and the rest of the team aboard the Helimed 1 chopper out of La Trobe were going gangbusters. They had already found *Solo Globe Challenger* that morning and had successfully completed the mission. Since then they had been assigned to searching and identifying some of the many EPIRBs that were still transmitting. By mid-afternoon it seemed things were quietening down, until AusSAR contacted them and asked that they investigate a flare from a one-man life raft that had been sighted about 80 miles offshore. Pilot Stef Sincich acknowledged the request and turned the powerful red and white chopper towards the target.

"We located it without a problem," said Robertson. "We looked at the raft and discussed the fact that it wasn't a one-man raft, it was bigger, but we still didn't know where it had come from or who might be aboard. The guys winched me down and I finned over to the raft and stuck my head in. I couldn't believe my eyes. There were four blokes inside, and they were very pleased to see me. The noise of the chopper was very loud so I yelled out and asked if there were any injuries. They all seemed OK. I told the guy closest to the door – it turned out to be Richard Winning – that I'd take him out first. I asked him if he was happy to get in the water so I could get the strop around him and he said he was. I told the other guys to collapse the canopy and get on top of it so the raft would be more stable if it got into the downwash from the chopper."

"Everything went really smoothly," recalls Robertson. "Just as we got clear of the water I yelled across to my first guy, asking if he was OK. He was. I also asked what yacht they were from and he said *Winston Churchill*. I couldn't believe it. I was shocked. It was a very special moment for me because a lot of people involved in the search were thinking *Winston Churchill* was lost and it was very doubtful that we would find any survivors. In no time at all we had all four in the chopper. I have to say it was a great feeling to know that we had got those guys. Sometimes you think it's a privilege to rescue people and that time it really was."

"It wasn't until we were up in the helicopter and could look down at the sea that we really appreciated what we'd been through," recalls Gould. "It was just a white mass of waves. It was an absolute shemozzle. We also realised how hard it had been for the poor guys in the search aircraft to find us."

The four survivors inquired as to the safety of their five other crewmates. They were told they hadn't been found – news that concerned them. At the same time the fact that they themselves had survived meant that the others must be safe and still in a raft somewhere nearby.

★

John "Steamer" Stanley and John Gibson had hoped to see search aircraft during the morning of the 28th. Their raft had disintegrated to a stage where it was little more than a black ring drifting on a savage black ocean. Many hours had passed since the yacht sank so the search area was now huge; and the cloud base was so low that visibility was little more than a few kilometres at the very best. Also, during their numerous capsizes, flares and other emergency equipment had been lost. In their estimation, they must have been at least 50 miles from where the yacht had sunk. As the day dragged on they began to think it was almost impossible that the other three crewmembers had survived. They were still hopeful of being rescued and knew there was an EPIRB in the other raft which would have been alerting the searchers. What they didn't know was that the aerial was broken and the device wasn't transmitting correctly.

"We were at the situation where we had to do something about staying with the raft because what we were left with was a ring," recalls Gibson. "If you leant on any one section of the ring it would submerge and the whole thing would flip over. We always had to be very careful about what we were doing. We had to work out a system whereby we could control what was happening, bearing in mind that John had very restricted mobility. The raft had lost all its shape. It seemed to take whatever shape it wanted. You couldn't put your foot from one side to the other. We worked out that if we positioned ourselves opposite each other, and John put his good foot in my crotch and pushed against me, we could then move our shoulders sort of above the wall of the raft and lock ourselves in. We were parallel to the arch so we could also hang on to that for support. Our bodies gave us some buoyancy with our backs pushed against the rubber. We took that position in the early hours of the morning and held it until we were pulled out at 11 o'clock that night.

"All I can say about the arrangement is that John now owes me a few beers because he got the good end of the deal. His foot was wedged hard against my balls and I can tell you that when it was all over the whole of my crotch was black. My balls were up underneath my eyes. We were hallucinating all the time. I remember thinking there was definitely a section of the raft that had a soft floor and that I could walk round and put my feet on it. Then I hallucinated about a solid floor. There was a corridor that I went down and I could simply just stand there. It was the most blissful feeling. We both saw buckets of ships and sailing boats; cutters and schooners. I went past millions of them.

"John told me exactly the same. There were vessels with lights on that went past us. I also spent lots of time with some of the lovely things in my life, particularly on the romantic side. I revisited all the beautiful people of the opposite sex I've known. I spent hours with them. It was a lot of fun and certainly helped pass the time, I won't elaborate except to say it was much better than counting sheep. I also thought about Jane, my wife of three years – they were beautiful, lovely thoughts. There was some conversation with John and, although he's a great talker, there were long hours of silence. I felt it was very important to have some sort of dialogue. I knew John was in pain and I was quite concerned about him."

Sometime during the afternoon a beautiful albatross landed in the water near the raft and looked sadly at the two forlorn sailors. It then flew over and sat right beside Gibson. Both agreed it was a good luck sign.

"We just lay there for a long time in silence. I remember thinking to myself, Jesus I'd better try and liven this up a bit so I said to John, 'Do you reckon we're on a steamer path here, a ship's path here?'. He said 'No Gibbo'. Then we just lay there in the water with the raft going splish, splosh, splash, splat.

"After a while I asked, 'Steamer, do you think any of the Hobart boats would come out here'?"

'No, mate.'

'Steamer, where do you think we are?'

'I reckon we're about 90 miles east of Eden.'

'Well Steamer there are no boats.'

'No Gibbo.'

'No yachts.'

'No Gibbo.'

'We're 90 miles off.'

'That's right Gibbo.'

'Mate, who gets to eat whom first?'

"There was no answer. Not even a grunt.

"We continued to drift along and I started looking at my hands. They were both oozing blood. Steamer then looked at them and then we looked at each other. We didn't say anything but we were both thinking the same thing – old 'Jaws' sniffing along behind the blood trail towards us. It was an additional part of the equation that we weren't ready for. We just dismissed that one altogether. The cold started to move through my body; muscle contractions, shudders and shakes. I distinctly remember as I attempted to shuffle my shoulders back up – to try and keep as much of my upper body out of the water as I could – that the effort needed to push against John for leverage was growing all the time. It was getting harder to do."

"Gibbo was trying to have a chat all the time – probably because he's a barrister," Stanley recalls. "But he never complained about his hands, not once. I suppose I didn't complain about my ankle either. Gibbo had lost his contact lenses and couldn't see, so I was his spotter for planes."

At around four or five o'clock in the afternoon Stanley and Gibson were convinced they had seen a fishing vessel, a big commercial trawler. They were also hearing aircraft. Then, finally, more than 24 hours after *Winston Churchill* sank, came their first real hope for salvation. Stanley heard then spotted a plane to the north of the raft. He waved frantically but was not seen. About 20 minutes later the plane returned but once again missed the raft. Stanley's efforts were rewarded sometime later. He saw a large aircraft at a low altitude coming straight at them and he shouted to Gibson to give him the yellow life vest. Stanley grabbed it and waved it in large, sweeping arcs over his head. He was desperately hoping that the vest would give a better contrast against the sea than the black raft. He kept waving furiously as the plane went past and was overjoyed to see the wing light flash.

They were little more than two yellow pin pricks in a vast expanse of bubbling sea but about an hour later the plane returned, accompanied by a helicopter, and both flew straight past them. Stanley and Gibson had not been spotted. The chopper was on its way to rescue the four others.

★

Darkness closed in on Stanley and Gibson for the second night in a row. They had no food or water yet were still, somehow, managing to hang on. At that moment new hope burst from the sky. The pair were roused from their near comatose state when they heard a search plane. They then saw it emerge from the blackness, its navigation lights flashing brightly. Gibson had a strobe light and Stanley had a Mag light which were both working. They aimed them at the plane and it flew overhead for about 10 minutes, indicating to them they had been spotted. As comforting as that sight was, the two sailors still had no idea how or when they would be rescued.

Then, above the roar of the storm, Steamer and Gibbo began to hear the deep-throated engines of a large helicopter approaching. It became louder and louder. A lumbering Navy Sea Hawk chopper emerged from the clouds with its searchlights blazing. The two sailors were elated.

★

The fact that the frigate HMAS *Newcastle*, manned by a skeleton crew, was in the area proved to be a springboard back to civilisation for Stanley and Gibson. It provided an offshore refuelling point for the Sea Hawk helicopter piloted by Lieutenant Nick Trimmer. He and his crew, Lieutenant Commander Rick Neville, Lieutenant Aaron "Wal" Abbott, and Leading Seaman Shane Pashley, had been searching offshore almost all day for disabled yachts and Glyn Charles who was missing from *Sword of Orion*.

"It was dark and we were heading back to Merimbula," recalls Pashley. "We heard an Air Force PC–3 Orion on the air. He was obviously searching using infra-red stuff. We heard him advise AusSAR that they had seen a light, a strobe in the water, and someone was shining a torch at them. Obviously it wasn't just an abandoned life raft but someone alive and in the water. He couldn't get a good enough ID on it with his infra red. He had also dropped a couple of flares in the water near the target. We judged that the target was abeam of our track into Merimbula, probably about 20 miles to the south. We waited to hear if any other aircraft were around and when it was obvious that there was nothing available we advised the PC–3 we'd come down and have a look. When we got closer to the search area the PC–3 dropped a couple of flares in the water for us, close to the life raft. Through the murk we started seeing the torch. It was still a few hundred yards away and hard to see. But it was there."

The crew aboard the Sea Hawk now had to work out the most effective rescue strategy. They knew the two stranded sailors had been in the water for some time, possibly were injured and most definitely were fatigued. This ruled out dropping the strop into the water and letting them fend for themselves. The only option was to winch Pashley down. He landed with a splash in the water and went straight under before popping up and flipping into the raft. He didn't realise the raft was bottomless and went straight down under again! Pashley was doing his first ever night-time sea rescue in conditions that he didn't want to know about. He was also concerned about the threat of a shark attack.

"He was an agile bloke and jumped over the top of the raft – straight into the water," recalls Stanley. "I had to shout to him, 'Watch out mate. We haven't got a floor. Be careful'. I told him to take Gibbo first because of his hands, and away they went. All of a sudden I saw the pair of them take off sideways, really hard and fast. I thought the pilot must have wanted to move them that way before he started lifting them. Regardless, I have to say that the guy who grabbed Gibbo, and the pilot, did a magnificent job."

"Just as I got the strop over the first man the aircraft had an auto hover failure and slid away a bit," Pashley recalls. "The wire just went tight and literally tore us sideways and out of the raft. It felt like you'd tied a rope around yourself, attached it to a car, and then the car took off at high speed. Gibbo went sort of backwards and sideways while I went forward and over the top of him. That's when my knife in the leg of my wetsuit caught on the side of the raft and carved into my knee, so much so that it subsequently needed surgery. At that time though, I could have lost my whole leg and probably not realised it. I also knew then that if either of us had had any of the wire wrapped around us at that very moment we would have lost a body part. It's fine wire. It would have ripped a limb off pretty quickly."

With the chopper now on manual hover Gibson and Pashley were winched out of the water. Gibson was placed on the floor of the machine, covered in a space blanket, given some water and a quick check over. It was then John Stanley's turn, but as Pashley prepared to go down he was advised the plan had changed. The chopper crew felt it would be too dangerous lowering Pashley again and thought that two men on the winch would work better. Pashley drove the winch while Abbott guided the aircraft into position using the little thumb control beside the door.

"I was surprised to see that the guy didn't come back down on the cable to get me," Stanley recalls. "They just lowered a ring to me. I thought they must have assumed that I was OK. He landed the ring right beside me and I put it on. I got my arms and shoulders through it but while I did that I must have tangled a rope from the life raft into the ring with me. He started lifting and all of a sudden I looked down and said to myself, the life raft's coming with me. I must have a rope tangled. I got to about 25 feet and thought, oh no, this is going to be dangerous so I just put my hands in the air and bailed out, straight back into the water. The next thing the guy just landed the ring about two feet away from me. I climbed back into it again. I remembered having watched these rescue procedures before; you don't put your hand onto the wire but lock your hands underneath the strop."

Stanley and Gibson were in remarkably good condition considering their 30-hour ordeal. They told the Navy crew everything they could about what had happened with their three mates the previous night, all in the hope that they might still be found alive. Pashley and Abbott talked to the two incessantly, knowing it was vital to keep them awake and alert to minimise any shock that might set in before they were in the hands of doctors.

★

Mallacoota, a tiny town on the south side of the NSW–Victorian border was, as the first four survivors of *Winston Churchill* were to find out, a town with exceptional community spirit and a very determined will to help those in need. From the moment they were helped from the rescue chopper, still wet and bedraggled, they were made to feel safe and comfortable. A local resident was allocated to each survivor, their role being to comfort and care for them. The Red Cross and local Volunteer Coastguard group were also on hand to help.

"They were just unbelievable," said Gould. "The hospitality, the way that community pulled together, they were just fantastic. They took our names and telephone numbers so they could call our families and reassure them we were OK while we were checked over and then taken to the showers. Dry clothes arrived for each of us. Nothing was a problem."

The joy of speaking with loved-ones on the telephone was followed later that evening with the news that the second raft had been found.

"We assumed, obviously being optimistic after our rescue, that all five of them would be on board," said Gould. "We didn't know how or when they would be picked up or where they would be taken to, so we had a beer in celebration and – because we could hardly keep our eyes open – went to bed. The sweetest thing on earth that night, after being jammed into a life raft with three others for so long, was to be able to stretch out my full six-foot-three-inch body in a bloody big bed."

★

Richard Winning rose early next morning to do a national television interview. When he went on air he was asked how he felt about losing three crewmates from

Winston Churchill. He had not heard the news. Mike Bannister and John Dean, two of his closest friends since they sailed dinghies as 10 year olds off Vaucluse, on Sydney Harbour, were gone. Jim Lawler, a friend in more recent times, was also gone. Winning bowed his head – deeply shocked and choked with emotion – and walked away from the interview.

Part Three

Eighteen
Racing to the finish

Many people have struggled to comprehend how the 54th Sydney to Hobart race could start so innocently then within 36 hours metamorphose into one of the world's worst ocean racing disasters. By the time the cyclone had cut its catastrophic swathe across the north-east corner of Bass Strait, viewers from Tasmania to Greenland were witnessing a horror story unfold. Graphic television pictures, newspaper photographs and interviews with survivors presented the perils of ocean yacht racing as it had never been seen before.

While all this was happening the massive rescue effort was continuing in earnest and the race – much to the surprise of those who did not understand the dynamics of the sport – went on. There were calls from some uninformed sections of the media to stop the race. It appeared that few, if any, behind those suggestions took time to consider what was really happening. Perhaps they thought it was akin to motorsport where if it rained too hard and the track became slippery, flags could be waved and the cars pulled into the pits. In reality, even if the race had been stopped, there were many yachts still 50 to 100 miles from safety – they would have had to have battled life-threatening seas and wild winds for a day or more to return to port. For some, friendlier skies lay ahead, not astern.

✮

The diligent staff at AMSA's Rescue Control Centre in Canberra were running on coffee and adrenalin. The second day of operation became a blur. The usual overnight workforce of five had soon quadrupled to 20 and as each staff member arrived they were briefed and deployed to fill another gap in the rescue coordination. Some would not leave their post for the next 14 to 16 hours. In a "normal" environment the RCC would not be dealing with more than two incidents at a time. Here they saw up to 17.

The AMSA public relations service was also under severe pressure as calls from families and friends of competitors plus countless media inquiries from all over the world flooded in. David Gray, Brian Hill and Robin Poke handled some 300 calls each in the space of 48 hours. They did live television crosses across Australia and into America and even did interviews to remote parts of Europe. Uncertainty and confusion were their worst enemies – most of the yachts had lost their communication capabilities and locating them was exceedingly difficult at times. Often the RCC would be relying solely on analogue mobile phones on board aircraft.

Assistant Operations Manager, Steve Francis, had difficulties in assessing and keeping up with the dynamics of the operation. At one stage the RCC was dealing with five beacon alerts simultaneously! When a helicopter was sent out with a homing capability, its on-board system was instantly overloaded, unable to cope with the volume of alerts. The search and rescue effort covered some 10,000 square miles and involved five civilian helicopters, 38 twin-engine fixed-wing aircraft, two Royal Australian Navy Sea King and two Sea Hawk helicopters plus HMAS *Newcastle*; and from the Royal Australian Air Force two PC–3 long-range Orion and two C130 Hercules aircraft.

While the weather continued to improve on the second day of the operation, it was not without incident. At one stage helicopters and aircraft were alerted that they may be rescuing one of their own – the NRMA. CareFlight chopper piloted by Terry Sommers had suffered an engine malfunction 80 miles offshore. Sommers advised the top cover SAR aircraft that they had a problem and were returning to the coast. Assistance was immediately arranged and they made it safely and securely back.

★

With CYC commodore Hugo van Kretschmar competing in the race aboard the yacht *Assassin*, former commodore Peter Bush had been nominated as the club's official spokesman. Bush was a veteran of 14 Sydney to Hobart races and was in regular contact from his Sydney home with club officials, monitoring the progress of the race the first night out. He suspected the fleet was going to cop some bad weather. He took a nap then headed to the club at 2.30am so he could monitor the 03:00 sked. Bush finally left the club more than 40 hours later. At around 12.30 on the afternoon of the 27th he heard *Rager* on the single side band radio in the sailing office report that they were in extreme winds of 70-odd knots. The club was soon inundated with phone calls from relatives and friends of competitors. Droves of media also began arriving, all determined to get a more powerful story than their opposition. Bush was feeling the heat so he arranged to stage a media briefing every two hours to pass on updates. The world, as well as Australia, hungered for news.

Around noon on the 28th *Assassin* returned to Sydney, having retired from the race. Bush had briefed van Kretschmar of developments by mobile phone while he was still at sea so he'd be somewhat prepared for the media firing squad awaiting him dockside. Van Kretschmar soon realised he should go to Hobart to take control of proceedings on behalf of the club. The media followed, always seeking answers. He held press conferences to update the media on each drama. He also found himself having to defend the sport and the CYC.

✯

By midnight on the 27th of December, 39 yachts had already retired with most heading into Eden. Seriously damaged boats, some with just the twisted remnants of what was originally a tall and proud spar, made a sad sight. At times ambulances seemed to be running a shuttle service to take away the injured. More yachts continued to wend their way into port that night while others which had avoided or miraculously managed not to be claimed by the most explosive forces of the cyclone, raced on towards Hobart.

The two fastest yachts, *Sayonara* and *Brindabella*, managed to avoid much of the storm's fury, but they still had their share of frightening moments. Amidst the terror and tragedy there were moments of humour.

"Our mastman, Paddy Broughton, was wearing a hydrostatic life jacket – one which automatically inflates after a few seconds of being totally immersed in water," recalls *Brindabella* crewman Andrew Jackson. "Because there was so much water going over the boat he decided the best thing he could do – to keep the water away from the automatic inflation device – was to put it on under his wet weather jacket and harness. At one stage when we were in Bass Strait, Paddy went up to the bow to haul in the No. 5 jib. The next thing the boat stuck its bow through this dirty big wave and the jib started being washed over the side. The wave was so big Paddy was underwater.

"When the water cleared Paddy was still there, flat on his back over the spinnaker pole on the foredeck and restrained by his harness. Next thing he started grabbing at his chest in apparent pain then before we knew it he had pulled out his knife and started stabbing himself in the chest – or at least it appeared that way to us. What had happened was that so much water had got inside his wet weather gear it had activated the life jacket inflation device. His safety harness wouldn't let the jacket expand, so his chest was being crushed. He had grabbed his knife to stab the jacket so it would deflate."

Due to radio problems the *Brindabella* crew weren't fully versed on the devastation behind them. The *Sayonara* crew had a fair idea, but they were still battling to cope with their own predicament. Larry Ellison and his 22 crewmembers ran into unexpected difficulties when they reached the north-eastern corner of Tasmania. There was a huge high-pressure system filling in against the low and the seas had yet again turned mountainous. With little warning they lost their secondary forestay, stanchions were being ripped free – the boat was coming apart piece by piece. Crewmembers were flung about like rag dolls and then had to deal with injuries on top of fatigue. Crewmember Phil Kieley was hurled through the air at one stage and snared his ankle as he went. "When I landed and looked down I thought my seaboot had come off because it was hanging out sideways from under the leg of my wet weather trousers. Then I realised my foot was still in it. There was so much happening around me right there and then it took a moment to realise my ankle was broken." *Sayonara* eventually tacked in towards the

Tasmanian coast, hitting the waves at a better angle and skilfully managing to stave off complete disaster.

⭐

The crew of *Foxtel-Titan Ford* were more than 60 miles offshore when they were forced to go under bare poles for more than five hours. To head for shelter on the mainland may have been more dangerous than to continue across Bass Strait. The crew were painfully aware the boat was untried since having the bottom rebuilt and the keel replaced. Their insurance came in the form of boatbuilder and crewmember Andrew Miller who, at the height of the storm, kept pulling up floorboards "to inspect the workmanship". Co-owner Peter Sorensen could have sworn he was scaling snow-capped mountains, not waves.

In the middle of the furore another of the owners, radio show host Stan Zemanek, was doing live radio reports despite being confined to his bunk with broken ribs and other injuries. Even though he had been sailing for 42 years he was a Hobart race debutante, and he vowed to his listeners that he would not be going a second time.

"We had a skeleton crew up on deck and all the time those of us below could hear them shouting 'IN-COMING, IN-COMING!' as though we were in Vietnam," Zemanek recalls. "We could only sit down below in this confined space and listen to the yacht being pounded. There was certainly a time where I thought, this is it, it's all over, and we're going to die. I started to think about my wife and my kids and all the family, thinking all the time that maybe I would never see them again. I'm not too proud to say I was praying and I'm sure everybody else on the boat was doing exactly the same thing. When you're sitting out there just helpless, like you're a cork in a bathtub, you have to rely on that spiritual belief. We all tend to believe we're big rough and tough sailors who can handle anything, but in the true scheme of things, when push comes to shove, when you're faced with the realities of life and you know this could be your last moment on earth, you start to think of family, and friends, and God. You also tell yourself you'd better start making amends."

For the third owner, and *Foxtel-Titan Ford*'s navigator, Julie Hodder, the fear of flying off waves was tempered by the reality of what had happening to other members of the fleet and by an especially eerie experience. She vividly recalls sailing through the eye of the storm, going from 70 to 80 knot wind to zero in a matter of minutes. Unsure of what to do, they waited for a few minutes then put up the mainsail with one reef in it, then shyly set the storm jib. Twenty minutes later the "eye" blinked and the storm slammed them again – but this time it was only 40 to 50 knots. Hodder was in charge of the radio and the infirmary below and was dishing out seasickness tablets, bandages and whatever else was required by the three injured crewmembers. She was also bailing furiously, second only to Tony Poole, and was on the radio, relaying information to Telstra Control on board *Young Endeavour.*

She and the other crewmembers were concerned about *Winston Churchill*'s position and condition. They knew almost everyone on board. Ian Kiernan and the crew aboard *Canon Maris* were also distressed as they made their way back up the coast towards Sydney. Every possible radio frequency was being monitored in the desperate hope that crewman Jonathan Gibson's father, John, who was aboard *Winston Churchill*, had been found. When the news came through John was alive young "Gibbo" grabbed the whisky bottle from the shelf and sculled about a quarter of the contents in one hit.

✫

Hobart was a city in mourning when the world's greatest maxi yacht, *Sayonara*, sliced its way up the Derwent River at around 8am on December 29. For 53 years the great race had brought national and international focus on this capital of Australia's island state, but this year it was an attention burdened with sorrow. It was supposedly the height of summer, but on this morning there was a distinct chill in the air as the white-hulled sloop broke through the finish line off Battery Point, immediately adjacent to the city's waterfront. And while the usual fleet of small craft was on hand to escort the first yacht into port, the elation that most often accompanied the moment was non-existent. The massive official welcome that had been planned – including daytime fireworks and a trophy presentation – had been cancelled as a mark of respect for those who had lost their lives. Aboard *Sayonara*, some of the world's most seasoned and professional sailors were shaking their heads in disbelief. Some just slumped to the deck.

Around 5000 people were crammed along the wharves to watch the first of the surviving yachts arrive. The *Sayonara* crew struggled to recognise the welcoming crowd inasmuch as the crowd seemed undecided whether or not it was right to celebrate *Sayonara*'s arrival. As the yacht docked alongside the pontoon specially prepared for the welcome, Ellison stepped ashore and was greeted by the waiting media throng. Immediately above him, colourful flags hung at half-mast. Ellison, his eyes reddened by tears and salt spray, spoke about his experiences.

"Never again. Not if I live to be 1000 years old will I do a Hobart race. This is not what it's supposed to be about. Difficult yes, dangerous no, life threatening – definitely not." After suggesting he might quit the sport he said there was only one word to describe the race – "nightmare". "It was by far the toughest race I've ever done in my life. It was horrible. The crew work was inspirational. Very bad things could have happened to us out there and these guys got us through. Guys were knocked down but they just kept getting back up and getting back to work. They kept doing what had to be done to keep the boat in one piece – and keep all of us alive. It was truly extraordinary. Anyone who signs up for this race expects a difficult race but no one expects a dangerous race. The seas were enormous and the wind made sounds I've never heard before."

World champion yachtsman Chris Dickson sat on the edge of the yacht, staring into space and listening to what Ellison was saying. His wife of one week, Sue, comforted him. "That's as tough as it gets," said Dickson. "Being here first sure is nice but being here at all is the big thing. Every member of the crew is thinking about those who are still out there and not thinking too much about how we have done."

Lachlan Murdoch was equally contemplative. "I think a lot of the guys in this crew have very strong mixed feelings about even finishing in this race at all. You needed to be out there to know just how bad it was. If you imagine any disaster movie you have seen before you have to double it or treble it."

Navigator Mark Rudiger, winner of the previous Whitbread round-the-world race with the team led by American Paul Cayard echoed the sentiments expressed by Murdoch. "The Sydney to Hobart lived up to all the fears I ever held about this race and then some. I was hoping I'd get away with an easy one but I didn't. At times it was worse than the Whitbread. It didn't last as long, fortunately, but at its peak the wind and waves we saw coming across Bass Strait were the worst that I have ever encountered."

✭

From the time *Sayonara* arrived until the last yacht crossed the line at dusk on January 1, the normally boisterous dockside scenes in Hobart were replaced by a respectful silence. Most activity centred around all the major television networks who had descended on the city, bringing satellite dishes, broadcast vans and spotlights.

Brindabella crossed the finish line almost three hours after *Sayonara*, followed by the battle-scarred remnants of what had been a strong 115-yacht fleet. With each arrival came incredible stories of survival, of unbridled courage, and of how fate had intervened. It was not until these crews got to the dock, saw family and friends and heard of the death and carnage in their wake, that they could completely comprehend the magnitude of events. One of the most remarkable achievements was that of David Pescud and his team of disabled sailors aboard *Aspect Computing*. As well as completing the course they were placed first in their race division. The motto for this crew was "Carpe Diem" – Seize The Day. Events in Bass Strait galvanised friendships, and there was none greater than that of two *Aspect Computing* crewmembers, the race's youngest competitor, 12-year-old Travis Foley, a dyslexic from Mudgee in NSW, and his blind crewmate, Mooloolaba's Paul Borg.

The bond was apparent when the two went to the podium to join Pescud in collecting their prize for being first in PHS Division. Young Foley was Borg's "eyes" onshore as they went forward to be saluted by the large dockside crowd. Borg already had 28-year-old Danny Kane to help him on the yacht over the previous 12 months. Kane was partially paralysed after suffering a stroke four years earlier. During the race Foley became part of that special team. "I was helping Paul whenever I could," said young Foley, "showing him where things were and helping him get into his wet weather gear. This whole crew are now my best friends." Foley, who was doing his first ocean race admitted he was scared, but added he'd do it again.

At the other end of the spectrum was 81-year-old Papa Tom – Sir Thomas Davis – former Prime Minister of the Cook Islands. He was the champion among the crew of 26 aboard the 83-foot *Nokia*. Despite the horrors he'd faced and the protestations of his friends, Papa Tom was more than glad he accepted skipper David Witt's invitation to join the yacht. His medical background had enabled him to assume the role of crew doctor and at the height of the storm he'd spent all his time below caring for the injured. He remarked he was by no means cured of ocean racing, but he was cured of the Sydney to Hobart.

★

The tragedies that had crushed the race also overshadowed an incredible achievement by the overall race winners, Sydney's Ed Psaltis and Bob Thomas with their 35-footer, *AFR Midnight Rambler*. This relatively small and lightweight yacht was tenth into Hobart, beating many larger yachts home. Declared the race winner on handicap, *Midnight Rambler* became the smallest yacht in a decade to take the major prize. It was Psaltis' 17th attempt to win the classic, his previous best placing being eighth with the even smaller *Nuzulu* in 1991.

"If there was an element of luck then it was that we got the worst of the weather during the daylight hours," he said. "We could see the most dangerous of the waves coming at us and because of that we had the best possible opportunity of getting the yacht over them. I guess you could say we didn't get 'that wave', the really big one that wiped out so many others. If it had been dark it might have been a different story."

*

On January 1, 1999, a large crowd, weighed down with sadness, watched in silence as six floral wreaths were cast onto the waters off Constitution Dock in Hobart in memory of those who would not race again.

Epilogue

Sailing has always been my passion and since leaving school that passion has also become my career. The 1998 race was the 30th Sydney to Hobart that I covered. In that period I had also managed three starts and three finishes in the classic. Being in Hobart in 1998 to report on the finish for television and newspapers saw me stretched – like so many of the race competitors – to the absolute limit of my emotional capacity. Suddenly my sport and my life had come face to face with fatalities.

For me, being ashore and knowing from some tough sailing experiences just how horrendous things were in Bass Strait, then trying to relay that in a composed fashion to the world, was not a pleasant experience. People had already died and I knew more would. At the same time I was trying to cope with my own emotional burden. Friends were the subject of searches. Were they dead or alive?

Then there was the fielding of a flood of telephone calls from anxious wives and friends. I had to try to assure them that everything would be OK, that they should have faith. It was almost as tough as being in the race. Those people desperately needed to know if their husband, father, sister, son or brother was coming home.

To speak with Robyn Rynan on the telephone that third night and confirm for her that her young son Michael – who was aboard *Winston Churchill* – had been found alive in a life raft was a bittersweet experience. I will never forget her torrent of tears, wavering voice and sobbing sighs of relief. It brought a realisation of what family bonds are all about. At the same time there was the thought of what other families – those that didn't know the fate of their loved-ones – must be going through.

Subsequent to this tragedy I have been regularly asked why we go ocean racing. For me one of the most appropriate answers is found in Sharon Green's great book of her sailing photographs, *Ultimate Sailing*.

"It is a romantic sport ... not carried out against the elements, but because of them."

Roll of Honour

This Roll of Honour has been completed to the best endeavours. However it is inevitable that many others were involved in this courageous rescue effort. Special thanks is also extended to each and every one of those people.

AUSTRALIAN MARITIME SAFETY AUTHORITY (AMSA)

Some 50 personnel were involved in coordination of all search and rescue activities from Australian Search and Rescue (AusSAR), Canberra, ACT including Rescue Coordination Centre Operations Officers, Management and AMSA Public Relations.

AIR SERVICES AUSTRALIA

HELIMED 1 AIR AMBULANCE
Captain Peter Leigh
Captain Howard Bosse
Captain Stefan Sincich
Aircrewman Steve Collins
Aircrewman Stephen Simpson
Aircrewman David Sullivan
Paramedic Cam Robertson
Paramedic Peter Davidson
Paramedic Terry Houge
Observer John Sloyan
Observer John Bailey
Senior Base Engineer Russell Gallattly
Operational Logistics Officer Wendy Civetta
SAR Observer Eddie Wright
Aviation Manager Ken Laycock

NRMA CAREFLIGHT
Pilot Dan Tyler
Pilot Terry Summers
Pilot Richard Nest
Aircrewman Graeme
  Fromberg
Aircrewman Steve Johnston
Dr Richard Cracknell
Dr Ken Harrison
Dr Arthas Flabouris
SCAT Paramedic Murray
  Traynor
SCAT Paramedic Steve
  Martz
SCAT Paramedic Ian
  Spencer
Engineer Mark Cruse
Co-ordinator John Hoad
Co-ordinator Ian Badham

**VICTORIA POLICE
  AIR WING**
Senior Constable David
  Key (Rescue Crewman)
Senior Constable Darryl
  Jones (Pilot)
Senior Constable Barry
  Barclay (Winch
  Operator)
Senior Constable Trevor
  Rim (Rescue Crewman)
Senior Constable Keith
  Fisher (Winch Operator)
Constable Chris Jameson
  (Pilot)

**WESTPAC LIFESAVER
  RESCUE HELICOPTER**
Illawarra Branch
Chief Pilot Jon Klopper
Rescue Crewman Peter
  Mangles
Air Crewman Douglas
  Smith
Air Crewman Matt Scott
Air Crewman Roger
  Graham

**ACT AMBULANCE
  SERVICE SOUTHCARE**
Pilot Ray Stone
Pilot Simon Lovell
Acting Base Manager Pilot
  Ron Maurer
Crewman Mark Delf
Crewman Matthew Smith
Crewman George Casey
Base Engineer Colin
  Hobbs
Paramedic Michael
  Abigail
Paramedic Paul Bibo
Paramedic Michelle
  Blewitt
Paramedic Paul Brooke
Paramedic David Dutton
Paramedic Grant Hogan
Paramedic Kristy
  McAlister
Paramedic Stephen
  Mitchell

Duty Superintendent
David Foot
Duty Superintendent
David Holdom
Acting Superintendent
Andrew Edwards
Director of ACT
Ambulance Service
Ken Paulsen
Chief Executive Officer
Emergency Services
Bureau Mike Castle

YOUNG ENDEAVOUR
**Royal Australian Navy
Crew**
LCDR Neil Galletly
RAN(Commanding
Officer)
LEUT Brenton Witt RAN
LEUT Ian Heldon RAN
LEUT Nathan Jacobsen
RAN
LEUT Debra Dunne RAN
CPOCSM(AC) John
Crawford
CPOMT Gregory
Goddard
POMT Paul Baker
LSCK Angela Miranda
ABWTR Sally Kingston
Supernumeraries
LCDR Ron Matsen RANR
LSPH Stephen Coates
Kirsty Boazman

CYCA Radio Operators
Lew Carter
Michael Brown
Audrey Brown
Youth Crew
Benita Ainsworth
Kathy Baker
Meretta Boyer
Katy Glenda
Catherine Habermann
Louise Keogh
Amelia Mills
Alethea Mouhtouris
Clare Omodei
Michelle Redden
Desiree Wilson
Timothy Davies
Richard Evans
Steven Hammond
Benjamin Harzer
Matthew Hosie
Jason Ives
John Moir
Steven Roberts
Angus Stevenson
Chris Daley

**THE NEW SOUTH
WALES, VICTORIA &
TASMANIA POLICE
FORCES**
Eden
Sergeant Keith Tillman
Senior Constable
Bradley Ross

Senior Constable Craig
  Baker
Senior Constable Nick
  Markulin
Merimbula
Sergeant Colin Bell
Bega
Sergeant Mark Welsby
Batemans Bay
Superintendent John
  Ambler
Inspector Rick
  Mawdsley

**WATER POLICE
  LAUNCH *NEMESIS*
  AND CREW**

**RAN SEA KING
  HELICOPTERS
  (HS817 SQUADRON)**
SHARK 05
LEUT Alan Moore –
  Aircraft Captain and
  First Pilot
COMMANDER George
  Sydney – Commanding
  Officer HS 817
  squadron, Second pilot
LEUT Philip "Wacka"
  Payne – Observer,
  (Tactical Navigator)
Petty Officer Kerwyn
  Ballico – Aircrewman

SHARK 20
LCDR Paul "Tanzi" Lea –
  Aircraft Captain and First
  Pilot
LEUT Chris "Ox" Money
  – Second Pilot
LEUT David Hutchinson
  – Observer (Tactical
  Navigator)
Petty Officer Brian "Dixie"
  Lee – Aircrewman
Duty Officer at HS 817
LEUT Scott Booker –
  Royal Navy (Exchange
  Pilot)
Maintenance Personnel
  HS817 SQN
LEUT Andrew Watson
  (Observer)
CPOATA Mario Cinello
CPOATA Tony Bouckaert
POATA Rohan Denman
LSATA Edson Flores
  (Observer)
LSATV William Miles
  (Observer)
ABATA Kieran Molloy
ABATV Jonathan Kick
  (Observer)

**RAN SEA HAWK
  HELICOPTERS**
TIGER 75 (HMAS
  MELBOURNE)

LCDR Richard Neville
LEUT Nick Trimmer
LEUT Aaron "Wal" Abbott
LEUT Richard Allen
POA Shane Pashley (HS816 Squadron)
CPOATV David John Larter
POATA Laurie Tomasinni
LSATV Zoran Dimov

TIGER 70 (HMAS *NEWCASTLE*)
LCDR Adrian Lister
LEUT Mick Curtis
LEUT Marc Pavillard
LSA David Oxley
POATV Jamie Edwards
POATV Henry Wakeford
ABATA Anthony Devenish-Meares

RAAF PC–3 ORION (NO. 92 WING)
FLTLT Paul Carpenter
FLTLT Mark Ellis
PLTOFF Mathew Taylor
FSGT Mark Wilson
FSGT Michael Makin
SGT Mark Koschenow
FLTLT Richard Wolf
PLTOFF Cecelia O'Leary
FLGOFF Andrew Gerkens
WOFF Mark Styles

FSGT Murray Walters
SGT Scot Bugg
SGT Shaun McConville
FLTLT Christopher Gall
CAPT Christian Martin
WOFF Christopher Kennedy
WOFF Andrew Ortlepp
FLTLT John Flynn
FLGOFF Simon Van Der Wijngaart
FLTLT Kevin Mulgrew
FLGOFF Colin Gray
SGT Andrew Kassebaum
WOFF Adam Tucker
WOFF Wayne Newberry
SQNLDR V Ludwig
SQNLDR G Roberts
SQLDR G Zidicky
FLTLT P Hay
FSGT Larry McLoud
SGT Jamie Burgess
SGT Peter Drury
SGT Gordon Tusti
CPL Ralph Bobart
CPL Paul Bonnar
CPL Scott Brady
CPL Barry Ramsbotham
LAC Michael Horner
LAC Adam Pannel
WOFF Pete Harte
SGT Garry Wood
SGT Mark Borchard
SGT Kim Nagel

CPL Vaughan Wilds
CPL Antony Hawkes
CPL Shane Drew
CPL Mark Bridewell
LAC Aaron Agnew

**RAAF C–130 HERCULES
(NO. 37 SQUADRON)**
FLTLT Paul Long
(Captain)
FLTLT Michael Rosenthal
(Navigator)
FLTLT Michael
Bannerman (Co-Pilot)
WOFF Joe Moellers
(Engineer)
SGT Kevin Reid
(Loadmaster)
SGT Scott Willacott
(Loadmaster)

FLTLT Mike Mayfield
(Captain)
FLTLT Andrea Harman
(Co-Pilot)
SGT Brad Horton
(Engineer)
SGT David Helmore
(Loadmaster)
WOFF Graeme Clark
(Loadmaster)

HMAS *NEWCASTLE*
CMDR SR Hamilton
(Commanding

Officer)
LCDR BJ Wheeler
(Executive Officer)
LCDR M Richardson
(Marine Engineering
Officer)
LEUT LD Van Stralen
LEUT C Dummett
LEUT L Brick
LEUT N Brett
LEUT M Harris
LEUT A Cox
LEUT NN Marshall
SBLT A Banks
CPOB PR Kiely
CPOET DA Stratford
CPOSN DJ Russell
CPOMT AE Vernon
CPOMT PT O'Keefe
POB PL Wood
POSY RMH Tadin
PORS SB Dummett
POCSS P Hassall
POSN M Hancock
POET RM Glover
POET GL Cruickshank
POMT AW Sims
POMT A Bowman
POMT DB McCelland
POMT MJ Jakes
LSBM SA Nesbitt
LSBM(SE) MJ Golding
LSBM(FF) SR Cannan
LSPT DA Hunt
LSCSO RP Pringle

LSSIG K Viant
LSRO SD Golder
LSRO DC McLeod
LSMED GJ Davis
LSET D Fielding
LSET JG Seguin
LSET MP Weidenhoffer
LSET D Levett
LSMT G Santini
LSMT J Strange
LSMT G Criado
LSMT P Armour
LSMT D Plummer
ABBM DA Low
ABBM DJ Brearly
ABBM RL Fealy
ABBM PW Beckwith
ABCSO CW Woodland
SMNCSO PA Keitly
ABCSO DA Wruck
ABCSO JD Allen
ABCSO DC Seaman
SMNCSO SS Allan
ABSIG J Upton
ABSIG G Judd
ABSIG L Hillier
ABRO MT Dwyer
ABRO PA Hunter
ABWTR P Aldridge
ABSN A Corr
ABSTD R Furner
ABSTD M Walker
ABCK J Holmes
ABCK G Janes
ABET GA O'Connor

ABET S Sandwell
ABMT P Marriott
ABMT A Walsh
ABMT G Beech
ABMT P Williams
ABMT N Thomas
SMNMT D Goodbun
ABMT S Atkins

ABC TV HELICOPTER
Gary Ticehurst
Peter Sinclair

IBIS AIR

AIR SAPPHIRE

AIR AMBULANCE VIC

**SOUTHERN REGION
  SLSA**

DIRECT AIR

**TASMANIAN AERO
  CLUB**

NATION WIDE

JOYCE AVIATION

AUSTRALIASIAN JET

**AUSTRALIAN AERIAL
  PATROL**

**GENERAL FLYING
  SERVICES**

SOUTH EAST AVIATION

**BRINDABELLA
  AIRLINES**

AIRTEX

TASAIR

VEE H AVIATION

**VESSEL *JOSEPHINE
  JEAN***
Owner Lockie Marshall
Skipper Olli Hreinsson and
  Crew

**VESSEL *MOIRA
  ELIZABETH***
Owner Joe Pirrello
Skipper Tom Bibby and
  Crew

Afterword

On June 1, 1999, the Cruising Yacht Club of Australia released the "Report, Findings and Recommendations of the 1998 Sydney to Hobart Race Review Committee". The report's key findings – summarised by Peter Bush, the committee chair, included the following:

- No one cause can be identified as being responsible for the 1998 Sydney to Hobart Yacht race fleet becoming involved in multiple incidents on 27 and 28 December 1998. As a result, there is no single change that can be identified for the future running of the Race that could preclude the repeat of such incidents. However, there is a series of incremental changes, that while on their own may appear of little significance, will together have a substantive and lasting impact on the organisation, running and safety of the event. These changes include a range of issues such as administration (processes and procedures), safety (education and equipment), communications and weather (forecasting and education).
- The Race Committee has the power under the "Racing Rules of Sailing 1997–2000" (RRS) published by the Australian Yachting Federation (AYF) to abandon the race. The Committee did not exercise this power. It was the Committee's view that Rule 4 ("Decision to

Race") should remain in each skipper's hands, particularly because of the fact that each yacht was in the best position to evaluate its own circumstances fully in the conditions.

- The competitors, while concerned about the 1998 SHYR itself, and being keen to pursue improvements, generally believe that the rules, safety regulations and safety equipment with which they raced, met their needs in the conditions. From interviews of 28 yachts, it is clear that skippers and crews do not see a single (or several) reason(s) for the incidents occurring and certainly see no basis to apportion blame to any particular group – organisers, Bureau of Meterorology (BOM), Search and Rescue (SAR) authorities etc. Furthermore, they do not see as a result, any need for wide sweeping changes to safety regulations and equipment.

- Yachts that experienced problems or encountered difficulties, and even those that continued racing reported that "exceptional" waves were responsible for inflicting the damage or causing severe knockdowns. These waves were always a minimum of 20% and up to 100% bigger than the prevailing seas and always came from a direction other than the prevailing wave pattern.

- Although the precise location, timing and depth of the low pressure system were not accurately forecast, the key issue relating to the weather was the gap in knowledge between the BOM's forecasts and the way they were understood by the sailors. The Bureau assumed that   its forecast winds would be interpreted as being up to 40% more than stated and seas up to 86% bigger. The fleet reported expecting winds and seas to be "as forecast" or a bit stronger/bigger.

- There is no evidence that any particular style or design of boat fared better or worse in the conditions. The age of yacht, age of design, construction method, construction material, high or low stability, heavy or light displacement or rig type were not determining factors. Whether or not a yacht was hit by an extreme wave was a matter of chance.

- The level of crew experience exceeded the requirements prescribed by race authorities and the AYF. However, many crews, despite having high levels of ocean racing experience, were poorly informed on aspects of safety equipment use and search and rescue techniques.

- After the 1993 SHYR, when only 38 out of 104 starters completed the race, the CYCA circulated a questionnaire to competitors. The results found safety equipment was satisfactory, but recommended that a series of actions be taken by the Club. These included the improvement of some safety equipment and the skill level and education of sailors in the use of safety equipment and heavy weather sailing. While some of the issues identified in the survey were addressed and implemented, many of the same issues emerged again during the investigations into the 1998 Race. These particularly related to training and education. The CYCA should have pursued these issues more rigorously.

The review committee recommended a number of changes for the race beginning in 1999. These include:

- Compulsory reporting of strong winds (above 40 knots) and high waves by competing yachts
- Compulsory assessment and report from each skipper prior to entering Bass Strait as to the boat and crew's capability of continuing
- Broadcast of additional "layman's" weather forecasts to the fleet
- Increase in the requirements for crew experience and an increase in minimum age of crew to 18
- Introduction of mandatory offshore qualifying races
- Compulsory attendance for at least 30 percent of a yacht's crew at weather, safety, and search-and-rescue seminars
- Compulsory use of the highly accurate 406–MHz Emergency Position Indicating Radio Beacons (EPIRBs)
- Upgraded personal safety equipment
- Improved race communications
- Handheld VHF radio carried aboard each boat as a last communications resort during a search-and-rescue operation

Every competing boat will be required to obtain an International Measurement System certificate of stability compliance whether the boat races under IMS, the Channel Handicap System, or the Performance Handicap System (PHRS).

About the author

Sailing has been Rob Mundle's life – his sporting passion and his career. Equally, the Sydney to Hobart has been part of that life. He has covered the annual classic on 30 occasions and has competed three times.

Born in Sydney, he was the first cadet journalist employed in the Sydney office of the national daily newspaper, *The Australian*, in its first year of publication, 1964. After training as a general reporter he created the ideal situation by combining his career with his sport. He is widely recognised today as a leading media authority on sailing.

As a sailing competitor he has won local, state and Australian championships and has contested many of the major offshore events overseas. He was responsible for the introduction and successful marketing and promotion of the Laser and J/24 classes in Australia.

In the 1980s he established a new career in television as a reporter, commentator and, at one stage, a prime-time news weatherman. He has reported on five America's Cup matches (including the live international coverage of Australia's historic win in 1983), three Olympics and numerous other major sporting events. In 1993 he wrote the successful biography, *Sir James Hardy, An Adventurous Life*.

Today Rob Mundle runs a media services and event promotion company, while continuing to contribute to newspapers and magazines around the world.